D1364024

# DEALMAKER

# DEALMAKER

## All the Negotiating Skills and Secrets You Need

**ROBERT LAWRENCE KUHN**

*JOHN WILEY & SONS*

*New York      Chichester      Brisbane      Toronto      Singapore*

*Library of Congress Cataloging in Publication Data*

Kuhn, Robert Lawrence.
    Dealmaker : all the negotiating skills and secrets you need.
    Bibliography: p.
    1. Negotiation in business.  2. Deals.  I. Title.
II. Title: Deal maker.
HD58.6.K84  1988      658      87-21543
ISBN 0-471-62465-9

Printed in the United States of America

10  9  8  7  6  5  4  3  2

# *Preface*

## THE JOY OF GOOD DEAL MAKING

My purpose for writing *Dealmaker* is to teach the skills and secrets I've learned in a career where the art of the deal is an everyday obsession. I am an investment banker. I arrange mergers and acquisitions, restructure companies, and develop new businesses. My doctorate is in brain science. I hold academic positions in corporate strategy and creative management. This background, I believe, helps me explain the hurly-burly world of deal making in a really useful way. Marketplace deals are what I do. Practical advice is what I give.

In many ways I see life as a deal. To live life is to make deals. Deal making is in constant session. From boardrooms to bedrooms, you can't avoid doing deals. You can either do them poorly or do them well. *Dealmaker* is about doing them well in business, professional, and personal life.

My objectives for you are to:

Learn the skills for finding good deals.
*Discover* the secrets for making them happen.

*Use* these skills and secrets to make your own deals.

*Win* by making better deals and having more fun.

*Enjoy* the stories of the best dealmakers in action.

Every aspect of deal making is exhilarating—the thrill of a new deal beginning, the satisfaction of a good deal closing. Making deals intrigues and inspires: the electric sparks of planning, creating, nurturing, and achieving. Nothing is as satisfying as a good deal well done (well, almost nothing).

It's not all roses and medals. Some transactions are bombs—good deals that never closed and bad deals that sadly did. Why do good ones fall apart? Why do bad ones come together? One learns from failure as well as success.

I've made some fascinating deals. I've negotiated in some strange situations. And I've worked with some of the best dealmakers in the country. These unstoppable dynamos pull off incredible transactions, dazzling allies and adversaries with their ability and agility, tenacity and temerity. They move in management, finance, and law—not to forget politics, academics, and religion. Sometimes rough and ragged, sometimes smooth and silky, these top pros are always bouncing and never beaten. I work with them and I work against them. But whatever the outcome I always learn from them. *Dealmaker* sums up what I've learned.

My emotions show. The examples presented are live. The people profiled I know. I combine novel ideas with basic applications to promote your deal-making prowess. I highlight crack dealmakers, the finest practitioners of the give-and-take arts. Peak performers are the input, the outstanding success stories from numerous deals. Creative strategies are the output, the tangible tools for active negotiators.

I tell you the secrets of master dealmakers. Vital principles are at work here. What the best dealmakers do, often by the feel of their gut, can be grasped, absorbed, and applied. You can do what they do. That's my point. Everyone can be a great dealmaker.

But to be a great dealmaker, you need perspective, insight, and techniques. So I must be provocative, impatient, and brusque. Intensity and guts must amplify strategy and structure. I seek action and get results. What's here is what works. What's here is what counts.

ROBERT LAWRENCE KUHN

*New York, New York*
*Pasadena, California*
*October 1987*

# Contents

*PART II:    DEAL-DOING SECRETS*
*How to Play the Deal-Making Game*

# *APPENDICES*

# DEALMAKER

# Overview:
# How to Become
# an Expert Dealmaker

*Dealmaker* is a lighthearted manual for self-improvement. It teaches, with a smile, the tools and techniques for finding and closing superior deals. In other words, you gain without pain.

Deal making emerges everywhere. No individual goes unaffected. No organization is immune. Since you must play the game, you should play it well. You should also have fun. How to have fun? Having fun means being good. How to be good? Get the skills and secrets and go for it. You'll enjoy deal making more, because you'll make better deals.

Compare the process to playing poker. Don't ante up unless you know the rules. That means *all* the rules, friend, especially the crafty ones. The difference between a cough and a comment may be as important as between a flush and a straight.

This book is not a mystery, so there is no suspense in which to keep you. Right up front I'll tell you the punch lines. Don't be fooled by their simplicity. The more you dig, the more profound they get.

*You must like people.*
*You must like deal making.*

Like them both and you're off to a good start.

How to use this book? Learn the skills, discover the secrets, live the cases, solve the problems, apply the principles. Competence and capability are what you acquire. A deal-making master is what you become. (Well, snip the hype, at least you do improve.)

What makes a deal doable? How to do good deals? These are two crucial questions we address. The first asks how to recognize deals that can close, so that your time is spent efficiently. The second asks how to shift deals to your favor, so that your work is done effectively.

This book is useful for making deals in all walks of life, from public agreements to private arrangements. Its principles will help you do better business and even make better love (the former is a promise, the latter a hope).

Deal making is fascinating. It encompasses all aspects of business and life. By using the skills and keeping the secrets, you can build your reputation, advance your career, and earn higher wages. You will buy and sell what you want, when you want, with terms and conditions you want—from house to hi-fi, new car to old company. This book will assist you with superiors and subordinates, peers and associates, and salespeople and attorneys. It will improve personal finance and help personal relations. Associating with friends, family, and spouse (current or potential) is also deal making.

## Deal-Making Skills and Secrets

The 10 Deal Skills and 40 Deal Secrets are all short, concise, pithy, and pungent. The multiple nibbles are designed to make digestion easier: Each Deal Skill or Secret is a complete capsule, a tasty morsel able to be savored in one sitting or, depending on appetite, devoured in one gulp.

Each Deal Skill in Part I and Deal Secret in Part II portrays one specific aspect of the deal-making process, showing what it means and how it applies. Useful practice is stressed. Cases and concepts are interwoven, to mold the heart as well as school the head.

The *Deal Skills* describe the general attitudes and concepts of finding, selecting, planning, and executing deals.

The *Deal Secrets* present the specific elements and components of deal making in give-and-take action.

Glance through the Table of Contents to get a feel for the course and flow of the book. Scan Deal Skills 1 to 10 and Deal Secrets 1 to 40. See what they're about. Sense their motion, direction, and relation. Appreciate how we peel apart the deal-making process, and how, step-by-step, we improve your deal-making proficiency.

Though reading, I trust, will be fun, you should keep an instructional perspective. Ask yourself, What should I *learn* from this specific Deal Skill? How can I *apply* this particular Deal Secret?

These secrets may not be mystical or arcane—but don't let their familiarity breed your contempt. Sometimes the obvious choice is the biggest mystery and the most-known idea is the best-kept secret. These secrets are the critical success factors for doing deals.

## Structure of the Parts

The Deal Skills and Deal Secrets should be read as presented. There is logic in the order; it is based on the step-by-step sequence of parts and pieces of the deal-making process.

The Deal Skills of Part I introduce the attitudes and concepts of deals and good deals, and the personality traits of good dealmakers. They show you how to learn the skills and keep the secrets in order to improve your deal making. They lay out the general framework for making good deals. They develop the foundation for formulating, evaluating, and implementing proper strategy and tactics.

The Deal Secrets of Part II dissect out the elements and components of the deal-making process. They describe the starting position in deal-making situations; and they present key issues of initial organization, composition, characters, and assessment. They reveal the kinds of broad maneuvers and operations, offensive and defensive, implicit in all bargaining activity. The Deal Secrets expose the kinds of detailed machinations and techniques that comprise the nitty-gritty of making deals and conducting negotiations. They illustrate games and gambits, plots and ploys, schemes and stratagems. Describing the Deal Secrets requires analogies to chess, sports, sex, and war.

At the end of each chapter, I'll throw a problem at you. These What To Do? cases are brief anecdotes from the annals of deal making. A perplexing situation is described, and the reader is encouraged to develop possible solutions and discern the best choice. Hint: The theme of that particular chapter must somehow apply. Your job is to expand options, extend boundaries, and break traditions. Experiment, be different, try the unusual. Suggest ideas you wouldn't dream of actually doing in real life. There are no right or wrong answers. Your suggestion may well be better than mine. If so, I'd be pleased. Expect to beat me as *Dealmaker* works its magic.

## Reader Freedom

Bored with my simple agenda? No problem. Bothered by the linear layout? No worry. If you are bored or bothered, forget my outline and devise your own. *Ignore* the structure I describe and access these bite-sized sections randomly, tackling them in order of personal preference, not author number. Enter and exit at any place you like. Skip ahead to any Deal Skill or Deal Secret. This book is not a novel: There is no harm in jumping to later chapters if that's the subject on your mind. Learning is best when motivation is highest.

The reader can wander and wonder through the various Skills and Secrets. They are designed for easy access, quick read, and simple application. Allow the diversity of the deal-making process to wash over you. Follow your interests. Grant rule to inspiration. Take charge.

# PART I

# *Deal-Doing Skills*

## HOW TO ORGANIZE
## YOUR DEAL MAKING

DEAL SKILL *1*

# *What's a Deal?*

## DOING DEALS IS HUMAN LIFE

When, in 1920, the Boston Red Sox traded a pitcher-outfielder to the New York Yankees for $125,000, that was a deal—although, as Babe Ruth would soon prove, not a good one for Beantown.

When, in 1986, General Motors bought back Ross Perot's stock for $700 million, and, just for good measure, added a little proviso that squelched the pesky fellow's irritating critique, that was a deal.

When the Securities and Exchange Commission agreed to a reduced penalty for Ivan Boesky in exchange for his cooperation, including the secret recording of friends and associates, that was a deal.

When companies buy and sell goods and services, when bonuses are given for exceeding quotas, when careers are advanced by undermining rivals, these are deals of the commercial kind.

When spies are traded across Berlin bridges, when weapons are shipped and hostages released, when missiles are limited and countries divided, these are deals of the political kind.

7

When *Dallas'* J.R. Ewing pays off police and politicians, when dating couples whisper sweet nothings to get you-know-what, when you starve all day to gorge at night, these are deals of the personal kind.

When you buy a car, sell a house, set your salary, or trade your stocks, you are also making deals. Ending a fight with your spouse, getting your kids home early, and convincing your mother to stop worrying are deals, too. Whether the exchanges are explicitly stated or implicitly assumed, such deals make the world go round.

Making deals makes human life, and life success requires deal success. You can't get around it. There's no other game in town. Want to achieve business goals? Build personal stature? Improve your standard of living? There's only one route straight and true. Virtually all achievement demands the successful selection and execution of transactions among individuals, groups, organizations, and institutions. Transactions take place in every corner of commerce and career. They occur all day every day. Like it or not, we are all dealmakers. And the best love it.

## Deal Fallacies

Let's start in reverse. What common assumptions about deal making are just plain wrong? What is real deal making *not*?

### Not Just Edge Getting

The popular press harangues us with getting-the-edge indoctrination. Predatory propaganda is the way of our world. If you don't know the craft of negotiation, you're a dolt and a doormat. If you don't conquer through intimidation, you're a pushover and a place mat. If you don't watch out for Number One, you're a flake and a dishrag. No one wants to be a blockhead, a pansy, or a nerd with a wet noodle for a backbone, so we are all compelled, actually bullied, to play the one-upmanship game.

But it's all so fugitive, so shortsighted. Today's quick buck chokes off tomorrow's thousand. Streams of dollars that could flow in the future are never seen. The irony is that what is not seen is not known; no negative reinforcement ever occurs, no long-term consequences of short-term actions are ever appreciated. Self-impressed edge-getters go blithely on their devious ways, smug that they have mastered the craft of negotiation, conquered through intimidation, and watched out for Number One—whereas, in reality, they have flubbed the deal, blown the negotiations, and flattened Number One.

### Not Just Negotiations

What constitutes a deal? Clever negotiations, if you believe popular wisdom. True—but not truth. Deal making requires greater talent and demands broader technique. Deal making means more than negotiating. Learning how to do deals means more than learning how to negotiate them. How to get what you want in trading and haggling is only part of our story.

Deal making describes the whole process whereas negotiations defines specific skills. Deal making involves far more than is usually assumed, and if you begin with techniques of negotiations, you've already conceded half the battle. Negotiations, if you think about them, start in the middle—taking for granted that a certain deal should or must be made. But *which* deal should or must be made? How do you know? It makes no sense to negotiate in a make-believe world, however nice the feathery fairyland.

*It is better, I tell you, to negotiate the right deal badly than the wrong deal well.* Think about that.

Many experts teach negotiations in seminars or write about the subject in books. I admire those who teach and write. But I trust those who *do*. ("Those who can, do; those who can't, teach.") This book is about doing.

### Not Just Tactics

Deal making is strategy as well as tactics, how to plan ahead as well as how to carry out. It is creative choice as well as shrewd manipulation. Choosing the right deal—knowing in advance which deals are doable and which are not—is more important than negotiating that deal. You need to be much more than a good negotiator to be a good dealmaker.

Not a clever negotiator? Not to worry. You don't need to be one to be a good dealmaker. Surprised? Read on. Certainly the skills of adroit bargaining are valuable. We will discuss them in detail—adding a few twists and turns sure to delight even the most jaded negotiator. But the facts are that one can be a good dealmaker *without* being especially wily in negotiations and that a smart negotiator may be winning minor victories on the wrong battlefield.

### Not Just Finance

Another common fallacy is to assume that deal making is limited to financial buying and selling, to the movement of money, and that the only people who do deals work in corporate finance or patrol the Street called Wall. The fact is that *everyone* interested in bettering themselves should learn better techniques for making deals. The principles apply in every facet of every life.

## Deal Making in the Bible

The Bible is a rich casebook of famous deals:

> God giving Adam and Eve the Garden of Eden paradise with the one condition being not to eat from the forbidden tree
>
> God's covenant with Abraham to make of him a great nation in exchange for his obedience and, well, a very small piece of very sensitive skin ("You want what..?!" "That's the deal, Abe, it's my best offer")
>
> Jacob wrestling with God and refusing to let go until receiving a blessing
>
> God at Mount Sinai offering ancient Israel blessings for obedience and cursings for disobedience

God granting David a choice of punishment for his sins (he chose to fall into the hands of God and receive a plague rather than fall into the hands of man and flee from enemies)

God allowing even the most wicked king (Manasseh) to repent and be forgiven.

Some deals worked for these biblical dealmakers, such as when Jacob bought his brother Esau's birthright for a bowlful of porridge. And some deals did not work, such as when Sarah gave Haggar (her handmaiden) to Abraham (her husband) in hopes of having the promised son through this surrogate mother (a particularly modern issue, only back then the insemination process was natural not artificial).

## Deal Making in History

Human history is driven by fighting wars and making deals. (The start of the former is often triggered by the failure of the latter.) Deals highlight all chronicles and records. Wherever we look we see deals. Many of the earliest annals from the ancient Near East are descriptions of trading transactions, mundane accounts of agricultural exchanges inscribed on cuneiform tablets.

Modern politics is nothing if not doing deals, a dense web of making and breaking promises, tough trading and constant trickery. Some deals literally changed epochs of history, such as the infamous non-aggression pact between Hitler and Stalin that ripped apart Poland and brought about World War II. Some deals are trying to stop an inexorable slide into oblivion, such as the strategic arms limitation talks and nuclear weapons reduction proposals. Some deals are bold and triumphant, such as the Camp David accord between Israel and Egypt. Some deals are foolhardy and naive, such as the attempt to buy hostage freedom with weapons for Iran. Finally, some deals are just good old pork-barrel politics, backslapping wheeling and arm-twisting dealing, with special favors being bartered and swapped in smoke-filled rooms.

## Defining a Deal

What, actually, *is* a deal? Let's frame some basic definitions. A little precision can't hurt. *A deal is an exchange of value and consideration among two or more parties.*

> *Value* means anything whatsoever that at least one side thinks has some kind of worth.
>
> *Consideration* means whatever things are used to purchase that value. A tangible or intangible "something" must change hands.*
>
> *Parties* means the participants in the deal.

The value and consideration of the exchange may include goods, services, assets, liabilities, cash, cash equivalents, promissory notes, stock ownership of all kinds, patents, rights, royalties, responsibilities, or commitments. Each side seeks to achieve specific objectives, and may include any combination of tangible and intangible value and consideration in the deal.

In a traditional corporate deal, one party exchanges cash to purchase the stock or assets of a company. In a less traditional corporate deal, a weak business might be exchanged solely for the assumptions of its liabilities.†

In a traditional personal deal, an employee gives his or her work time and effort to a company and receives a salary and other benefits in exchange. In a less traditional personal deal, an indicted criminal plea bargains for a less severe punishment in exchange for admitting guilt and/or cooperating with authorities.

---

*Value and consideration can be *tangible* (i.e., items that have physical substance) such as property, plant, equipment, and inventory; and they can be *intangible* (i.e., items that lack physical substance) such as copyrights, brand names, customer lists, and licenses.

†Assumptions of liabilities to acquire businesses can be worse for the acquirer than paying an equivalent amount of cash, since it introduces more uncertainty and risk.

# Deal Complexity

Complexity is a killer in deal making. It sucks time and saps strength. Dealmakers should fear its ominous advance.

There is an *inverse* relationship between complexity of deals and probability of closure. This means that the more complicated the deal structure the less likely it is to work. The KISS principle—Keep It Simple, Stupid—is as valid with giant corporate transactions as it is with small personal arrangements. (In fact, small deals are no easier to make than big deals. Sometimes they are even harder, since personality and ego can more easily foul up the air and choke off progress.)

Transactions may be disarmingly simple or tortuously complex. A purchasing agent and a vendor can agree on price without need for written confirmation. Some corporate mergers cannot close without consuming hundreds of turgid legal documents. But a deal is a deal is a deal, and every point in every transaction must be sifted and selected, dissected and analyzed, considered and decided, no matter how large or small the numbers.

# Deal Components

Stripped to basics, all deals are similar. Simple or complex, all deals look the same inside and underneath. Reaching agreement with your kids on their weekly allowances is analogous to hammering out terms of a line of credit with your bank—both of which parallel discussing a raise with your boss.

All deals have common components: distinct parties with differing interests, value and consideration to be exchanged, terms and conditions to be discussed, a process of negotiation, a closure or consummation event, and an execution or implementation of the agreed-upon terms and conditions.

Mutual agreement is the key idea. Easy to say. Hard to do. Determining terms and conditions is the crux of most deals. It is the area of greatest conflict, yet it offers the most opportunity for dynamic creativity—for bridging unbridgeable gaps and climbing unclimbable cliffs.

A first step in devising good terms and conditions is to understand their composition. The following seven questions should be answered before the deal terms and conditions can be established. (A more complete description, with a corporate and personal example, is presented in Appendix A.)

1. *What Kind of Stuff?* What is the nature and character of the value and consideration being exchanged?

2. *How Much of the Stuff?* What are the amounts of the value and consideration being exchanged?

3. *What's the Stuff Really Worth?* What is the relative benefit of the value and consideration being exchanged?

4. *What's the Stuff Really Like?* What promises and assurances (representations and warranties) are given to the value and consideration?

5. *What's for Sure and What's Not?* Which terms and conditions cannot change (noncontingent) and which can change (contingent)?

6. *How to Assure Compliance?* How to provide for each side living up to its side of the bargain?

7. *What's the Timing?* What is the schedule for completing the transaction?

## Deal Domains

Different deals have different traits, and different traits require different strategies. When a factory manager negotiates with Ford, it's not the same as when Toyota does the talking. Deals can be viewed from various perspectives, or "cut" from various angles. Three different ways to size up deals—deal participants, deal locus, deal sector—are given in Appendix B. Mood and feeling, the fuzzies and tinglies, are at issue. Make no mistake: How your stomach is churning influences how your head is working.

# What's a Good Deal?

*GOOD DEALS ARE GOOD FOR ALL*

Good deal making is like good love making: When both parties are satisfied, each party enjoys it more—and wants to do it again! Being satisfied, however, does not require being satisfied at the same time, to the same degree, or in the same manner—on either side of the analogy. Deal making, again like love making, involves a complex mingling of personality and passion, a mysterious mixture of ego and desire.

A good deal means different things to different parties: To a company enjoying high growth, a good deal might mean a 25 percent annual return on investment. To a company threatened with bankruptcy, a good deal might mean selling off inventory at a loss to generate survival cash. To an independent consultant, a good deal might mean selling services at low fees to establish a reputation. To a governmental agency, a good deal might mean speeding up spending to justify a larger budgetary appropriation.

Larry Hagman (J.R.) gets paid bundles for each original episode of *Dallas*, but shares none of the residual income from reruns of the hit series. Lorimar, the production company, loses substantial money on each first-run episode but amasses fat profits from syndication of those reruns. It's a good deal for both sides. The actors take no risks and pocket their cash up front; the producers take high risks (since most series are not hits and losses are never recovered) and hope to score big later. That's the nature of deal making: lower risk for lower reward and higher risk for higher reward. (Although here the actors' "lower" reward is hardly skimpy!)

In the short run, a good deal is whatever makes *you* happy. In the long run, a good deal is whatever makes *everyone* happy. Short run boosts egos; long run promotes careers. In making deals, one often chooses between ego and career. It's a tough call: Conceit never likes second place.

## When Bad Means Good

In the language of the street, *bad* (pronounced something like "Bhhaaaaayyd") means *good*, something tough and strong; and *good* means mediocre, something soft and weak. The same reverse sense applies in evaluating deal making. A good dealmaker is often glamorized as a ruthless manipulator, a cold-blooded predator of the concrete jungle who devours all without mercy.

By some quirk of character, evolutionary or social, we admire the tough guy. Macho is cool. The masculine image is steel and ice, not satin and silk. The feminine image is warm and sensitive, and few dealmakers have the ego strength to survive such compliments.

How to win accolades and respect in this media-blasted world of saber-toothed virility? Pressure and squeeze the other side. Better yet, pummel and pulverize them. To trick your opponents and seize more for yourself is the touchstone of success, the proverbial pot of deal-making gold at the end of the shrewd tactician's rainbow. Building the business takes a backseat when personal ego does the driving.

Too many businesspeople pride themselves on besting their buddies. They must twist an advantage to feel productive; they must feel the turn of the screw to sleep satisfied. You know the type. A fair price is never fair. Grinding never stops. Agreements are changed constantly. Power plays never end. An agreed-upon deal is altered on signing. Payment is delayed deliberately. Simple meaning is confounded by calculated obfuscation and legal pyrotechnics. The pounding is relentless.

Some of these characters browbeat and coerce. Others prefer to dupe and deceive—the former like to see you squirm; the latter enjoy the painless slice. Priorities are always inverted, objectives pulled inside out, goals flipped upside down. Getting the edge is the goal and shaving points is the game. Edge-getters are often haughty and swell-headed ("legends in their own minds") with more vanity and arrogance than acumen and smarts. When these types fancy themselves dealmakers, they are often more addicted to the clever kill than to the extra meat. What counts is not the spending power of the bigger payoff but the puffing power of the smoother stroke. It's the edge itself that's sought, not necessarily the amount—the intoxicating elixir of Darwinian dominance brewed with sublimated sexuality.

Cutting a deal with a 1 percent nick is almost as gratifying as one with a 10 percent gouge. But whatever the hit, the entire deal becomes more tenuous and closure less sure. Commitment is weakened, confidence is shaken, and time is lost. Problems can erupt, days are wasted, deals delayed, relationships ruptured, and reputations ruined—all silly sacrifices on the high altar of ego worship and gamesmanship.

Morality is not the issue here. Straight pragmatics is what we promote. We count numbers and keep score, with no special points given for being fair or nice. Know, however, that the race we run is a marathon—our time frame extends well beyond the close of the current deal—and what will be remembered as a good deal tomorrow defines what must be considered as a good deal today.

# Describing a Good Deal

*A deal is good when it optimizes objectives.* This general definition means that solutions must be found for most problems under consideration. But *optimal* is different for each party and for the deal as a whole. From each side's separate viewpoint, a good deal fulfills most of that side's wants and needs—irrespective of the impact on the other side. In other words, as long as your side is content, it matters not a whit how the other side comes out.

A "best" deal, then, is the maximum you can reasonably expect to get combined with the minimum you can reasonably expect to give. This is what you give in deals:

The value and consideration, the cash and stuff you paid or received

The risks assumed, such as the potential default by the other side

The opportunity costs incurred, such as the lost chances to do other deals

When both sides of the deal are assessed at the same time, a deal is good when it optimizes objectives of both parties. A deal is "best" when it achieves the maximum total goals of every side while sustaining minimum risks all around. Using this collective definition, a good deal is not all that common and a best deal is indeed a rare find. Most deals have uneven value to the opposing parties. A best deal for one side is likely to be only a good deal for the other.

Good deal making is a means to an end, not an end in itself. Though it is satisfying to do good deals, the source of that satisfaction should be the higher goals being attained—not a showcase for advancing ego. All parties to a deal should be satisfied on signing, enthusiastic during execution, delighted on completion, and pleased on reflection. Sets of solutions that achieve nonconflicting objectives are always present in deals and should be sought aggressively.

A deal can be considered good when it fulfills at least minimum goals of all participants. A good deal is as good 10 months after closing as it is after 10 minutes. Good deals should stand the test of time and be remembered fondly 10 years hence.

## Unequal Roles in Good Deals

Don't misunderstand. We build no safety nets under weaker parties. Social support has no place in this definition. Bleeding hearts are barred. The toughness of the marketplace must dominate. Dealmakers must consider the other side simply because in the long run it makes smart business sense—not because it is a nice thing to do. This point is vital.

Unequal outcomes result from unequal positions. Each side is seeking good, better, and best for itself. The contest is adversarial and win–lose (i.e., if one side gets $1 more, the other side has $1 less). The rules of the game, even when known, are not always fair. You play dealmaker, therefore, very much at your own risk. Final decisions are yours alone.

A good deal does not require each party to play an equal role, to achieve the same success, or even to make money. Natural power is distributed according to preexisting patterns. For example, if a liquidator buys end-of-season merchandise below cost the manufacturer seems to lose money. But if the manufacturer's overall costs are covered, the conversion of the unsalable inventory into ready cash produces a benefit.

In another example, when a company with a tax-loss carryforward and low profits pays a whopping price to purchase a company with substantial profits, the deal can be good for both sides. The buyer thinks in terms of the acquired company's pretax income (which it shelters from tax) and the seller thinks in terms of receiving top dollar.

How about a more extreme example? Assume you are able to purchase a company in serious financial trouble by assuming only part of its outstanding liabilities. The previous owners wind up with residual debt and a negative worth. Is this a good deal by our definition? The answer is yes, if it is the best arrangement the sellers can construct under the circumstances. (In these dire situations, good dealmakers like to give something positive to the other side. Here a multiyear, personal consulting contract is one possibility.)

## Relativity Makes Deals Good

Variety in deals is endless. No two are exactly alike. Good deals, however, have one facet in common: Comparisons are always made and assessments are always relative. Satisfaction is achieved to the extent that each party feels relatively positive about the outcome. The key word is *relatively*. To find out what it means, we explore a peculiar aspect of human nature.

Human beings are creatures of comparison. We react emotionally to recent events, even when it makes no sense to do so. Consider the following situation.

You own 1000 shares of a stock selling for months at $20 per share. On Monday you hope but don't expect the price to rise. Suddenly, on Tuesday, there is a rumor of an unfriendly takeover and the stock shoots up to $30. You are elated. You are also $10,000 richer, at least on paper. You tell your spouse, kids, relatives, friends, perhaps plan some long-wanted pleasure purchase—you're a hero. Then, on Thursday, the target company sues and the raider backs off. While there may be other suitors, no one surfaces and the stock drops to $24 where it closes on Friday.

You are depressed. *Even though you are $4000 richer on Friday than you were on Monday,* you feel terrible—after all, you just "lost" $6000. This emotional relativity is what we mean by saying that humans are creatures of comparison. Your mental attitude with the stock at $24 is controlled by your mental attitude when the stock was $30 (however momentary the event) and not when it was languishing at $20.

Now, for the sake of argument, we make the middle of the week disappear. There is no dramatic announcement of an unfriendly raid. Rumors of merger build slowly. The company states it might begin negotiations. The stock moves smoothly from $20 to $24 over the course of the week. And on Friday, you are feeling fine—after all, you just "made" $4000.

The same relative emotions dominate in deal making. Absolute assessment of transactions carries less weight than logic would suggest. "Good" is appraised, consciously or unconsciously, in relation to other real or imagined alternatives. The closer you think your deal is to the best deal, the better you feel. The better you feel, the likelier you are to make that deal.

There is another, invidious kind of comparison skulking around deal making. This is the comparison *between or among* parties. All too often, one side blows a superb deal simply because it feels that the opposing side is getting a "better" deal. The truth or falsity of the attitude is irrelevant. Judging motivations of the other side is impossible. Furthermore, it doesn't matter how successful the other side is if your objectives are achieved. Nixing a deal because of ego imbalance is akin to cutting off your nose to spite your face. Good dealmakers evaluate what *they* get, not what others get. They like their noses uncut.

## Why Deals Get Done

At first blush, doing any deal would seem unlikely. How can human nature allow it? Agreement on terms and conditions appears impossible. Yet dozens of healthy-sized deals, hundreds of mid-sized deals, and thousands of smaller ones are consummated every day. Deals get done because, ultimately, each side comes to believe that it is getting more than it is giving. Making each side emerge a winner is the critical essence of doing good deals.

## Why Work Good Deals

Good deal making is the way of dynamic action, potent growth, and competitive edge. This is the frontier, the comparative advantage for contemporary businesspeople. Good deal making is intense, gutsy, spirited, and aggressive. Good deal making, in short, propels companies and catapults careers.

Edge-getters, however, often wind up with few deals and fewer friends. They can be found spinning endless hero stories of long-forgotten transactions. In deal making, if you will pardon one more love-making analogy, you can play by yourself, but it just isn't as much fun.

DEAL SKILL $3$

---

# What's a Good Dealmaker?

*GOOD DEALMAKERS HAVE LONG LEGS*

You, a good dealmaker? No fooling, friend, read and believe—it's what you can become.

Inherited talent is not a necessity. Nor is Wall Street work in any way required. Desire is important, no, *very* important. So is drive. And never forget dedication and persistence. (Don't worry, I won't let you.)

Attitude. Substance. Skill. These are the three pillars that support good dealmakers. *Attitude* is personality of the dealmaker. *Substance* is content of the deal. *Skill* is deal-making technique. In this chapter, I offer some thoughts about skill and attitude. Substance comes in Part II.

## *Image versus Reality*

What's the classic picture of a superb dealmaker? What image pops into your mind? Probably a sophisticated banker type, a denizen of New York's financial district, bedecked with three-piece suit, expensive jewelry, styled haircut, and big cigar.

Despite the visual stereotype, many of these folks are truly outstanding dealmakers. They have to be. Whatever their external appearance, they know how to cut a deal—exacting maximum value and consideration while risking minimum fracture and rupture. They are intense, smart, single-minded, committed. Investment banking is a a deal-making profession, with the largest financial stakes on earth, and those who rise to the top are the cream of the crop. How these deal makers conduct their craft, how they work their wonders, forms the foundation for this book. The principles of Wall Street can apply for you.

A sharp businessperson is a sharp dealmaker—someone who formulates, evaluates, and implements various transactions; someone who works with sensitivity and finesse. Such a person plans, organizes, strategizes, and structures the interchange of products, services, and financial considerations between companies and people. Such an animal, common wisdom assumes, survives in the marketplace jungle by wit and scheme—these being claw and fang—with only raw cunning providing protective cover. Yet the best businesspeople live by reputation, the evidence of past deals done well, the image of personal integrity long lasting.

Good dealmakers defy stereotype. They cannot be easily classified. They can be female, minority, young, or old. They can be doctoral graduates or high school dropouts. They can work in large companies or off by themselves. The sole distinguishing characteristic is their capability and compulsion to do good deals. To fulfill this one passion, they are united by drive and determination.

## *Involving the Other Side*

Charles Hurwitz,* a well-known financier, has a basic principle for developing large real estate properties with potential partners. He insists that the top executive of the possible joint venturer see the property *personally* before beginning serious negotiations. Sure, the lieutenants have to go first. Sure, the numbers have to work. But Hurwitz won't start the deal-making process until Number One on the other side has actually trod the earth. "I want to see personal commitment, even enthusiasm," Hurwitz says. "I don't want to be three months down the road and then suddenly he finds something better to do. I also want to eliminate the excuse of 'Well, you know *I* never actually saw the site.'"

Good dealmakers want the other side to know what they're doing. If your opponents aren't knowledgeable, it is more likely they may back out later—after you've expended money and effort and, most costly of all, forfeited other opportunities.

This rule, as you might expect, has exceptions. The idea of intimately involving the chief decision maker of the other side only applies when your property is first-rate. Your stuff is hot and you won't waste time with lookers and tire kickers. However, when you are trying to unload, shall we say, inferior merchandise, you play a different game.

If the top guy gets involved too soon, the deal could be history. The "sunk cost" principle applies here. You want the other side to invest their time, money, effort, and ego in examining the deal. Nothing dishonest, mind you. Just let them sell themselves. Let them take

---

*Charles Hurwitz of Houston, Texas, the chief executive of MCO Holdings and United Financial Group, is a superb dealmaker. He is a business associate and a personal friend. This brings up the whole issue of conflict of interest, whether to write about people and companies with which one has financial relationships. For someone with both commercial and literary interests in business, the dilemma is a delicate one. Though my writing rewards, relatively speaking, have been more psychic than pecuniary, this in no way diminishes the strict responsibilities of the profession. Yet to expunge all traces of conflict would strip the manuscript of personality, warmth, and spirit. Insight can only be derived from real-world experience, and there is no substitute for having done it yourself. Better, I finally decided, is to tell good stories and make full disclosures.

their time. Then, with higher costs already sunk, they may not scuttle the junk. They're less likely to fold the hand and more likely to see the next card. After all, they have to justify their already-gone investment. More about sunk costs in Part II.

## Action Principles for Good Dealmakers

I like *four* action principles that mark good dealmakers: choosing deals wisely, developing common interests, achieving personal objectives, and building personal careers. I use these principles myself and recommend them to others. They are effective guides for making deals happen.*

### Choose Your Deals Wisely

Don't squander your efforts. The most critical moment in making good deals is often overlooked. The decisive point comes up front, right at the beginning, *before* you start negotiating. I've said it once and I'll say it again: *It is better to do a good deal poorly than a poor deal well.* Your chances of success are affected dramatically by the type and nature of the deal you've chosen to do. Sensing "doability" of a deal is an art developed through insight and experience. (We promote the former with principles and the latter with cases). Time, too, is a valuable resource and it cannot be squandered on unlikely prospects. The tick of the clock is a dealmaker's primary asset. Time allocated is the highest cost of doing business.

### Develop Common Interests

Don't ignore the needs and wants of the other side. The best deal makers have a keenly developed sense of "people assessment." They

---

*Note that these four action principles cut across the themes of subsequent chapters that describe specific deal-making skills and secrets. Use these principles for flavor and accent; use the later chapters for food and substance.

just seem to know where that elusive bottom line falls—the absolute minimum that various parties must have for the deal to happen. They can separate necessity from desire. They can decide when to give something to their opponents and when not to. Power relationships shift as deals develop, and you must be able to make similar judgments—necessity versus desire—for your own side as well.

### Achieve Your Objectives

Don't polish your ego at the expense of doing your deal. The best dealmakers keep their goals clearly in mind and never allow personality conflict or narcissistic intrusion to deflect a straight run for the gold. Don't worry what others get. Don't worry what others think. Just know what you want to accomplish. Keep your eye on that ball and don't allow extraneous pressures to distract you. A good dealmaker is constantly enhancing his or her perceived power. The trick is track record. Everyone wants to associate with a winner.

### Build a Career, Not a Caper

Don't misjudge the point of good deal making. It's not about personal puff before peers or press. It's not about gambits and games, strokes and schemes, sophistry and duplicity. It is about accomplishment and triumph, winning big and winning long. Constructing a career is a long-term program; copping a caper is a short-term heist. If you plan only one deal, go read the one-upmanship books and play the intimidation game. A fast-talking huckster, said to be "veneer all the way through," was fabulous at one deal, and maybe a second, but inevitably the bubble would burst and his deals would self-destruct.

## Personality Characteristics of Good Dealmakers

Personality is vital: Good people make good deals. The reverse is also true: Good deals are made by good people. Demeanor, disposition, and manner are critical success factors for deal makers. A would-be dealmaker who stubbornly maintains poor character traits starts every inning with two outs, two strikes, and a knuckleball zigzagging toward his leaden bat. Why start a tough game at such a disadvantage? The following seven categories of personality characteristics are important for being (or becoming) a good dealmaker. They are exemplified in the best dealmakers working today.

### *Achievement and Accomplishment*

Good dealmakers are like successful entrepreneurs. They are motivated more by inner needs than outer show. They have a never-ending sense of urgency and are attracted to challenges, not risks. Power is important, but it is the power to make things happen, not the power to boss subordinates. They would rather consummate a deal from their makeshift garage office than command a huge corporate division from an elegant executive suite.

### *Commitment and Dedication*

Good dealmakers invest themselves in all their deals. Psyche and soul are always on the line. They consider their current deal, whatever the size or substance, to be the most important thing in the world, and on it alone does the sun rise and set. The day begins early and ends late. Fervent conversations with other deal participants proceed virtually nonstop. There is tension, insistence, and compulsion. The commitment must be wholehearted and the dedication monastic. These traits won't assure deal success; but omitting them can guarantee failure.

### *Focus and Intensity*

Good dealmakers shoot rifles, not shotguns. They define tight targets and never allow their eyes to waver from the bull's-eyes. To change the metaphor from shooting to fishing, hook good dealmakers on good deals and they'll swallow the line and sinker as well as the hook. They may miss other deadlines or appointments, but they blaze a one-track path for doing their deal.

### Patience and Perseverance

Good dealmakers never give up. They are bulldogs; they do not rest until every avenue and alternative is explored to exhaustion. A lost deal must be lost long before it is lost forever. They know how to wait, but they don't know how to quit. They have an exquisite sense of timing and have learned through experience that acting too quickly is as dangerous as reacting too late. They can read the verbal and nonverbal signs of deal participants on both sides of the table. They can discern the right moment for movement. Professionals know that sometimes no action is the most aggressive and powerful action that can be taken. The hardest thing for novice dealmakers to do is nothing.

### Sensitivity and Perceptiveness

Good dealmakers read people well. They translate emotions and feelings into plans and programs. They appreciate the negative impact of seemingly innocent suggestions and off-handed remarks. They rarely have personality clashes and never turn opponents off. They find and push the "hot buttons" of allies and adversaries. They genuinely like people and thereby achieve competitive advantage.

### Integrity and Consistency

Good dealmakers can be trusted. They say what they mean and perform what they promise. They are not volatile or mercurial. They know from experience that truth is easier to remember than fiction, and that a reputation for honesty is the best advertisement for future business.*

---

### Creativity and Innovation

Good dealmakers try new tacks if old ones stall. They are never at a loss for fresh suggestions to circle obstacles, bridge gaps, scale walls, and a bunch of other tiring cliches (pardon the pun). They use diverse techniques to devise unexpected responses to troublesome situations (see Deal Secret 30). Originality in deal making becomes both process facilitator and content contributor, stimulating helpful interaction among people as well as suggesting specific ideas to resolve deal points.

# Worried about Competition?

What happens when my readers develop into vibrant new dealmakers? Am I concerned that the cluttered marketplace will make my own deal-making life more competitive? No. The more really good dealmakers are working, the more really good deals are made.

Good dealmakers do not require bad dealmakers as their natural prey. Rather, good dealmakers on both sides of transactions increase the overall quantity, and improve the overall quality, of deals being done. Good deals enhance the reputation of all dealmakers. I look forward to meeting you.

---

*There is an Armenian proverb that asks whether one can trust "going down into a well" with the person in question "holding the rope." With a good dealmaker you can descend deep.

# DEAL SKILL 4

# *How to Learn the Skills*

## *SKILLS GIVE BROAD STRUCTURE*

What makes Sandy Sigoloff, chairman and president of Wickes Companies, such a good dealmaker? How did Sandy negotiate his company out of flat-on-the-back bankruptcy and into high-flying acquisitions? First we will learn the skills; then we will learn about Sandy.

Learning deal-making skills is easy—if you know what you're doing. Reading *Dealmaker* should help—if you know what to look for. What to do? What to look for? That's the purpose of this chapter.

As noted in the overview, this book is organized by Deal Skills and Deal Secrets, the former presenting deal-making frameworks, the latter describing deal-making elements. To become an effective maker of deals, you must appreciate, remember, and apply these frameworks and elements. Hit it hard. Such proficiency requires the knowledge of essential attitude-building concepts called "idea–skills." Keep them in mind while reading subsequent chapters.

## How to Learn Skills and Secrets

Consider three steps in learning to use deal-making skills and secrets:

1. *Understand*. Understanding the deal-making skills and secrets means more than reading the words. It means knowing the essence. Picture how each would be worked by professional dealmakers. Play with the skill or secret. Examine how it behaves under different deal conditions (e.g., when the stakes are large or small) and explore how it affects diverse deal situations (e.g., when negotiating with good guys or bad guys).

2. *Image*. Imaging the deal-making skills and secrets means picturing how you would put each one into productive use in your own deal-making life. Project yourself into potential negotiations and watch yourself employing each specific skill or secret smoothly and suavely. Feel comfortable and free, wholly at ease. See the actual image in your mind's eye and hear the actual dialogue in your mind's ear. Construct give-and-take exchanges; gauge your responses and monitor your emotions. (This process of pretending is called *simulation*—doing something, as it were, without actually doing it.*)

3. *Utilize*. Utilizing the deal-making skills and secrets literally means putting each one into practice. Don't fear failure—learn from it. Fear is the only thing to fear. Sure, you'll feel awkward at first, but just as with learning a foreign language, you must use it to know it. Concentrate on two or three skills or secrets at a time, no more. If any don't work, figure out why—and then try it again. Remember, the more you use them, the better they work.

## Five Idea–Skills for Deal Making

These following five deal-making idea-skills set apart leading negotiators from haggling hacks. They should live inside you and form

---

*Simulation is how pilots practice realistic flying while grounded safely on solid earth. They use computer-controlled trainers that create the entire effect with all the right sights, sounds, and movements. It's how professional athletes, such as tennis players and golfers, image their strokes and improve their game.

the core of your natural deal-making instincts. These idea–skills should become second nature, loading automatically into your subconscious whenever you commence deal-making behavior.

### Know the Attitudes and Elements of Deal Making

Knowledge builds confidence and competitive edge. Your effectiveness in using each deal skill and secret will increase as you appreciate the structure of the deal-making process. Picture this image: Each deal skill and secret is a tree and the deal-making process is a forest. Your task is to see how each tree builds and blends with the entire forest and how the forest gives context to each tree. Seat-of-the-pants deal making is fine for some sharpies, but most mortals need some assistance in grasping the subjective aspects of each deal skill and secret.

### Know What You Want to Achieve

It's self-defeating to judge by comparison. Jealousy and envy are diversions for dealmakers. They erect obstacles for making good business. Worry about yourself, and let the other side worry about itself. Don't get hot over what your opponents get and don't be bugged by their apparent satisfaction. Be pleased with what your side gets and be content with your own satisfaction.

Good dealmakers can segregate their own needs and wants from those of others. However, to do so, you need preparation and self-confidence. For instance, if you sell your business at the price you want, you should have no gripe when the buyer makes even more money over time.

### Discern What the Other Side Wants to Achieve

Project yourself to the other side of the table. Float down into the seats of those with whom you are dickering. What are their real requirements? What's on their wish list? What are they looking for in the deal—bottom line—and how important is it? Most critically, what are their priorities?

Often, giving others what they want will *not* take away from what you can get for yourself. But gaining such insight does not come quickly or easily: You must develop sensitivity to people and aware- ness of situations. For example, if the owner of a closely held com- pany wants to sell out in order to retire, there can be meaning beyond money. Maximum price can become secondary to special terms and conditions. Such an owner might well sell the business— a beloved "baby"—to a buyer offering a lower price if the owner be- lieved that these new managers would take better care of the family legacy (including employees, products, customers, community, and reputation) than those offering a higher price. The best dealmakers always go for the emotional heart of the other side's interests—espe- cially when it's not price.

### Seek "Win–Win" Solutions

Search for areas where each side can achieve certain of its goals without adversely affecting the other side. In the language of game theory, such sectors are called *win–win*, since one side is not com- pelled to lose (i.e., gives up something it likes) whenever the other side wins (i.e., gets something it likes).

How to find win–win? Establishing common ground is key. Exam- ine each aspect, element, and component of the deal. Go through all the pieces and particulars of the transaction several times—you never know where these optimal regions will turn up. Win–win intersections can be surprisingly broad if one has the foresight to search for them, the insight to develop them, the perception to rec- ognize them, and the resolution to employ them. When one struc- tures deals with innovation and intelligence, win–win solutions emerge constantly.

For example, a company acquiring a family business might replace some of the cash purchase price with its own equity stock. Such a modification may win for the selling parties by giving them a sense of participation and continuance, and win for the buying parties by diminishing the amount of cash they must dish up and fork over. What happens here can happen often: In a very real sense, the buyer pays less and the seller receives more.

### Think Alernatives and Solution Sets

The best dealmakers multiply their options. They think on several levels at the same time; they plan for contingencies. The unexpected they expect; the unimagined they imagine. They are constantly watching over their shoulder with one eye and over the horizon with the other.

Experienced negotiators keep diverse alternatives always in readiness, like having several relief pitchers always warming up in the bullpen. They play what-if scenario games, devising creative responses to dummied-up problems. Expecting surprise at all times, good deal makers are never surprised. They know how to hit curve balls even while waiting for sliders.

Solution sets suggest a family of related ideas available for bridging gaps and resolving conflicts. No professional ever relies solely on one perfect solution to negotiating disputes. Perfection is impossible in the crazy-quilt world of human bargaining. Total control can never be exercised in deal making. There are too many issues, too many people, too many agendas—many of which can be hidden and all of which can be contentious. Dealmakers who think in terms of solution sets are better able to fine tune their deal structures. Optimizing the interests of both buyer and seller is the objective. That's the meaning of win–win.

## Sandy at the Bat

When Sanford C. Sigoloff took the chief executive post at Wickes it was the second largest Chapter 11 bankruptcy in U.S. history with almost $2 billion in debt. Wickes emergence after two and one-half years, followed by its aggressive acquisition moves (not all friendly), has been hailed as a triumph of turnaround. Sigoloff's deal-making skills played no small part in the transformation.

In a Chapter 11 proceeding (called a debtor-in-possession), creditors and company are often adversarial. Both want the highest payback, making the best of a bad situation. Creditors, already burned, want quick cash. The company, seeking survival, wants to rebuild. Though creditors would get more of their money back if they waited (assuming that the company was successful in its rebuilding), they are usually scared of tomorrow and anxious to get what they can today.

Early on as the new CEO, Sigoloff determined that he would not allow Wickes to be sucked dry of funds and mangled into an economic cripple. The creditors, for their own good, would have to be patient. "I never allowed uncertainty on this issue," said Sandy. "There was no debate in anyone's mind: I was not going to decimate the company. Feeble companies help no one."

Sigoloff combined toughness and fairness, keeping creditors imtimately informed but resisting their natural bent for curtailment and liquidation. He stopped the current hemorrhaging by closing divisions that had no future (laying off, with personal trauma, hundreds of loyal, long-time workers). He built for the future by expanding divisions that had significant potential (using capital the creditors sought for themselves). He came close to confronting creditors in court. But, in the end, with debt repayment and stock ownership, Wickes' creditors came out better.

> Sigoloff says: You always have an imaginary line. It is a point of honor beyond which you will not go, and most negotiations have that point. It could have been construed as insulting to claim that the smaller creditors believe us and the larger ones do not. It may have been intimidating to threaten to go to court. But there is a time when normal negotiations are effectively over, and management must go about the business of rebuilding the company.

# How to Keep the Secrets

SECRETS GIVE SPECIFIC STRATEGY

What are "secrets" in deal making and why should you keep them? Labeling Part II's chapters Deal Secrets is my way of directing attention to real deal making in real situations. I like the concept. It stresses knowing and doing, remembering and applying. More particularly, it underscores the *active* accumulation of deal-making knowledge and the internal storing of fresh ideas. Practice, not theory, cuts ice.

You must feel it inside. Often there's just no time for studied response. If you stop to think, you've stopped forever. If you hesitate, you could be lost. Dealmakers must be driven by instinct to react properly under all circumstances. How to train those instincts? You need right reflexes. That's the message here.

In this book, the word *secret* has two meanings.* First, since the ideas presented here are often ignored by our deal-making popu-

---

*What follow are not secrets in any slanderous or secret-agent sense. There is no expose or espionage involved. I offer no juicy gossip. I tattle no tidbits. I expect no trouble from any

lace, they are, in a sense, secret. Second, you can gain relative advantage over other dealmakers, especially in the long run, by keeping these ideas secret.


# Seven Instinct-Secrets for Deal Making

The following seven deal-making secrets train your instincts for rapid response.


### Be Fair But Be Frank

Some of the toughest businesspeople are also some of the fairest. Getting the upper hand should be gotten out of your head. But *conceding* the upper hand should be stricken from your mind. Don't seek personal domination. But don't appear frail, fragile, feeble, or flimsy either. Remember, doormats get stepped on. Place mats, eaten on. Dishrags, wiped with. None of these textile-types do good deals (the soles of shoes, bottoms of plates, and dirt from dinner don't build negotiating strength).

Being fair does not mean being weak. Weakness, in fact, disrupts deals by tempting the other side to expand expectations and swell demands. Creating false hopes—building appetite without satisfaction—is not conducive to good deal making.

Let the other side realize that you know the nature of their game, the way they change the rules, and what their players have in mind. For example, if you decide to do business with a certain company regardless of price, be sure that they know that you know the score. If that supplier thinks they've pulled a fast one this time, they will try to pull a faster one next time. The price, already high, will go even

---

governmental agency for unauthorized disclosure. I will receive no journalistic award for investigative reporting. There are no scandals uncovered here, no deep throats, no charges and countercharges. I am not a muckraker. However, I do intend to make you a better dealmaker. And I need these secrets to do so.

higher. (As in the jungle, weakness is attacked mercilessly, and the nick will swell to a gouge.)

However, if the supplier realizes that you know what's going on—that you've decided to do business *in spite* of the high price (for whatever reason, say quick delivery)—they will respect your strength. You may get a more reasonable price the next go-round. Respect encourages fairness.

### Heave Hype

Hype helps? Well, that depends. Hype can sometimes sell a first deal, but never a second. (Fool me once, shame on you; fool me twice, shame on me!)

Exaggeration is a short-term, rapidly depleting asset—and a long-term, quickly accruing liability. Hype is usually either a bad habit or a desperate act. Be advised, neither is good for deal making. Just try negotiating again with someone you've jiggled. The French Resistance was no tougher than what you'll face.

If all you have is one deal to make, be my guest, make my day—have at it. Though I admit I've done it myself, I don't recommend hyping it; nor have I ever met a person who has only one deal to do. So give hype the old heave ho.

### Be Conservative

Always be moderate in projecting your most likely results. Make reasonable and restrained public pronouncements. Aim forecasts below center. Strive to exceed a pessimistic projection rather than fall behind an optimistic one.

### Develop Alternative Scenarios

Allow the other side choices in assessing your analysis. (This transfers some of the burden.) Give them room—and keep your options open.

What impact would various internal surprises or external shocks have on your company? For example, what might happen to cash flow if sales rose or fell 10 percent, 20 percent, or 30 percent? What if competition pressured prices? What if interest rates escalated? What if two surprises or shocks hit simultaneously? Such sensitivity analysis is particularly apt for buyers and sellers of businesses and for lenders and borrowers of debt.

Sensitivity analysis should also be used to examine the position on the other side of the table. Such appraisal will probably be more descriptive than numerical, providing more insight than facts. What are best guesses of your opponent's current position and possible options? Are they really at the wall or can they be coaxed just a bit further back?

### Admit Uncertainty

Don't be afraid to profess doubt about parts of your package. Point out, for example, where some of your numbers or statements may be slightly suspect. Business information cannot be that perfect or that precise. Honesty enhances credibility, and careful admissions can be most disarming. (Try using such high-powered honesty when battling a cynic; it can melt the most hard-bitten dealmaker.)

In preparing a proposal for bank financing, for example, a company should enumerate all assumptions precisely, pointing out areas of difficulty or ambiguity. Potential problems should be exposed by design, rather than be hidden by default. The honesty shown will be a potent force for augmenting confidence.

I've not advocating, of course, spilling the beans, singing like a canary, hauling skeletons out of the closet, picking through your garbage, turning over all the rocks, and other such tattletale clichés. Taking truth serum is not the idea here. Improving credibility is.

You don't have to tell the whole truth, but be sure that whatever you do tell is in fact true. Dealmakers are grown-ups. The rules of the game assume each side carries its own weight.

### Address Questions Nobody Asked

Use this deal-making secret for surprise. But use it cautiously. Few moves are more impressive than when one side brings up sensitive subjects regarding its own position that the other side has not considered. It enhances believability enormously—not to mention how the shock value can disorient the other side.

Such superfrank actions are good counterattacks to credibility problems. Say your company has fallen behind its sales projections and as a result your bank is beginning to question everything. A daring technique is to show your account officers something *else* they missed about the company, say a collection problem with minor accounts. Such credibility enhancers can become credit enhancers. (This technique, be advised, is a bit of brinkmanship; there is danger that your new admission will undercut an already shaky house.)

One must be careful not to go overboard. Most people are conditioned to assume that their deal-making opponents aren't telling the whole truth, anyway. Some dealmakers always shave (haircut) projections by 10 to 30 percent. By giving a pessimistic reading as your most likely case, you run the risk of having this low-ball projection subjected to the same financial clippers. A double haircut you don't need; baldness in transactions does not mean deal-making virility.

### Think Image, Not Ego

Act as if your deal opponents are your public relations agents. In a way, they will be. No matter how confidential the negotiations, no matter how secret the deal, other people will hear about it. Regardless of how you envision yourself, what circulates about you is how others see you. Your reputation is cast by the look in their eyes when your name is mentioned. Dealmakers' reputations are their most valuable asset. Such an asset is not to be hidden away but made manifest openly.

It's in poor taste to parade your supposed superiority. Such conceit will boomerang and slap you on the backside. Whatever you dish out, so will you be dished. It comes down to this: What's your thing, getting the edge and puffing your ego or building the business and promoting your career? You can win the battle of making one deal, and still lose the war of making many.

## *Secrets of Author and Publisher*

Let me break tradition and tell you my secret. How I negotiated the contract for this book makes an interesting case, and if my editor doesn't mind, I'd like to tell you about it. It's more the story of what went on inside my head than what happened at the bargaining table.

Money was secondary. Few make it in Manhattan on the strength of publishers' payments (the wages of sin, sure, but not the royalties of writing). Books are a vital part of my life, though authoring them hardly pays an admittedly high rent. I am an independent investment banker. Deal making is a subject about which I wanted to write. It had been coursing through my cranium for years and was now ready to gush out.

John Mahaney, my editor at John Wiley & Sons, caught the idea. I liked how he positioned the budding book and enjoyed working with him. So I agreed to go with Wiley without ever having shown the outline to any other publishers. Up-front advance payments— often the key criterion by which authors select publishers—meant little. Company commitment was far more important. Wiley would push the book. My energy was escalating.

Then I got the contract. My heart sank. Its terms were below expectations. The offer was barely better than my first Wiley book, *To Flourish Among Giants: Creative Management for Mid-Sized Firms* (which had received excellent reviews and publicity, was a book club main selection, and was translated into Japanese). The suggested agreement undermined my ardor and verve. I felt a trifle taken advantage of— and that wasn't good for a writer's soul. My spirit, much more than my wallet, was the issue here. How could I keep convincing myself of *Dealmaker*'s importance with such a mediocre contract sitting in my files? How ironic, I thought, to negotiate my negotiating book. I was uncomfortable. I wanted to write this book—not haggle over it.

I decided to suggest several modest but necessary changes in the contract. I did not go stratospheric in order to allow ample room for compromise. I recommended the right level immediately. I didn't ask much and wouldn't take less. In the spirit of the relationship, my points were accepted and the project begun.

# 6 *DEAL SKILL*

---

# How to Find the Ideas

*MULTIPLE OPTIONS MEANS HIGHER EFFICIENCY*

"Finding a new deal is like looking for my lunch," the street-smart cab driver informed me. "I know it's somewhere, maybe in the fridge, maybe in the microwave—I'll spot it if I just keep moving."

Some people assume that deal making is a black art, draped in secrecy and cloaked with mystery. Many novices, it seems, search for dark sayings, the one special incantation for wrapping up negotiations and finishing up deals. The quest for deal making's holy grail is, regrettably, a vain one.

## No Deal Is a Snap

Never underestimate the difficulty of doing a deal. Closing a contract, even a small one, can be frightfully complex. Many things can misfire: Changing conditions can trigger valuation disputes; person-

44

ality clashes can incite emotional conflict; new options can cause second thoughts.

Always be on guard. Gremlins abound to muck up the works. Assume there are legions of deal-smashing demons lurking around. Most are not rational, but all are out to get you. Anything that can go wrong, says a famous lawmaker, probably will. Deals rupture with the slightest provocation. Busted transactions are more the rule than the exception.

The window for completing a deal is often small and narrows quickly. I'm often asked to estimate the probability of making a particular deal happen. My answer usually hovers in the 10 to 20 percent region *if* all parties have already agreed to *all* significant terms and conditions! Surprised it's so low? (Note that we speak of a time *before* attorneys become involved, which, by the way, explains part of the high failure rate).

I'm often amused to watch amateur dealmakers splitting the spoils of undone deals. They deplete energy, waste time, and strain ego arguing over who gets what percentage—when the transaction hasn't a hope of actually working. Believe me, if you're ever tempted to call any deal easy, bite your tongue.

## *The Critical Moment*

The most important part of deal making comes right up front, *before* any negotiations begin. When you start negotiating a specific deal, you've already made your biggest decision. Choosing which deals to try, and which to pass, determines the end result more than all other factors combined.

How do you pick the best deals? The first step is to procure more prospects. Efficiency in deal making means selecting the most doable deals. Such efficiency is increased by enjoying a large number of possible transactions. Expand opportunities. Augment alternatives. Multiply options.

## *How to Find Deals*

Finding deals is fun. You always await the next lead with eager anticipation. It is also frustrating. You get to run, it seems, all the blind alleys.

Generating ideas for new deals is not as important as recognizing them when they smack you in the face. It's easy to seek a certain deal, and not so easy to find what you seek. And if you do, perchance, discover the end of your rainbow, what spate of arrogance makes you think you'll negotiate reasonable terms?

Major investment banks, representing corporate clients, use sophisticated methods to screen merger and acquisition candidates.* However, comprehensive computer searches often just generate paper, not to mention fees. Better, in our tightly wired world, is the grapevine.

Who's around and what's happening? The more you talk, the more you learn. Lawyers and accountants are a good source of tips and leads; they keep in close touch with their clients and know who could be ready to deal.

Whenever you hear something that might have potential, don't hesitate—follow up. The worst you can get is a cold "no, thanks." But even a negative reply can lead to, "It's not for me, but I'll keep you in mind. . . ." Or, better yet, "I'm not interested, but I'll tell you who is. . . ."

The game is called networking; it really works and you should learn the rules. Networking is not just for big-time executives and lawyers on the one hand or for ex-hippies and swinging singles on the other.

---

*Computerized data bases now contain virtually every conceivable number on every industry, every public company, and many private companies. It is possible to set extraordinarily specific criteria, generate a list of potential candidates, and have the hard copy on your desk in minutes. For example, you can call up all firms that do 50 percent or more of their business in health care, have revenues between $20 million and $150 million, have at least two years' profitability above 5 percent (pretax) but below 15 percent (to keep the price down), have minimal inside control (below 5 percent of the voting stock), and are located in California or the Northeast.

It is a generic technique that simply makes sense. The more people you know, the more people who know you, the greater your chances for making something happen.

## Kinds of Ideas

Generating fresh ideas is the key for multiplying options in deal making. The more alternatives from which you can choose, the greater your chances to make good choices. When jousting in the deal-making arena flexibility means strength.

Good deal makers are effective and efficient when:

Choosing which deal to do
Using skills and secrets to do the deal

The key here is to provide real alternatives. Don't get caught with one deal being a critical necessity. Be independent and a bit remote. Such autonomy and distance is a spine stiffener and bully stopper, a bulwark against high-pressure shakedown.

## Whether Buy or Sell Side

Buyers and sellers have different attitudes about the sale. When selling something, whether a company asset such as a factory or a personal possession such as a house, the more potential buyers the merrier. After all, enlarging your net and extending its reach increases the odds of catching the biggest fish.

But when sellers attract numerous proposals, how close in price are the offers? Usually they fall within a tight range of one another. Almost inevitably, however, one or two bidders will ante up additional chips. Why do they stretch? For diverse reasons, from business necessity to personal interest—but motivation doesn't matter. What does matter is locating these premium players.

As a seller, the more you listen the more you learn. There is no substitute for up-to-the-minute, in-the-trenches marketplace information. But there is a point of diminishing returns. Progressively more input produces progressively less output. Once you've learned what you can learn, efficiency craters.

The same principles hold true on the buy side. Shopping around, kicking the tires of various deals and getting a feel for current conditions, is vital.

## Receptivity to New Ideas

Original ideas have two purposes in deal making:

Discovering new deals

Discerning new ways to do old deals

Fresh thinking enhances each element of the deal-making process. Always be ready to intervene with a new thought to break a deadlock, bridge a gap, change an attitude, or shift the power.

At this stage of deal making, it is important not to overanalyze or dismiss any notion too quickly. When multiplying options allow no negative thoughts. Admit no worry about working. If you don't devise some off-the-wall ideas now, you're shooting too low. (See Deal Secret 30 for the mechanisms, tools, and techniques for generating fresh ideas.)

New ideas mean nothing in themselves. What's the sense of coming up with novel thoughts if nobody will listen to them? Being receptive to new ideas sounds simple. It is not. Much of our social conditioning fights flux and change. Old ideas have high inertia. It takes a strong force to put them in motion and an even stronger force to throw them out. We are brought up to fear being wrong. An error is an insult. Such defensiveness is devastating to creativity and counterproductive to deal making. Being wrong is the natural result of being creative. Being wrong is not bad. Being scared to be is.

Improving receptivity to new ideas, then, is an important aspect of deal making. The following methods will help.* They apply whether the new ideas are discussed on your side alone or with both sides together.

## Paraphrasing

Paraphrasing is a method through which the listener uses his or her own words to repeat the new idea back to the original speaker. Stay faithful to the essence of the idea and the important specifics. Check your understanding with the speaker ("Let me see if I grasp your point . . ."). Keep the paraphrase free of evaluation or opinion. The task here is twofold: (1) to define a mutual starting place and (2) to keep the idea and its originator actively engaged.

## Developmental Response

The development response technique guides the new, raw idea toward a more workable solution. First, state the pros of the idea—the elements you want to preserve. Next, explain how each pro is useful. Be specific and genuine, listing at least one pro more than comes easily. Often a valuable contribution comes from this last, hard-to-give pro. Then state the cons, phrasing each one to invite solution. As you consider and correct each con separately, the modification process will transform the original idea. The final solution may not even resemble the original suggestion. No matter what the outcome give initial innovators credit, whichever side they're on.

## Expert Sessions

Expert sessions, which were pioneered by Innotech,† use specialists from widely divergent fields to brainstorm issues and problems. For

---

*See Harriman, Richard. "Techniques for Fostering Innovation," in *Handbook for Creative and Innovative Managers*, Robert Lawrence Kuhn (Ed.) (New York: McGraw-Hill, 1987).

†Innotech is a creativity facilitating company located in Turnbull, Connecticut. See Gamache, R. Don. "Toolbox for Practical Creativity," in *Handbook for Creative and Innovative Managers*, Robert Lawrence Kuhn (Ed.) (New York: McGraw-Hill, 1987).

example, a session searching for a painless blood sampling device included experts on mosquitos, acupuncture, magic, hypnosis, and electronics—medical doctors, pointedly, were invited out.

The creative sessions ask developing questions about new ideas ("What's good about it?"). Generally, the most sparkling gems are not noticed or appreciated when they appear. The ideas generated must be sifted and weighed afterward like small nuggets of gold buried in heavy beds of mud.

### Nonexpert Ideas

We are all too quick to reject simple-sounding words from simple-sounding people. Listening to nonexperts takes effort. Why should we pay attention to inexperienced folk who don't know anything about the subject? The history of human knowledge tells a different tale. Many radical breakthroughs were made by nonexperts shattering tradition. Remember, a nonexpert is not encumbered by years of entrenched thought patterns, nor burdened down with predictable approaches to obstinate issues. When a deal is stymied by technical problems, say inventory evaluation or financial matters, a nonexpert can sometimes find a novel solution.

### Ideas Couched in Question Form

This technique recognizes that people frequently float queries as trial balloons. Questions are a comfortable way for introducing radical ideas that may sound absurd. The pattern occurs because people have been burned by harsh rejection of new thoughts. They are gun shy. You must draw out the ideas from behind these questions. By being sensitive to such suggestions, and by encouraging the questioner to develop the idea further, you can tap into creative gold.

# How to Make the Choices

*THE RIGHT DEAL IS AN EASY DEAL*

Stephen J. Cannell, creator and producer of *The A Team* and other television series, had to choose his deal. Universal Studios had offered him a huge annual salary plus royalties to continue working for them. The alternative was to start his own studio, which, at best, would be fledgling, undercapitalized, and cash flow negative. Every logical argument cried out to play it safe—but Cannell chose to go it alone.

Why did he do it? Why risk bankrolling an independent studio? Why chance disaster? Though Cannell points to the tremendous leverage of owning a hit series in syndication, one is not convinced by comic claims of avarice. Sure, monetary reward is part of the story, but it's probably not the best part. Cannell plunged for different reasons.

He made the choice because playing ball in the big leagues was his ambition, and Cannell bought his franchise with smarts, guts, and chutzpah. When Cannell could say that he had more hours on television than all but one major studio, or that his batting average for turning pilots into series was 1.000, these words meant more to him than the megabucks lining up for his bank account. ("Take away the money and I'll still be at my typewriter 6:30 tomorrow morning.")

## Skills for Choosing Deals

How do you know whether a deal is likely to work? How can you develop your deal-making nose to sniff out doable deals? There is only one answer: wisdom and insight undergirded by knowledge and experience.

The key to selecting the best deals is rigorous evaluation—the tough, tight analysis of the deal ideas, alternatives, and options that were generated in Deal Skill 6 and Deal Secret 30. The main criteria for deal evaluation are discussed in this chapter.

## Evaluation Questions to Ask

Efficiency in deal making means choosing those deals most doable. *It's better to do the right deal wrong than the wrong deal right.* This is the first principle of good deal making (I told you I'd say it again). The following series of test questions address the deal strictly from your side's viewpoint:

Is the deal identifiable and clear, easily understood, and readily explainable? (Deals should be simple.)

Does the deal seem workable and practical, able to be put into practice with minimum hurdles to jump? (Deals should begin uncomplicated; even the plain ones become complex enough.)

Does the deal take advantage of any competitive advantage? Does it maximize any distinctive competencies or play up any special capacities? (If not, where's your edge?)

Is the deal internally consistent with your side's goals, strengths and weaknesses, functional capacities, financial capital, human resources, and timing requirements? (Lack of internal consistency is the prime killer of deals.)

Are the personal values and aspirations of your side's senior players being satisfied? Will the deal stimulate managerial effort and engender corporate commitment? (Good deals light your fire.)

Does the deal consider the diverse participants of your side? (You don't need dissension when doing deals.)

Can the deal be consumated and executed with the present organizational structure? If not, can the required alteration be handled? (You must assess the consequences of closing as well as how to get the deal closed.)

How does the proposed deal affect other deals currently being negotiated? What about any deals already consummated? (Deals that adversely affect each other are a double negative.)

What is the risk–reward trade-off? Are the risks acceptable in economic and personal terms? (What are the consequences, for example, of a deal well bungled?)

Can doing the deal trigger any unpleasant side effects, say a price war from competing bidders? (Deals that can bite back need a long second look.)

Can the deal be assessed up front? Can its viability be checked? Can you forecast the effect of a closed deal *before* you actually close? Can you discern early indicators of results, such as market reaction? (Good deals reduce uncertainty.)

Is the time sequencing of the deal elements realistic? (Good deals need clear deal-making paths.)

Is the deal flexible enough to adapt to changing conditions arising during negotiations? How tight are you locked in? (Good deals are malleable, able to meet new situations.)

Are you betting the company—or your own career—on the success of the deal? (The rewards of good deals must far exceed their risks.)

# Evaluation Techniques to Use

Consider a powerful rejection rule for deal evaluation: Any strategy or deal that does not either create or exploit an asymmetry in the environment constituting an advantage for the firm or the individual must be rejected. There are four tests in the evaluation procedure:* the Consistency test, the Importance test, the Structure test, and the Smell test.

### The Consistency Test

Is the deal internally consistent? Any deal that contains any conflicting or contradictory goals, objectives, or implications must be rejected. Thus deals that require more cash than the company can pay, or will change the direction of the company in undesirable directions, are not good choices.

### The Importance Test

Does the deal concern areas of relevance? Any deal that does not involve major and meaningful goals must be rejected. The relevance test highlights the consequences of issues—not the solving of problems. One must be sure that the deal involves the right values and consideration. Discriminating between importance and unimportance is the essence of deal-making wisdom. Thus deals that enhance a company's current market share are more important than those that develop totally new businesses.

### The Structure Test

Is the deal properly organized to enable successful completion? Any deal that is too diffuse or too constrained must be rejected. Unless

---

*I like to apply Richard Rumelt's rules for strategy evaluation to deal evaluation (to assess both which deal to do and how to do each deal). He stresses discovering "asymmetries," the lack of

there's real potential for completing the deal to your liking, trying to force it is wishful thinking and wasting time. Deals hung out as bait should be avoided.

### The Smell Test

Is the deal likely to work? Any deal that is not likely to close must be rejected. Use your nose. For example, deals offered by dealmakers with reputations for obstinacy or disruption are smellier than those offered by dealmakers known for their reasonableness. Take a deep breath before plunging into a deal opportunity.

# What to Do?

A family that owns and operates a successful regional magazine group made an offer to purchase a similar group in a different area of the country. Although combining the two publishing companies is expected to yield substantial competitive strength, heavy financing is required from an outside source. Since the company is their only source of wealth, some family members are arguing for a more conservative strategy. Suddenly another regional magazine group enters the bidding. What to do?

Magazines are expensive properties and the limited capital here is stretched too thin. A bidding war is inconsistent with financial resources and family harmony. Try forming an alliance with the other regional magazine group—if combining the two gives a competitive edge, combining the three might be better still. Such an alliance

---

equality and evenness, in the environment. Under conditions of absolute equality, he says,"no one can predict which of two identical armies or corporations [or competing dealmakers] will prevail . . . the winning strategy is always the same—play only those games in which you have an advantage . . . one wins games by exploiting asymmetries that make a difference." Rumelt, Richard. "Strategy Evaluation," in *Strategic Management*, Dan Schendel and Charles Hofer (Eds.) (Boston: Little, Brown, 1979).

might take any of the following forms: (1) A joint venture between you and your competitor to buy and run the target group; (2) a full merger of the three groups under shared management; (3) an acquisition of your company by the third company.*

*In the actual situation on which this case is modeled, the third alternative was chosen. The business was sold, satisfying family objectives. Lucky, too, since a subsequent economic downturn would have made the go-it-alone strategy precarious.

# How to Set the Goals

*WHERE TO GO DETERMINES HOW TO GET THERE*

Goals are the most discussed and least understood part of making deals. When dealmakers plan their transactions, goals are often overlooked as obvious and simple and not worth worry or concern. Strategy and tactics are studied, but strategy and tactics to accomplish what? The setting of deal-making goals, not so obvious and not so simple, drives the deal-making process.

## *What Are Goals*

Goals are planned positions. They are results to be achieved, desired situations to be attained. By definition or default, deal makers must have goals. If a dealmaker does not set formal goals, they are set nonetheless by neglect. A smart dealmaker always sets formal goals. Figure 8.1 lists some characteristics that distinguish good goals from

57

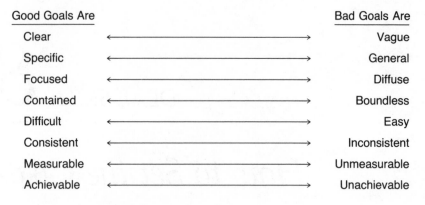

| Good Goals Are | | Bad Goals Are |
| --- | --- | --- |
| Clear | ←——————————————→ | Vague |
| Specific | ←——————————————→ | General |
| Focused | ←——————————————→ | Diffuse |
| Contained | ←——————————————→ | Boundless |
| Difficult | ←——————————————→ | Easy |
| Consistent | ←——————————————→ | Inconsistent |
| Measurable | ←——————————————→ | Unmeasurable |
| Achievable | ←——————————————→ | Unachievable |

*Figure 8.1. Goal Content Characteristics*

bad goals. From a corporate viewpoint, goals serve several purposes at the same time. For example, they

Serve as guidelines for directing strategy

Function as guidelines for suggesting tactics

Assign team players to specific tasks

Focus the team on coordinating its efforts

Motivate the team and guide its behavior

Act as yardsticks with which to measure results

Provide the basis for feedback and control

## Deal Goals

Dealmakers bring diverse goals into a negotiation. Some are more productive than others.

1. *Satisfying Your Own Needs.* This is a healthy, productive goal. You know your own bottom-line needs—the minimum requirements you demand—and you seek to get them or better them.

2. *Thwarting the Other Side's Needs.* This goal is not so healthy or productive. Success is defined in the negative—stopping the other

side cold. Your mission is to prevent them from achieving their bottom-line needs. Sometimes, of course, you can't help it, such as in adversary proceedings (e.g., when creditors seek to liquidate bankrupt companies).

3. *Maximizing Your Desires.* A sound approach. Go for highest personal benefit. Seek to exceed minimum requirements. Start by establishing hard-to-reach goals.

4. *Optimizing the Other Side's Desires.* The best approach. Go for highest mutual benefit. Even in bankruptcies, both creditors and debtors gain from a successful turnaround.

5. *Getting a Bargain.* An emotional approach to goals. Few can resist a bargain—even when it's something you don't want and can't afford. Some dealmakers will only buy a bargain. They will not close a transaction unless they believe they've gotten such a deal that they can't refuse. What's a bargain to these birds? Getting the lowest price around. Getting a hefty price reduction (forgetting where the price began.) Getting the last item (it must be good). Getting something else thrown in free (whether you want it or not). Finally, the comparative test: if someone else says you got a bargain then you got a bargain.

## Goal Components

Consider the various parts of a goal. Being conscious of each element helps set good goals.

*Position.* Where in the corporate or personal hierarchy does the goal fit?

*Content.* What is the nature of the goal?

*Measure.* What is the criterion of the goal?

*Level.* What is the amount of the goal?

*Period.* What is the time constraint of the goal?

The following example shows how this goal dissection works. Here, the situation is (1) a search for the right acquisition candidate and

| Deal Component | 1 | 2 | 3 | 4 | 5 |
|---|---|---|---|---|---|
| Position | Corporate | Divisional | Marketing | Manufacturing | Research and Development |
| Content | Financial return | Absolute dollars | Product scope and control | Facility use and overhead absorbtion | Innovation synergy |
| Measure | Return on equity investment | Contributional income | Increase in market share | Increase in utilization rate | Technology transfer of new products |
| Level | 20% | $1 million (increasing) | 5% (30 → 35%) | 15% (75 → 90%) | 4 |
| Period | Year | Year | Season | 18 months | 24 months |

*Figure 8.2. Goal Components of an Acquisition*

(2) the proper negotiation of the deal. The acquiring company is a large conglomerate that seeks to strengthen one of its divisions, a medium-sized manufacturer of telecommunications equipment. Figure 8.2 shows how each component contributes to, and defines, the whole goal. Observe how the goals guide which deal to do and how to structure each deal. The five goals are picked by position in the corporate hierarchy.

1. A *corporate* goal might be a financial return of 20 percent per year on shareholders' investment. (This suggests a certain price limit, below a specific price/earnings multiple, and possibly a certain debt structure, allowing leverage of equity.)

2. A *divisional* goal might be an increasing amount of contribution income of $1 million every year. (This suggests certain revenue expansion and/or cost reduction opportunities.)

3. A *marketing* goal might be an increasing market share of 5 percent in the first season by incorporating the new acquisition (raising total market share from 30 to 35 percent). (This suggests that new and old companies must not cannibalize each other's sales.)

4. A *manufacturing* goal might be increasing the utilization rate of current facilities 15 percent (from 75 to 90 percent) within 18 months, thereby absorbing additional overhead burden. (This suggests purchasing the target company's products and marketing resources, but not buying its manufacturing plants and equipment—an important, if difficult, negotiating strategy.)

5. A *research and development* goal might be developing innovation synergy between the companies by technology transfer of four new products over 24 months. (This suggests that the research and development capabilities of the target company must be a vital part of the deal analysis.)

By so dissecting your goals, you cut a clearer image of what you want to achieve. You may not get all you want, but you'll understand what you want, and thereby come closer to your ideal.

# Politics of Goal Setting

Goals would seem to be logical statements. In the real world, this is not necessarily so. Gone is the fiction that goals are set rationally and logically.

### The Goal Setting Process

Good procedures include: general commitment, especially by principals; belief in the meaningfulness of the outcome; easy communication up and down the deal-team hierarchy; feedback of results; healthy and spirited competition among peers.

But often, deal-making goals are set on the basis of power and position—just like other business decisions. The general rule is that each person or area seeks to maintain (or increase) his, her, or its relative strength and authority. Corporate politics (i.e., which individual or department will exercise control) is a major factor in setting deal-making goals.

### Organizational Politics

Whoever has the boss's ear has a good grip on the company soul. Jockeying position and maneuvering people is the corporate bargaining game, and it's played hard and tough in deal making where the stakes are high and the prestige is powerful.

**Individual Politics.** Familiar with organizational politicians? We all know them. What makes them tick? At the top of the list, these people fancy themselves as dealmakers, influencing goal setting whenever possible. They have consummate knowledge of company systems and people—not how these systems and people work on paper but how they work in reality, the informal relationships. Organizational politicians track the opinions of superiors, senior managerial successors, even current sleeping arrangements. Their favorite position? Controlling the flow of information. They are not too hot on authority; responsibility too soon can get them knocked out early. They are always seen with the right people (lunches are visible), and the "CEO–secretary game" is played well. They choose their tasks carefully, selecting only those that will work and win.

**Departmental Politics.** Departments, too, are creatures of politics. They act as if animate. Mere boxes on organizational charts, they have an uncanny sense of their own existence. It doesn't matter who's operating the shop, managers can come and go, there is constant pressure to sustain power and position, to maintain the established routine, and to keep the status quo. Departments will do anything to maintain their mystical being.

Deal making is both the greatest threat and the strongest ally of organizations. Deals are disruptive. They alter power and position, break up the established routine, and demolish the status quo. Organizations, or subgroups within organizations, will kill to control deals and the deal-making process.

# How Expectations Affect Goals

1. *Power of Expectations.* What you expect will happen influences what in fact does happen. The strength of what you anticipate alters both your strategy and the commitment with which you carry it out.

2. *Changing Expectations.* When anticipations change, deal making becomes less sure. Confidence in goals is shaken; strategy becomes unstable and enthusiasm is sapped.

3. *When Expectations Differ.* A deal-making team with different goals is both weaker and stronger. Weaker in that strategies may conflict and dissension overflow. Stronger in that there is spirited discussion of issues, and "group think" (when everyone supports the same wrong-headed policy) is less likely.

# 9 *DEAL SKILL*

# *How to Plan the Strategies*

*STRATEGY IS MORE THINKING THAN DOING*

Strategy is an ancient term derived from warfare. It depicts the fighting plans of battlefield commanders. One can envision generals hunched over detailed relief maps, moving armies as if pawns. One can visualize wars being won and lost by subtle shifts of thrust, parry, and feint.

Strategy in deal making is a directed plan. It defines the approach. It links overall goals with operational tactics. It has specific, clear-cut objectives and describes the actions and reactions of decision makers to the shifts and changes of conditions. Strategy for a deal-maker is like a hammer for a carpenter or a bat for a baseball player. It is the tool that gets the job done. The better your strategy, the better your deals.

In this sense, strategy is the search for *competitive advantage,* for areas of relative strength that can coax, coddle, or coerce favorable outcomes. Competitive advantage seeks to capitalize on your *distinctive competencies*, those aspects of the deal-making process where your side excels or can excel compared with the other side.

Assessing mutual strengths and weaknesses is the key to devising the best deal-making strategy. Compare your strengths and weaknesses to those of your opponent in the context of the deal issues. The result of this assessment is a series of alternative strategies. These various options for deal-making direction are then evaluated for probable outcomes, and the best are chosen to put into action.

> *Creativity* promotes strategy formulation
> *Consistency* directs strategy evaluation
> *Structure* controls strategy implementation

There is, however, a dark side to strategy. Its presence can fool dealmakers into thinking they've got a good grip on a situation when they haven't got a handle on anything. The more the strategic sophistication, at times the stronger the strategic illusion. The mirage of control is the problem of strategy.

It has been said that corporate strategy is like a ritual rain dance. It has no effect on the weather that follows, of course, but it makes those who do it feel they are in complete charge. Often when we use strategic planning, we are laboring to improve the dancing, not the weather.

# Ways of Thinking: Incremental versus Strategic

Strategic planning is not sorcery; strategic hocus-pocus will not conjure up instant deal closing. Strategic planning is just a way of thinking about a transaction. It can be best understood in contrast to its opposite, incremental planning. The best dealmakers function well in both modes. While the strategic process leads to original thinking in devising alternative options, the incremental mode can be fertile soil for the spontaneous sprouting of "aha" insights.

### Incremental Thinking

Operating in the incremental mode, the dealmaker begins *reactively* by recognizing an immediate problem, some unexpected shock, whether opportunity or threat. The dealmaker then searches selectively through a restricted variety of potential solutions, making marginal movements from the status quo, evaluating each tiny step in order. Deviations from current policy are considered sequentially and widened progressively until the first satisfactory solution is found. Such an agreeable answer is accepted immediately and all other alternatives, even if potentially better, are ignored.

Herbert Simon's idea of *bounded rationality* controls here.* Dealmakers can't ever know *everything;* so if they want to do *anything,* they must replace *optimizing,* finding the best answer, with *satisficing,* finding an acceptable answer. According to bounded rationality, problems in the real world need only be solved satisfactorily, not perfectly.

### Strategic Thinking

Operating in the strategic mode, dealmakers begin *proactively* by defining general goals and setting specific objectives. They scan the deal-making environment seeking opportunities and threats and analyze both sides for relative strengths and weaknesses. The key here is deal-making strengths and weaknesses in the light of the opportunities and threats in a search for competitive advantages.

What emerges from this dynamic, creative process[†] is a set of alternatives. Each is evaluated for probable consequences. Strategic choice is made with the guideline of internal consistency: Which set of strategies best matches goals and strengths? Implementation (including step and time sequencing), feedback, and review complete the process.

---

*Simon, Herbert. *Administrative Behavior* (New York: Free Press, 1976).
[†] See Deal Secret 30 for specific techniques for generating creative alternatives.

It is a common misconception to judge incremental decision making bad, and strategic decision making good. Each is good, but in its own arena. One would not resolve an ugly personality clash in the strategic mode, just as one would not formulate a comprehensive plan in the incremental mode. Learn when to stay incremental and when to jump strategic.

## Strategy and Surprise

Strategic thinking, to be truly strategic, must deal with surprise. The unanticipated must be anticipated; the unforeseen, seen. If everything is assumed to be known, if your deal-making future is expected to emulate your deal-making past, then the process is simple extension (trending), and strategy is playing no part. Strategic deal making must be concerned with radical change, discontinuity, sharp breaks with the past, even violent twists from current paths. Deal-makers must plan for the unplanned.

## Scope of Strategy

Strategic thinking works for individuals as well as for companies. People can apply the thought processes for making personal decisions and planning personal deal making. For example, you can use the strategic method to resolve whether to push for a still higher salary at a prospective job or to negotiate a better position at your current job.

An honest assessment of your strengths and weaknesses in light of the employment opportunities and threats (e.g., the prospective vs. current job) can be a critical part of the process. Careful consideration of diverse alternatives in light of overall lifetime goals is certainly worth the effort. (One would not, of course, need strategic thinking to make the vast majority of daily deals. Lifetime goals are irrelevant for buying a car or settling time-to-bed arguments with kids.)

# When Planning Strategy

What to do first when planning your strategy? When negotiating or structuring a deal, do *not* focus on conjuring up tricky tactics. Gimmicks do not achieve. Plots sicken as they thicken.

Devising the plan must come first. Where do you want to go, and how will each step of the process help get you there? See ends from beginnings. Have a clear vision of the proposed path—even though that path will twist and turn often. Keep ultimate results in current focus. After each step of the deal, try to reconstruct your objectives. Are you proceeding on target? Or have you drifted? If you've strayed off course, can you get back on? Or should you now consider altering your objectives to conform to the new reality? Negotiating deals is a continuous series of course corrections and target shifts.

# Strategic Attitudes

There are three general kinds of strategic attitudes in deal making. They are: (1) simple and direct, (2) press and push, and (3) cool and aloof.

### Simple and Direct

Come right to the point. Say what you mean. The straight-forward approach may be startlingly effective, disarming the other side and driving to quick resolution. Go simple and direct when

You've worked with the other side before

The deal is bogging down

Immediate closure is a goal

### Press and Push

Here's where the shoving starts. Sensitive points are squeezed. To be effective, the pressing and pushing should be subtle. If the other side thinks that you are twisting arms they will become resentful. Pressure is not some evil, alien torture. It is often the mechanism to get a deal closed.* Press and push when

Your side is stronger

The other side needs a quick close

You want to assess limits

### Cool and Aloof

This approach uses reverse psychology. Play hard to get. Let the other side sell themselves. It can be marvelously effective. If you give points too quickly, if you're too compromise minded, the other side may worry that they've undershot their potential. (I've been there, kicking myself when the positive response came a mite too easily.) Avoid tempting your opponents: Awakening latent greed is not smart. The key here is making the other side work when exacting the concession. Be cool and aloof when

The other side is stronger

Your side is under time pressure

You have other alternative deals

## Tactics to Consider

Attitudes and approaches to negotiating vary. In some situations, the "drip" is preferred, letting out demands little by little so as not to scare off the other side. In different situations, the "drop" is pre-

---

*On arrival in the United States, my father-in-law had to be pressured and tricked by a real estate agent to make an excellent purchase of a small apartment building. Having been buffeted by the business ways of his old country, my father-in-law was highly skeptical of everyone. There's no doubt that, left unpressured and untricked, he would have never bought any-

ferred, with the whole load being dumped at once. The following 12 tactics are used commonly in negotiations. They give flavor for the 40 Deal Secrets in Part II. If you choose to use them, know how to thrust. If they're used against you, know how to parry. Consistency is vital here: Tactics must be matched to strategy.

1. *Patience.* You wait. However anxious, you don't show it. Patience is a devastating weapon when the other side is highly volatile. When you set the pace, you control the deal.

2. *Slow Agony.* The deal moves at a crawl. Every issue takes inordinate amounts of time. Delays are frequent. Slow agony never says "no"; the deal never actually stalls. This is an interesting defense against high pressure.

3. *Apathy.* Overt concern is minimal. Whether the deal goes or blows appears immaterial. You request without energy and respond without passion. Apathy defends against high pressure.

4. *Empathy/Sympathy.* Concern is shown for the other side. This is a powerful tactic for breaking deadlocks and bridging gaps. Such feelings should be genuine. Do not feign personal concern; compassion as a ruse is off limits. Use empathy/sympathy when you mean it.

5. *Sudden Shifts.* Whim and caprice do not build solid reputation. Consistency is important, but sometimes it equals sluggishness, even obstinacy. When talks are turgid and momentum has dissipated, unexpected changes can dislodge blockage and overcome obstacles. You have nothing to lose by shaking the tree.

6. *Faking.* Dealmakers are like football halfbacks, able to feint one way and run the other. Faking is more trading than lying. Fake when you want to protect a particular point. For example, you might insist on all cash in selling your home (or business) just to be able to maintain your price when you finally "concede" some seller financing— which you planned to concede all along.

7. *Walking.* Closing your briefcase and leaving the room. A dead deal. This tactic is less extreme than it looks. After all, you can al-

---

thing. His investment of $15,000 grew to over $400,000 in 15 years, not to mention all the years of income, free rent, and meaningful work.

ways reopen negotiations (though some of your credibility is lost). Walking works when the other side has more basic power and has pushed too hard too long. Quitting is the ultimate leveler.

8. *Fait Accompli.* The threat to take unilateral action. The deal, or something about it, would be irrevocably changed. For example, when a financially troubled company negotiates with creditors, each side can threaten to file bankruptcy proceedings—which would put all decisions in the hands of the court. Use fait accompli when you control a critical issue—but use it cautiously.

9. *Salami.* Cut a little here, a little there, and soon the salami is all gone. Some negotiators grind for small gain—but they never stop. The deal's never done. You must stop these people. Strict limits are the antidote for salami tactics.

10. *Limits.* Allow the other side to go so far but no farther. Setting boundaries can be imposing, even riveting. Don't do it often, but always make it count. Set your limits once and stick to them. Use this tactic when the other side keeps pushing.

11. *Deadlines.* Countdowns are contentious. Calendar pressure is troublesome. One must never make a hasty decision under time constraint. Try to force yourself to go even a bit slower than normal. If the deal evaporates, it evaporates. It's far better to pass a dozen good deals than to make one bad one.

12. *Antagonism.* Not a good tactic. More is accomplished by seeking personal harmony even during professional disputes. Nonetheless people are antagonistic, some deliberately as a technique, others because that's just the way they are. Disarm the antagonism by sidesteps, not body blocks, by leveraged angles not frontal assaults. Direct confrontation rarely works. Try gentle correction, tinged with humor. "I see the new day hasn't brought forth a new attitude." "I can't toughen my position because you can't get more upset."

## What to Do?

You are a buyer negotiating to buy a new home. You currently rent an apartment and have no pressure to move quickly. The sellers, however, have serious concerns. They have moved to a new city and have already bought another home. What to do?

Time is a strength to you and a weakness to them. Draw up a series of alternatives related to time. You might give a short deadline for your offer if you feel pressure is the right tactic. Conversely, you might grant extra time to the sellers. Evaluating the different options requires careful analysis of the personalities of the people. The high-pressure strategy might be more effective if the sellers are unable to maintain two mortgages or cannot be bothered with unfinished business in their old city. The sympathetic strategy would be more effective if the sellers show appreciation by making an easier agreement. It is also possible to hedge your bets: Try one approach, and if it doesn't work, shift to the other. (Think carefully about the order.)

# How to Build the Structures

*YOUR PRICE, MY TERMS*

You've been a grand potentate setting glorious goals (Deal Skill 8). You've been a field marshall plotting dynamic strategies (Deal Skill 9). Feeling pretty powerful? Well, now comes the hard part: Making those strategies work and reaching those goals. This is the moment of truth when words and papers are transformed into deeds and action. This is when machinery gets rolling and hands get dirty. I trust you're ready.

Structure in both process and content is needed to make the deal work. Thus, in deal making, structure has two meanings:

It is the mechanism for putting the strategy into action during negotiations (process).

It is the actual way the deal is put together, the terms and conditions as they ultimately turn out (content).

## Structuring Your Strategy

Structure is to strategy as form is to function. Each is dependent on the other. Each can cause the other. Start with a specific strategy and the structure needed to implement it is defined. And if you start with a specific structure the proper strategy is described.

Watch for strategy-structure relationships in deal making. For example, if a seller's strategy calls for an exceptionally high purchase price, then the deal's structure will probably have to include some noncash consideration (e.g., contingent future payments or seller financing). If, however, the deal's structure demands all cash, then the strategy must allow for a lower price.

The principles are parallel for personal deal making. Take salary negotiations. If your strategy is to absolutely maximize the amount of money you could conceivably put in your pocket, your structure might require a lower base salary coupled with a higher incentive bonus. If your structure requires a higher guaranteed amount, your strategy would have to accept a lower ceiling.

## Structuring Your Negotiations

The stages of negotiation are important. Though seemingly static, stages modulate pace and control direction. Good dealmakers understand stages; they recognize when they occur and what they should do in each. The boundaries between these periods can be indistinct. Nevertheless, any negotiation can be dissected into five independent stages.

   *1. Deciding.* Don't jump into the middle of a battle without choosing the right war. Too many people forget the preliminaries and lose the game before it begins. Determining whether and what to negotiate usually controls more of the outcome than all the strategies and tactics combined together (Deal Skills 6 and 7). What are your long-term goals and short-term objectives? Verbalizing what seems to be obvious may reveal elements that are not so obvious.

2. *Preparing.* Good lawyers write detailed briefs. Good scientists plan careful experiments. Doing your homework is essential. Maximum data should be accumulated early on, condensed down into concise information, and then transformed into critical knowledge—all before actual negotiating sessions are begun.

Understand the other side's positions and postures. Separate superficial stances from fundamental necessities. Get your hands on all possible information—numbers, public reports and statements, press clippings, even private opinions. Do a self-analysis as if from your opponent's point of view.

Note the distinction between data (raw facts), information (facts that are organized and categorized), and knowledge (facts that have meaning and implications). The problem in organizations is often too much data, not too little. The need is for better data reduction, not more data collection.

3. *Initiating.* At the beginning of negotiations, positions are presented and images are portrayed. Healthy self-interest demands proper mutual respect. Good dealmakers put priority on establishing good rapport at the outset. Power plays of meeting location, seating arrangements, first proposals, and instant deadlines are common. These opening gambits are generally more irritating than effective. What you want to establish is common ground.

4. *Continuing.* Keep going and don't despair. Persistence and patience are assets in protracted deal-making discussions. Progress will never zip along in straight lines, so don't expect the impossible. Watch out for emotional ploys, gambits of sudden disruption (or sympathy-attracting weakness), and trumped-up issues. Remember, neither high speed nor straight direction is in the cards. Be satisfied with minor movement.

Good dealmakers can overcome frustration. Obstacles can be circled, hurdles can be jumped. Go back to the beginning and ask why you are there. Reiterate your initial objectives. Sticking points are often the result of artificial ego hindrances. Saving face often means losing deals. Novelty is an effective win–win tactic. Try generating fresh sets of alternatives to overcome inertia, especially when negotiations stall.

5. *Concluding.* Have the good sense to finalize when finished. Many deals have been ruptured after having been made because one side did not stop pressing for advantage (which is often more cosmetic than substantial).

What is your attitude when seeing your opponent fulfill needs and achieve goals? This is a marvelous test for the professional dealmaker. If you can kick yourself for not asking more, you're still in the amateur ranks. If you feel genuine satisfaction, you're well on your way to making it in the pros.

## Structuring Your Deals

"Your price, my terms," is a classic phrase attributed to various legendary dealmakers. Essentially, this saying sums up an entire philosophy about structure in four easy words. It speaks volumes about deal making.

### The Other Side's Price

As a seasoned buyer, you like to give people their price. Why? Not good-heartedness, though compassion is no vice. By delivering their price, you know you can beat competition and make your deal—and that's surely a virtue. Price is a solid number, easily remembered and simply repeated. When getting their price (or close to it), people feel good about themselves because they achieved their goal. The fact that terms of payment weren't exactly as anticipated is no major matter—especially when the story is recounted to friends over drinks at the club.

### Your Side's Terms

Also as a seasoned buyer, you want to provide substantial margins of safety. You like to maintain maximum flexibility—time to work in the new operation and room to maneuver should things go awry. Good dealmakers are usually willing to pay more in exchange for postponed payments. If sellers wait, they get more; if they can't (or won't), they get less—this is the rule of the deal-making jungle. The buyer is happy to pay interest. Where else can you get a nonasset-supported, nonguaranteed loan on a risky business? And it is especially true when the future payments are contingent on performance.

Good dealmakers will always give up a good portion of the upside to gain real protection on the downside. Proportion is not the issue here. It's worth much to a buyer to make a deal less likely to explode. The difference between major success and modest success is small compared to the vast difference between minor success and major failure. A dealmaker likes to sleep at nights.

### Mutual Victory

Structuring deals is the best route to win–win resolution. It is the mechanism by which opposing interests have a chance at harmony. When I'm asked to structure a deal, I focus on how or where I can get more for my side without taking away a similar amount from the other side. My opponent's hide is the last place I look to gouge (or slice). Improving the deal is infinitely easier when both sides gain, even if one side (my side) gains a little more.

For example, if you are buying some products from a vendor, look for other products offered by that same firm that you might need. Determine prices for each item separately, giving the impression that if you buy anything at all, it'll be one or the other, certainly not both. After working the best price for each individually, and maybe walking away for a while to show the serious possibility of buying nothing, then suggest buying both together. What's the additional discount, you inquire? It must be healthy, for sure. Vendor reaction to your surprise request, even more than their specific answer, gives insight into how much play really remains in the price.

# PART II

# *Deal-Doing Secrets*

## HOW TO PLAY THE DEAL-MAKING GAME

# Balancing the Power

POWER SKEWS DEALS

In physics, power is the energy needed to do work. In deal making, power is the force needed to shift odds and skew results. Skew—it's what you want to do; it means weighting outcomes in your favor. Everyone wants advantage. No one wants equality—not unless starting out behind. Power gives capacity to create advantage, or if behind, to catch up quickly.

Power is the essence of deal making. It is strength; it is control. It establishes the opening positions, and determines the end game. Power means winning.

How do you assess power in deal making? Not easily. Strength and control are not simple judgments. Much lurks beneath the surface. The bigger, brawnier side may not have all the marbles.

## Power Is Relative

A young, single friend of mine, a successful investment banker, reasonably good looking and not without charm, found himself sitting beside an attractive young woman on an airplane. He was returning from a trip where he held the power to do or undo a $200 million transaction. The young woman was also single, a struggling artist working as a waitress in a backwater restaurant. For the entire three-hour flight, though my buddy tried every imaginable negotiating trick, he could not get that woman's last name (much less her phone number). He just didn't have the power.*

Power is determined by balance, how much on one side versus how much on the other. Negotiations between corporations over terms of a joint venture has similar power structure to discussions between children over which movie to see. When assessing power, the critical issue is which side has more.

Absolute levels of power mean nothing. Relative power is all that counts. If your side's got it, exploit it (but, as we'll see, carefully). If your side doesn't have it, figure out how to foul up your opponent. Real power players don't put on parades. Show-offs show out. Crass displays of power bristles backs, stiffening, not softening, resolve. Real power players get their way quietly before anyone realizes what's happening.

## Symbols of Power

People look to assert power—over things, events, and other people. Power is a primary human motive. To some, the substance of power is all that matters. To others, the appearance is the shining crown.

Power symbols are more appearance than substance. It's fun to consider power dressing, power eating, power puffing, power living,

---

*Robert Meisel, an officer of TSG Holdings Inc., was rather ambivalent about pinning his name to this little story. At the author's goading, he finally put social amusement over macho power—a brave decision for any investment banker.

and power talking—but they really have minimum impact. (Appendix C gives a brief description of each.)

## Pieces of the Power Puzzle

Power in deal making is not calculated without complication. There are at least 15 pieces of the power puzzle. Identifying which are most important and assessing their relative strength is tricky. Traditional factors alone can be misleading. For example, a bankrupt company may threaten a fire-sale liquidation in negotiating with creditors—and thus tip the balance of power. In the same way, an employee can threaten to quit a vital job—and gain the upper hand in dealing with a boss.

To assess power in deal making, pay attention to the following power pieces. Be subtle when applying power: When you've got it, use it; when you haven't, hide it. Power in deals promotes your side and retards the other side. It is always being weighed and balanced, tested and shifted. Power, remember, skews deals.

### Size Power

*Which side is bigger?* The larger side has more power, if only psychologically, since size is always a threat. Size is the clearest indicator of potential force, whether that size be financial, legal, market, or the like. If you're on the bigger side, don't flaunt your girth. Size power looms larger if veiled—the most powerful arrow is the one still in the quiver. If you're on the smaller side, exploit the slowness, sloth or stodginess of your opponents. Try quick changes to rattle their cage. (A flea can make life more difficult for a dog than a dog can for a flea.)

### Need Power

*Which side requires the deal more?* The party that has greater necessity to do the deal is weaker throughout the process. A small vendor supplying a critical part to a large manufacturer can demand and receive a healthy premium.

### Priority Power

*Which side considers the deal more important?* The party that puts higher emphasis on doing the deal is stronger, especially in competitive situations. When doing deals, put a premium on the top of the list. If doing multiple deals, think like a computer and "time share"; each deal gets your full, undivided attention, as if it were the only deal on your plate, for short bursts of time.

### Focus Power

*Which side is concentrating more on the deal?* The party that zeros in more intently on this one deal is stronger. Dispersed, fragmented interests sap deal-making strength.

### Passion Power

*Which side likes the deal more?* The party that has more desire to make the transaction is weaker. When an acquiring company's chief executive officer (CEO) is enamored with your business (or your industry), hold out for more goodies. When the CEO buys by the numbers, and has wide selection of acquisition candidates, get what you can—take the money and run.

### Resource Power

*Which side has greater muscle?* The party that can throw more dollars, people, and lawyers at the deal is stronger. When confronted by greater resources, strive for straightforward simplicity and sure-footed speed. "Let's keep these eggs unscrambled," is your line.

When the greater resources are in your pocket, don't mind some foot dragging and omelet eating.

## Sunk Power

*Which side has made the larger investment?* The party that has sunk more costs into the deal—time, money, effort, ego, and image—is weaker. If you are a private company and your opponent is public, a premature press release describing the deal, especially if glowing, puts more pressure on them. In some cases, sunk power can be used to encourage the other side to invest in the deal-making process by holding meetings, analyzing data, visiting factories, retaining accountants, and cranking up lawyers. (Note: Sunk power and focus power can pull in opposite directions. This illustrates the complexity of power analysis.)

## Flexibility Power

*Which side has more options?* The party that can shift and move in more directions is stronger. A dealmaker with only one way to work is forever running uphill.

## Unity Power

*Which side is more together?* The party that has greater internal agreement is stronger. There is nothing more disrupting than lack of unity among a deal-making team.

## Personal Power

*Which side has the better people and personalities?* The team that has more knowledgeable players is stronger. Knowledge in deal making includes: content data, legal technologies, tax expertise, negotiating techniques, and the like.

## Political Power

*Which side wields more influence?* The party that can bring greater external forces to bear on the deal is stronger. If a negotiator on one side knows the boss of the negotiator on the other side, he or she has implicit political power. (This type of power is there even if never used—especially if never used, since it's probably more perceived than real.)

## Reward Power

*Which side can help the other more?* The party that can aid the other to a greater degree in affairs beyond this one deal is stronger. If your company can provide additional business to the company with which you're negotiating, whether directly through additional orders or indirectly through recommendations, you've got a leg up.

## Punishment Power

*Which side can hurt the other more?* The party that can inflict higher relative damage—be it economic injury or insult to prestige—is the stronger. When one side is a heavy customer of the other side, there is an implicit commercial threat of general cancellation. Even a weak company can command high ground by supplying a difficult-to-replace product or service. If your opponent can tarnish your reputation more than you can blacken theirs, they are stronger. Poison, sadly, is easy to spread.

## Knowledge Power

*Which side has more information and understanding?* The party that has more relevant data and deal-specific comprehension is stronger. If you've got it, use it. Knowledge is a powerful intimidator.

## Logic Power

*Which side has more sensible arguments?* The party whose points are more defensible is stronger. The careful, concentrated use of good reasoning, without a cocky, know-it-all attitude, can effectively control deals.

# What to Do?

Dr. Barry Munitz,* a first-rate dealer with people, had been eyeing an interesting chess set in a store window for some time. He liked the overly large pieces and the simple, modern design. Munitz watched while the sticker price was reduced over several months from $1400 to $1100. He didn't want to pay an exorbitant price, but he also didn't want to lose the set. What to do?

When the price was marked down to $1000, Munitz could stand it no longer. He wrote out a check for $800, gave it to his secretary, and told her to tell the store owner that he was out of town and that the $800 was "take it or leave it." Well, the owner took the $800 fast. Need power, sunk power, and resource power were all working against the store owner, with only mild passion power working against Munitz. But the owner took the check *so* fast that Munitz, although proud to own the set and pleased that he paid $800, not $1400, couldn't help but wonder, what if he had written out a check for $600 or. . . .

*Dr. Barry Munitz, a personal friend, is president of Federated Development Company and former chancellor of the University of Houston. His father was a high-ranking U.S. chess player.

# 2 *DEAL SECRET*

# *Pegging the Parties*

*DIFFERENT PARTIES MAKE DIFFERENT DEALS*

The parties to the deal are the entities making it. Good dealmakers understand who and what they are up against. They know how to classify the other side of the deal. They can distinguish among diverse parties—who they each are, what they are each about, what they each want and how they each act. The objective is how best to handle each type, how to match strategy choice to party type. We consider three ways to classify the other side of the deal, to peg the parties: identifying the entity, assessing the need, and locating the key decision maker.

## *Identifying the Entity*

What parties are participating in the transaction? Their nature and composition can suggest purposes to fulfill and hot buttons to push.

1. *Individuals.* Solitary people have complex motives. They are driven by various factors: mission, wealth, ego, and power. When individuals are party to the deal, be sensitive to the relative strength of their driving motives.

2. *Groups.* Groups are individuals who band together to achieve specific objectives. Motivation can become less complex as the group grows larger. When working with groups, either close the deal by targeting the central objectives or confuse the deal by appealing to fragmentary issues.

3. *Companies.* Companies are profit-making entities whose goals are to increase earnings and equity. Yet, though the principal in the transaction is a company, never forget that you deal only with people—and people think as individuals. When negotiating with companies, understand profit objectives, but don't ignore people purposes. For example, assume you are purchasing several products from a distributor. You can probably lower your overall costs by buying some slower-moving items in exchange for additional discounts on your primary products. The salesperson becomes a hero and you save some bucks.

4. *Institutions.* Not-for-profit organizations strive to accomplish specific missions. When dealing with such institutions—whether religious (churches), humanitarian (charities), or cultural (museums)—any hint of goal agreement can facilitate your deal making. But don't be overly sweet: Too much sugar is sickening.

5. *Governments.* These bureaucratic organizations seek survival and status quo. When dealing with public sector agencies or entities, assume they are risk averse, protective of the current state, and upset by disruptions. There is high inertia to change; lots of force is needed to alter the existing way of doing things. Government employees, remember, can fail more easily than they can succeed.

## Assessing the Need

As we've seen, need power is a critical power piece. The relative strength of each party's need should be assessed.

1. *Anxious parties* are what you like to see sitting across the table. They want the deal done more than you do. They are desperate, fearing failure. Any reasonable costs are acceptable. But you can only push anxious opponents so far. Be careful, these types can be volatile; push them over the edge and they'll blow off.

2. *Interested parties* want to do the deal—but not at any cost. You have to use more logic than pressure to coax the deal to closure. These people can walk without worry.

3. *Indifferent parties* can take it or leave it. They have other alternatives and will spring only for a good deal. Patience is a virtue here. You can't be overly aggressive with indifferents. Try playing hard to get to induce them to do the chasing.

4. *Browsing parties* are time eaters—the worst of the bunch. They are lookers, professional tire kickers, deal-making hobbyists who might check out 100 situations and not do a one of them. Browsers are the bane of a dealmaker's life. They sap energy and destroy efficiency. Develop your nose: Sniff out these temporal parasites and give them short shrift.

## Locating the Key Decision Maker

Deals are closed when some person or group from each side gives a final thumbs up. You know the key person or persons on your side. The trick is to find him, her, or them on the other side. It's always helpful to find the desk on which the buck stops.

1. *Table Person.* When the key decision maker is active and visible in the negotiations, assessment is simple. You look the decision maker in the eye, make your moves, and see who blinks.

2. *Closet Person.* Here the dealmaker is not present. He or she is hiding, as it were, in the closet, never present but always there. Sometimes you know who the person is and sometimes you do not. The people at the table are basically messengers. How to handle this situation? Smoking out a closet person may be helpful, though it may be better to allow the other side comfort in their little secret.

Don't knock the ploy of leaving the decision maker in the closet. Since it is an effective way to avoid making instant decisions, it may be a good strategy for your side. This is why a president and a chairman should rarely be in the same deal-making meeting at the same time. Each provides the other with a convenient reentry. When both are present, each is on the spot.

3. *Heavenly Group.* In this decision-making structure, only a high-level group, such as an executive committee or a board of directors, can give final approval. Life is difficult for dealmakers on both sides. The people with whom you are negotiating are not in control of the deal content or process. Be sensitive to their frustrations.

4. *Amorphous Group.* This is the worst case. Disasterville. No one is responsible and no one can take responsibility. This situation is characteristic of government bureaucracies and commercial companies in organizational transition. What are the signs of amorphous decision making? Watch for uncertainty in response time, vacillation in response content, mixed signals on deal points, contradictions in terms, and open disagreement among same-side participants. If you are faced with an amorphous group, try to determine if different or disputing forces are involved. Then play directly to those who seek the deal more avidly. For example, if one signal demands a higher price, and the other requires complex conditions, try countering with an upgraded price and even simpler conditions.

## What to Do?

A group of investors I represent were considering helping two entrepreneurs start a new business. The investors would not only do the seed funding, they would also promote an early public offering to raise substantial sums. The two founders were distinguished investment bankers earning very large incomes. For them to forsake their established careers, they had to see very substantial rewards. There was good compatibility between investors and entrepreneurs, except for one thing. The investors thought that the money should get

80 percent of the equity, and the entrepreneurs would not consider less than 60 percent for themselves. How to bridge the 80 to 20 percent versus 40 to 60 percent gap? What to do?

These parties were interested, not anxious, and had strong individual motivation. The key to the deal was not the initial funding by the investors, but their ability to float the public offering. I therefore recommended that we reduce greatly the initial funding levels, so that the entrepreneurs themselves could coinvest with the investors, and in this manner build their share up to 60 percent. (Money was still getting 80 percent, but now half the dough was coming from the entrepreneurs). The investors, under this scenario, would be putting in little cash. However, if they were unable to raise the additional sums through the public offering, they would lose their cheaply purchased shares.

# Psyching the Characters

## CHARACTER TRAITS SUGGEST STRATEGIC POSTURE

Personalities of dealmakers vary dramatically and influence how they make deals. Learn to recognize the traits and types of deal-making characters and thus plan your strategies. Even when parties to transactions are large organizations, particular (and sometimes peculiar) human beings make those deals happen.

How to assess personality traits of dealmakers? How to match strategic response to personality types? Effective dealmakers must be good judges of character. They are quick studies of people. Getting a good sense of personality helps the proper planning of strategy.

How to classify the people with whom you deal? Categorize each character according to a basic understanding of makeup and manner. Use the character scales discussed in the following sections. Most people fall somewhere in the middle of each category. Don't take this rating system too seriously. Try it a few times, just to get the hang of it. Normally, your assessments will be rather informal.

## Top Banana or Errand Boy/Girl

What kinds of decisions can the person make on his or her own? How much independence does an individual have? In other words, are you dealing with a principal who can make decisions or an agent who can only transmit them?

Good dealmakers play principals and agents differently. For example, irritation or outrage is only rarely expressed to a principal. It's just not done unless circumstances are extreme. Hitting an agent hard, however, is perfectly acceptable (as long as social decorum is maintained). You know full well that the message will be reported back to the boss accurately and quickly. Hot buttons of top bananas, the ones you push to get results, are normally greased with vanity.

## Veteran or Virgin

How experienced is the person? Does he or she have a long track record of making deals or are you initiating a greenhorn? Is your opposite a grizzled-old buzzard or a fuzzy-faced fledgling? With veterans, you play it straight—and you watch for tricks. They are usually either forthright and direct or cunning and crafty.

Novices are noisome, virgins the pits. Both hide their inexperience behind a facade of awkward toughness. They think flintheadedness, even rudeness to older people, portrays fortitude and confidence. They are wrong, but you must still deal with these upstarts.

With virgins, there are two approaches. The first allows them to bolster their weak self-image through bluster; they may calm down into good dealmakers. The second approach is to pull them up short. Let them know that you know the script and can read their lines. Tell them that bravado is not bravura. Show them the carrot and the stick. They can either make or break the deal, and bask in the former or give account for the latter.

# Egotistical or Action Centered

What's the person's primary objective? Is it accomplishing the task of puffing the self? Egotists who fancy themselves consummate deal-makers can be spotted in a microsecond. Some telltale signs: the number of "I's" in their conversations and the ring of constant condescension in their tone. Check how they speak in meetings, act in front of others, handle subordinates, even write their names or answer the phone.

How to deal with egotists? Direct confrontation is a last resort. It can always be tried but if it flubs all other efforts end.* Instead, you can deflect the egotist by appealing to his or her baser instincts. Give the braggart something to crow about. Skew part of the deal to puff the person, as long as it costs you nothing. For example, trade away public recognition (with no authority), additional features thrown in (cosmetics only), and inflated purchase price (watered way down with extended payments and little interest), or a hefty special payment (subtracted from the real purchase price).

Action-centered people are fulfilled by closing good deals; they seek the straightest and clearest route to success, irrespective of personal prestige. Don't be fooled by their pleasant manner. They work hard and tough and can be smooth and slippery. You can give away more than you should and feel good about it. Deal making is not philanthropy. Be on guard here.

# Self-Willed or Team Player

Does the person play ball with a group, or is he or she a loner? Can he or she share responsibility, authority, and credit? Self-willed principals should be handled one-on-one. Don't worry about alienating the team; they don't count, anyway.

---

*Taking a finesse in bridge is an apt analogy. It may or may not work, so you try other alternatives first. Then, if all else fails and you need the finesse to make the hand, take it.

Self-willed agents are messy for both sides, and are likely to cause confusion. If you've got an uncontrollable ego representing the decision maker, communicate directly with the principals. (But don't antagonize the overblown messenger.)

Team-playing principals tend to rely on one or two special associates. Determine the favorite counselors and find their soft spots.

It's a mistake to assume that team players are all good news and self-willed types are all bad. Self-willed principals can make fast decisions, even ones to your liking, and not wait around for others to critique them. Team players may be indecisive, and waste everyone's time while they grope with their group.

## Intense or Relaxed

Is the person uptight or at ease in the deal-making setting? Intense people show little patience and drive linearly for clear objectives. They are less flexible in thought and deed. Relaxed people are apt to find more creative solutions. They tend to take themselves less seriously and don't mind looking a little foolish as they search for new answers. Your task, in general, is to induce a more unruffled, easygoing atmosphere, to encourage a calm, positive posture in the deal-making process.

Innovative problem solving is nurtured when parties are less high-strung. Humor is a good technique, especially good-natured kidding of opponents combined with light deprecation of oneself. Try comments like, "We're acting like this deal's important. A million years from now, who'll care?" Or, "Nothing kills a good deal like hard heads on stiff necks—on both sides."

## Objective or Subjective

Is the person influenced more by logic or emotion? Will he or she conform to the traditional solutions or seek the unusual? Which appeals more, converging to a solution or diverging with more options?

Objective types are more analytical, rational, and focused. They generally conform to traditional ways of thinking and behaving. They like to converge ever closer to stark solutions. Proceed step-by-step with these folks.

Subjective types are more passionate, abstract, and daring. They are generally more nontraditional and iconoclastic. They seek to explore new areas even if confusing and risky. This type of personality is often more flexible in deal making.

Subjective types are great at bridging gaps and breaking deadlocks. They are not great, however, at closing deals. It's hard for them to come to a final agreement because they can always find something else novel or better. In order to consummate a deal, objective types should be in control. To do good deals, especially if they're complex, have both objectives and subjectives on your team.

## Consistent or Capricious

Is the person reliable in both promise and practice? Can he or she be trusted to follow a predictable path? You can deal directly with consistent thinkers. Moves can be planned well ahead. When dealing with capricious characters, you must focus more on the present. Nail down agreements in detail, even on small points, before moving on to new subjects. With unpredictable personalities, sit lightly and never rest. Always expect change.

When there's a real impasse in a deal, however, roles may reverse. Capricious types are often better at unblocking problems. They can jump higher hurdles, though you can never predict how, where, or when they will land. Consistent types, those who think step-by-step, have a harder time overcoming obstacles.

## Likers or Haters

How does the person see people—as individuals to know or as objects to exploit? Likers see the good in people and forgive their faults. Haters see the bad and carry grudges. Likers enjoy doing deals with friends. Haters prefer getting even with foes. Likers and haters are polar opposites, and the look on their faces is often a dead give-away.

Doing business with haters is no fun. You never know when you've tripped their tightly strung wires. Disarming a hater is like defusing a bomb. Confrontation, while tempting, is the technique of desperation. First, try showing that you do not take yourself, or the deal, too seriously. It's hard to hate someone who just doesn't care. Make small talk. Try to establish a relationship. Friendliness can be contagious.

## Normal or Strange

Once in a while you come across a head case. Be careful. Normal rules of the road don't apply. Deal making as a profession attracts diverse characters. A few are real oddballs. You expect to contest large egos, and you learn to handle them (if not like them). But occasionally you'll meet an ego so massive that it's almost comical. You never know when that mental mass is going to explode. An innocent remark taken wrong, an inadvertent slight blown out of proportion, and we have a fireball.

It's hard to prescribe a proper response, short of a graduate degree in abnormal psychology. Your primary task is to recognize what you are dealing with and to take care not to react strongly to any provocation. If you are patient, it may be possible to make your deal. But if it works it will probably come in an unexpected manner.

## What to Do?

You are the principal negotiator in a critical deal for your company. Suddenly, the principal negotiator on the other side becomes caustic in her personal attacks. You are being belittled and insulted publicly. Your team members are waiting. What to do?

You must make a rapid judgment call based on a character assessment. If the individual is only capricious, her rudeness is a tactic—confront the boor and thwart the trick (see Deal Secrets 26, 27, and 28). If, however, she is a hater or is strange, you must say nothing and await developments. Your relaxed, slightly bored countenance will be most aggravating. If she calms down, you will have gained ground. If she continues her tirade, just disengage. There is no way to win against such irrationality. Your quiet withdrawal from the maelstrom—and the deal—throws the ball directly into her court.

# 4 *DEAL SECRET*

# *Surveying the Turf*

## *THE MEDIUM IS PART OF THE MESSAGE*

How do settings of deals affect their substance? How does environment influence the way deals get done? In deal making, signals are always being sent. Your side sends them; the other side sends them; even the setting sends them. Telltale signs abound. Conscious awareness may or may not be involved. You may not recognize these hidden communications. Like infrared and ultraviolet light, unseen at both ends of the spectrum, they are always there.

## *Metamessages*

Signals are "metamessages": nonverbal feelings, projections, impressions, connotations, and influences. They bias the actual messages with their subliminal tugs and pulls. Consider the following examples:

When a principal will not speak without an attorney beside him, you begin to wonder. The literal message is that your opponent is one careful person. The metamessage may be that your opponent is uncertain, unsure, nervous, worried, or frightened. (Ask yourself what he is so afraid of.)

When one side of the deal volunteers to take a crack at writing a first draft of an agreement, the literal message is, "We'll do the work and cover the expense." The metamessage is, "We know the deal better than you do," or "we will control procedure from now on."

The subsequent sections are metamessages regarding "turf," subliminal signals about the setting of deals. Watch for these subtleties in your deals.

## Home Court Advantage

There are two general rules of thumb regarding meeting place. The first describes relative power: Home court gives control (meeting location indicates positional strength). The second describes relative desire: The one who wants, walks; the beseecher travels to the territory of the beseechee. (Accountants and advertising executives, for example, usually meet at their clients' offices.)

Often, the meeting venue is a matter of mutual convenience, not game-playing tricks. However, be aware that some dealmakers deliberately use the home court advantage. I prefer to concede the place of meeting and have the other side assume that I come in a weaker position. (I like defying convention when it comes to power.) I also like to see the home grounds of my opponents. You never know what you can learn. For example, if there are lots of vacated offices, this could mean that business may not be as rosy as it's being pictured.

On a personal note, I hold many meetings in my home. The atmosphere is private and relaxed. It is always conducive to serious business with a creative touch. I never thought of this practice in terms of any psychological advantage until a foreign dignitary told a friend that I must be exceedingly important, since I had invited him to come to see me. Indeed, by agreeing to meet at my home, rather than at his hotel, the dignitary was reaffirming my preeminence in his mind.

## Seating Arrangements

Remember how long it took just to decide the *shape* of the negotiating table at the Vietnam Peace Conference? In your deals, does the primary principal take the head seat? If not, does that indicate real dominance and high confidence? If the principal is not present, who takes the chief spot—and does that person take the lead? Either way you gain insight about the power behind the throne.

A curious thing happens in organizations. You sometimes find that meeting rooms fill up in reverse, from the rear forward, so that the last one in must take the uppermost seat. Such an external show of meekness can be more artificial pretense than true humility. It can also mask political conflict boiling below the surface.

## Telephone

Where would we be without telephones? I am fascinated by their power. You can get to "see" people by phone whose offices you could never even approach. An urgent meeting with a person who might have traveled across the country can be interrupted by a casual call from across the street.*

When asked whether I like to travel, my snappy answer is, "Sure, by telephone." Phone calls—especially conference calls—are highly

---

*Why is the telephone so invasive? I think it's the mystery of the sudden ring, the arresting intrusion of the unknown, perhaps the easy access to instant gratification. Something's happening, you don't know what, but to find out all you do is pick up that piece of light plastic. It's intoxicating.

efficient. They compress time and promote a get-down-to-business attitude. Actual geography is becoming less relevant for business. When I'm staying on the West Coast, I can often do my East Coast business better. My day starts earlier, 20 minute phone calls replace two hour meetings, and efficiency is improved. (Don't tell the phone companies, but communication costs are one of the best bargains in contemporary society.)

Telephone talk doesn't work in all situations. For example, it's too easy for the other party to say no to the mouthpiece; the impersonality makes for an easier turndown. The medium also promotes rapid-fire response, not a positive if you want the other side to reflect on your ideas or proposals.

There is no slighting direct contact in deal making. You often need to see reactions and expressions. This factor is especially important when making and responding to proposals. The telephone cannot communicate body language.

Deal making on the telephone has special character. For example, advantage is achieved, however slight, by the one who makes the call. Readiness is key. The caller is obviously ready; the one who receives the call is obviously not. Some people just do not take many calls, preferring to return calls at their discretion. Secretaries and answering machines are good filters. If, after a secrtary asks your name and says "Just a moment," you are told that the person you are calling is "unavailable," become suspicious. But you always learn something, even the fact that your opponent is not ready to speak with you.

As another example, facts are more literal on the phone. The specific details of offers and counteroffers are uncolored by atmosphere and aura. Sometimes this is good for your side, sometimes not. It depends on your current position and intended strategy.

Telephone tricks are common. Lawyers like to bill out a minimum of seven to 12 minutes of their time for each call made for clients, irrespective of whether the call was much shorter or even whether the person was actually there. Since these calls can average well under a minute, such a lawyer can rack up several hours worth of billings in less than 60 real minutes. (Some would call this system efficient; others would use a less kind word.)

Ducking calls is a required skill; to some it's a new art form. Let's say you want to avoid giving a final answer to a prospective buyer because you'd rather test some other offers first. But you don't want to turn them off, since they might be making the best deal. If you talk, and if they catch you before you're ready, you're in Trouble City. It's like the proverbial mouthful of scalding soup: The next thing you do must be wrong. You don't want to say yes (you want to check those other offers); you can't say no (theirs may prove to be the best offer), and any hesitation will betray your fence-sitting. The situation is a delicate one. Calling back during low likelihood office hours—such as lunch time or early evening—is a favorite technique for slipping people without making it too obvious. Using secretaries to leave messages is another. Ducking can't work for long, of course, but it might buy a few precious days.

## Informal Settings

While deals get concluded in more formal settings, they usually get started in more informal ones. Business meals are a favorite. Watch protocol here. Signals are sent by what restaurant is chosen and who picks up the bill. It is inappropriate, for example, for a start-up entrepreneur to cavort with investors at an expensive nightspot. Likewise it doesn't sit well for a struggling company to entertain its bankers at a swanky watering hole.

I often apply a story my father told me. In the go-go 1960s, when his private apparel company was being courted by a conglomerate, he was invited to lunch at an extravagant restaurant by the division president. This executive made lofty promises with great fanfare and flamboyant gestures; but when it came to check-paying time, his hands developed sudden rigor mortis—as did, I might add, his deal.

Sporting events, spectator and participatory, are good catalysts for building relationships. People get to know each other as individuals instead of objects. Emotions are less inhibited by social convention and you get a glimpse of the real person hiding beneath the hand-tailored suit.

Such personal knowledge is invaluable in understanding the characters in the deal-making process, and it is essential if the deal involves a continuing relationship. The golf course is a legendary place for making deals. The relaxed atmosphere stimulates expansive thinking. (You also get to see how the other fellow functions in the rough, in the traps, and when four-putting a short green.)

## *What to Do?*

You are a senior executive contemplating joining a new firm in a top management position. You've met the chairman and president of the company in their offices and seem to get on well with them. But your entire career hangs on this decision and work relationships are vital to the job and to you. What to do?

Suggest meeting the senior executives, especially the person to whom you will report, out of the office, preferably away from business clothes and formal manners. Seeing the families of those with whom you work is another way to gain special insight.

# 5 DEAL SECRET

# Gauging the Size

*SIZE IN DEALS MEANS MORE THAN SIZE OF DEALS*

Remember back when $100,000 salaries were the stratosphere for sports superstars? It seems that a certain well-known athlete was offered $100,001. When asked if the extra dollar was symbolic, he reputedly answered, "Hell no, a buck is a buck."

## How Size Influences Deals

Why is size important? What aspects of the deal-making process are affected by the amplitude, volume, and weight of transactions? No doubt the number of dollars exchanged is critical—size is surely measured in green. But there are other colors to the deal-making rainbow—size counts in more ways than one.

Size can sway the intensity of negotiations, the length of discussions, and the difficulty of agreement. It can slant the visibility of outcomes, the public image of results, and the reputation of participants. It can determine the level of management doing the negotiating, the attention paid by senior executives, and the orchids or onions reserved for the dealmakers.

## Relativity

Size, as most things in business, must be judged by comparison. Relative balance is more important than absolute standard.

1. *Deal Size Relates to the Size of the Parties Making the Deal.* It is nonsense to speak of $20 million as a large deal. To General Motors, it's microscopic. To Paul's Pontiac dealership, it's mammoth.

2. *Deal Size Also Relates to Other Options Available to the Parties.* A $50 million deal would have been small to Carl Icahn when he was contemplating taking over Trans World Airlines. Similarly, a $100 million suit against Texaco would not have made much of a ripple when they were busy appealing the $10 *billion* judgment for Pennzoil.

## Factors of Size

What parts of a deal determine its size? Dollar value is the obvious answer. But must a $10 million deal always be 10 times larger than a $1 million deal? Not necessarily. The fact is that the latter, even in the same company, can be even bigger than the former. Remember, there is more to size than numbers.

### Positive Kick

A small deal with a large customer may be a test case. Upside potential can be enormous; the future can dwarf the present. Do a good job on this one and the sky's the limit. In some industries, for example, where expertise is hard to judge up front, smaller contracts are generally given before larger ones. Likewise with government programs, where you must work your way up the procurement ladder. Confidence must be built slowly.

### Negative Kick

Mess up a smaller deal with a current customer and you foul up an ongoing relationship. Downside danger can be serious; the present can disrupt the future. A $10,000 order from a $500,000-a-year customer deserves more attention than a $20,000 order from a $50,000-a-year customer.

### Visibility

The public presence of a transaction, inside or outside the company, influences its magnitude. A special $50,000 corporate image project for a company chief executive may be more important to an advertising agency than a $500,000 media buy from that same company. Similarly, a contract to dispose of dangerous chemicals, no matter how small, risks a nasty public relations spill if not handled correctly.

### Strategic Value

A small deal that helps achieve your longer-term objectives can exceed in size a larger deal not so relevant. A $2 million research and development (R&D) contract for a technology company may be larger than a $20 million production order. Sure, the $20 million means higher profits—but that may be a one-shot deal. The R&D contract may build expertise that could produce continuous profits. (Give a hungry man a fish and you feed him for a day; teach him how to fish and you feed him forever.)

*Symbolic Value*

What a deal means affects how it is perceived. A small matter with large implications can be a big deal. A company that talks innovation and funds tradition digs credibility gaps. Nothing speaks louder than the movement of money, and a pilot project in a risky new area looms large in the corporate consciousness.*

# Strategies of Size

So you can gauge the size of your deal—big deal! Now what? How does such knowledge help make better deals? Certain strategies work better under different size conditions. Several follow.

## What to Do when the Deal Is Large

The following should be done when the transaction is big:

Put your best people on the case.

Focus on the deal—don't be distracted by trivia.

Provide proper resources; recognize that investment is necessary and don't skimp on legal, accounting, and consulting fees.

Pay attention to details; small points in large deals can cost bundles.

Build human relationships; a light touch can ease protracted negotiations with heavy stakes. The high tension in huge mergers and acquisitions is reduced when opposing sides eat pepperoni pizzas together in all night sessions.

---

*Symbolism is especially critical in religious organizations. In a certain Bible-believing group the observance of a specific holy day (Pentecost) was changed from Monday to Sunday; the move was enormous, as was the prior controversy, since it represented biblical fidelity and a willingness to admit error, both of which were claimed as vital group attributes.

### What to Do when the Deal Is Small

The following should be done when the transaction is little:

Prime your negotiating team—it's easy to go into small deals unprepared.

Be sure your people do not consider the job beneath them; look for ways to show your team the importance of the deal.

Stay alert even if you aren't excited.

Give credit to your dealmakers; it's often just as hard to pull off a small deal as a large one.

### What to Do when a Corporate Deal Is Mismatched

Consider a situation where a large public corporation is negotiating to buy a small private company.

When you're the larger corporation, don't bully or condescend; treat your potential deal partners with dignity—after all, you want what they've got.

When you're the smaller company, don't cower or show anxiety; handle your suitors with equality—after all, you've got what they want.*

### What to Do when a Personal Deal Is Mismatched

Consider the relationship when superiors and subordinates make deals in the workplace, for example, the negotiation of salary or position.

Each side must maintain its mutual dignity. The superior's tactics must not intimidate or humiliate, and the subordinate's tactics must not embarrass or beguile.

---

*Bullying and cowering provoke equal and opposite reactions and are not conducive to making good deals. Bullying raises resisting hackles; cowering invites aggressive attack.

When you're the superior, use questions to draw out ideas, showing real interest in your subordinate's opinions.

When you're the subordinate, offer ideas and information, asserting confidence in your convictions.

Be careful that criticism is always constructive; the superior should not feel compelled to pull rank, the subordinate should not fear to be firm.

Each side should lead through proper example.

# What to Do?

You are the head of marketing and sales for a consumer product in a large manufacturing company. Your product broke all sales records this year but bonuses will be severely curtailed because the company as a whole had minimal profits. Furthermore, the prospects for next year look grim. Morale is starting to suffer. Your boss, the divisional vice president, states that while your department will not receive bonuses, you will be rewarded handsomely. What to do?

Incentive compensation is important for most employees, but it is critical for marketing and sales personnel. Without bonuses, your department could be decimated. Plan a twofold attack.

1. Suggest to your superior that your people will take *lower* base salaries next year if they can exceed even their normal bonuses with exceptional performance. The proviso is that the department's bonuses will be determined by its own performance, not the company's.

2. Take a chance. Distribute part of your personal bonus this year to your people. The size of the bonus will exceed its dollars. It will inspire employees and build personal loyalty. The combination will make waves and perhaps shake up senior management.

# 6 *DEAL SECRET*

# *Valuing the Stuff*

*WORTH IS IN THE WALLET OF THE HOLDER*

Vincent van Gogh produced over 800 paintings, but during his life-time he could only sell one—for $25. Recently, one of those unsold paintings sold for $40 million. So much for absolute value.

"Stuff" is the value and consideration being traded in a trans-action. Stuff is all kinds of things; in fact, it's anything changing hands in a deal. How you value stuff is important.

If beauty is in the eye of the beholder, then worth is in the wallet of the holder. Cash is about the only thing with a fixed value. The value of virtually everything else depends on who is the owner or poten-tial owner, what are the conditions, and who is the judge. Absolute value is a myth.

## *Principles of Relative Value*

Value is a moving target—subjective and ever changing. When, as well as who, affects outcome. Scarcity, need, and social values all

112

contribute to the perception of worth. I am reminded of Woody Allen's incisive insight in *Stardust Memories*. Allen plays an enormously successful filmmaker who has become rich and famous from making funny movies (semiautobiographical). When he meets a childhood friend who drives a cab, Allen consoles him by saying something like: "So our society puts high value on humor. If we were Apache Indians, I'd be at the bottom of the totem pole—jokes weren't important when chasing buffalo—and I can't ride a horse. . . ."

I like to define value relatively, in comparison with other things. In this sense, the real value of your stuff can be defined by the value of the other side's stuff. "How much is some *X* worth?" is not the best question. I prefer, "Which would you rather have, the stuff you're giving or the stuff you're getting?"

A good technique for valuing stuff is to ask yourself constantly which side of the trade you like better. Ask the question every time the deal changes. Another objective is to discover your *indifference point*—that special place where it doesn't matter whether you do the deal.

Relative value affects each side differently. One side may look simply at financial data—the generally accepted market value—while the other side may consider what business advantages it can gain by ownership.

Your task is to assess relative value on both sides. Get at underlying motivations. First, understand how your side values the stuff. Then, perceive how the other side does its valuing.

## Polarity of Value

In general, there are two categories for assigning value:

1. The positive benefits to be achieved by having or owning this stuff. (Obvious.)

2. The negative costs that can be avoided by not having or owning this stuff. (Less obvious.)

Each category has its own subtleties. Positive value means that you want to do the deal because, if you do, the stuff will increase your worth or wealth. A company whose high-growth division could command a massive multiple of earnings would sell for a premium price. Negative value means that you want to do the deal because, if you do not, the stuff will decrease your worth or wealth. A company whose cash-hungry division could drive it into bankruptcy would sell for a discounted price.

Desire, greed, and lust differ from fear, anxiety, and dread. Would you do a deal if you had 9 chances in 10 to make 20 times your annual salary but had 1 chance in 10 to lose your right arm? Most people would refuse (even lefties). What about 50 times your salary? A hundred times? A thousand times?

Most people are *risk averse;* that is, they would rather play it safer than mere odds would suggest. Avoiding negative threat, therefore, carries heavy weight in valuations.

## *Valuation Under Competition*

Bidding in auctions can be dangerous to your financial health. When a joint venture between Phillips Petroleum and Chevron won offshore drilling rights in 1981 they were shocked to discover that they paid more than double the next highest bid. The four other bids ranged from under $1 million to $161 million. These pros paid $333.6 million—$170 million more than necessary—and suffered what has become known as the winners curse among oil lease auction victors.

Research has shown that bidders are usually overconfident about their ability to assess value, often generating a huge gap between the highest and next highest bids. The phenomenon is strongest when involving unproven values (e.g., defense contracts for new technologies, leases in new shopping malls, and mineral rights). Factors affecting price, in addition to true value, include the number of bidders and the structure of the auction. Sealed bids with many bidders induce the wildest frenzy. (See Deal Secret 9.)

# Appraisal Process

Few things have an unconditionally fair value. Lots of values may be fair, although some may be more fair than others. It depends on whom you are asking and why you are asking them. In general, beware the appraisal process.

Appraisers have notorious reputations for skewing valuations according to their client's objectives. Purposes affect outcomes. Whether the appraisal is for sale purposes (on the upper hand) or tax purposes (on the lower hand) will influence how a real estate appraiser values a piece of property. When the government appropriates forest lands from a company, appraisers for each side make their best case. You can be sure the government's appraisers assign a far lower worth per acre than do the company's, even though both appraisers may be expert and honest. (Reverse the clients and watch those appraisals flip.) You get, it seems, what you pay for.

# What to Do: Corporate Example

I know a company that wanted to sell. How much should they ask? How should they establish the right purchase price? What to do?

We analyzed the business and categorized five kinds of buyers who would be interested in an acquisition—each would have a different number; each would use a different method.

1. *The cash-flow buyer* would look at the profits generated, targeting the net free cash; they wouldn't care one whit about the products, process, or people. They might offer $40 million for the steady stream of dollars.

2. *The asset-based buyer* would assess the fair market value for the company's net assets—the dollar amount of all assets sold off in orderly fashion minus all liabilities. They could offer $25 million for the liquidation rights.

3. *The replacement-value buyer* would consider what it would cost them to set up an equivalent facility, the production plants and marketing organization they needed. They could offer $50 million for fast and cheap entry into the business.

4. *The synergy-value buyer* would view what they could do with the company by integrating it into their own company, how the new entity would enjoy increased market share and lower average costs. They might offer $55 million for the increased effectiveness, efficiency, and market dominance.

5. *The defensive-value buyer* would envision what their rivals might do with the new business, controlling the market and driving others out. They could offer $60 million to keep competitors at bay. (Need I say which one we accepted?)

## What to Do: Personal Example

Let's go close-to-home—setting your salary at your job. Consider the five following methods of valuation. (Compare these categories with those in the corporate example.)

1. *A net-dollar-value salary* is pegged to the incremental gross profit—the fresh bottom-line dollars—that you bring into the company. A salesperson who could generate $3 million in new business might be worth $100,000+.

2. *A market-value salary* is a collective valuation of what people with your general skills and experience could expect to command in your field or industry. This valuation is *not* individual.

3. *A replacement-value salary* is the company's total cost of finding and paying someone else to do your job if you were no longer working. Job interruption costs (downtime on your tasks), job disruption costs (interference with the tasks of others), search expenses, and subsequent salary must be included.

4. *A synergy-value salary* is what a company would pay you considering the added benefits that other aspects of the company could derive from your talents and participation. For example, a salesperson

who covers Illinois for the shirt division of a large company might also be able to represent the suit division of the same company in the same region.

5. *A competitive-value salary* is what a competitor might pay you to join their firm. Your presence would not only help the new firm, your absence would also hurt the old one.

# 7 *DEAL SECRET*

# *Appraising the Stakes*

*STAKES VERY HIGH OR STAKES VERY LOW*
*MAKE DEALS VERY TRICKY*

Everything you do in deals is colored by relative significance. When stakes are high you act one way, when low another way. The gravity dictates attitudes and approaches.

Stakes are high when deal success would contribute dramatically to company progress or personal career. Stakes are also high when failure would severely undermine organizational viability or professional path.

## Anxiety and Stakes

Anxiety is a good indicator of stress and stakes. The degree of apprehension can signal the level of the deal's importance. Anxiety is a general sense of foreboding, an unspecific fear of the future. You are afraid, but you are not sure of what. Anxious behavior includes overeager reactions, exaggerated responses, and inappropriate demeanor.

People function best with moderate levels of anxiety, and worse with very high or very low levels.* High levels of anxiety disturb and distract. Low levels allow ramble and roam. Moderate anxiety is ideal. It is enough to maintain and preserve interest but not enough to sabotage and subvert attention.

## Stakeholder Analysis

Stakeholder analysis is a technique that helps analyze how each side views the deal. Uniformity is out. Neither side is considered homogenous; the parties are not all cut from the same cloth. Instead, each side is seen to be composed of individuals with special motives and interests. Thus each person has his or her own private agenda, a committed interest (or stake) that each group member maintains (or holds). Your task is to discern the special stake of each individual in order to determine the group's overall thrust. Organizational behaviorists believe that stakeholder analysis—getting at personal motivations—is vital for understanding why groups act the way they do.

## How to Judge the Stakes

Certain signals help in evaluating the stakes in deal making. Knowing these signs can give your side an advantage:

*Level of Key Person.* How high in the organization is the prime negotiator? The higher the person the higher the stakes.

---

*Proven by research in various areas of human performance, from athletic events to academic exams.

*Focus of Key Person.* How much attention does the prime negotiator give the deal? The greater the focus the higher the stakes.

*Level of Activity.* How responsive is the other side? Are your phone calls returned quickly? Are requests for information fulfilled promptly?

*Frequency of Meetings.* How often are meetings scheduled? When are the next steps planned? Do days float by without concrete progress?

*Degree of Pushiness.* Which side is setting the time schedules and deadlines? The active party generally has higher stakes.

*Conscious Behavior.* Are there any obvious signs of stress and anxiety, such as exaggerated reactions, hair-trigger tempers that are out of character, or wide (and wild) swings of moods?

*Unconscious Behavior.* Are there any telltale signs of stress and anxiety? Fidgety, nervous habits and rapid, high-pitched speech suggest very high or low stakes. (By the way, don't forget to monitor—and mask—your own reactions. The other side might have read this book, too.)

## When the Stakes Are High

When you play "bet the company" or "wager the career" on a particular deal, mental attitudes are complex. You are tough because the deal is important; you are soft because you fear the deal won't happen. Your posture can be volatile, with violent shifts in moods and positions.

As a result, you are likely to react quickly and simplistically to tricks and trades by the other side. Cool is hard to be when your feet are on fire.

When negotiating a high-stakes deal, concentrate on reducing your levels of stress and anxiety (if only their outward show.)

Slow down your speech

Do physical exercise to soak up that awkward energy

Use breathing exercises to induce relaxation

Try faking calmness; artificial serenity can induce real serenity

Stakes in a deal can be reduced by finding another option outside the deal. Assume the deal is broken and consider what to do next. Don't actually do anything, but think of alternative action. If you can develop independent choices, stakes lower, anxiety drops, and deal-making behavior improves.

## When the Stakes Are Low

When you do not care about a deal, you get sloppy. Lack of attention breeds mistakes of fact and errors of judgment. Control slips away and advantage is lost.

When deals degenerate, deals disrupt. Sometimes, in a belated attempt to salvage a decaying deal, the negotiator will make a sudden shift in position. Unfortunately, the surprise move may trigger outright rupture.

When negotiating a deal where the stakes are low, concentrate on raising your levels of stress and anxiety (if only their outward show).

Speed up lazy speech

Force yourself to pay strict attention to details

Don't dawdle over issues

Try faking fervor; artificial intensity can induce real intensity

If, however, you find it impossible to generate even modest anxiety, you may be the wrong person for the job. Find another person to negotiate the deal and find another deal for you to negotiate.

# What to Do?

How about playing some high-stakes corporate poker? At the table we find Pennzoil and Texaco squaring off. The game is five-card stud, four cards up, one hidden in the hole. Pennzoil is showing three-of-a-kind; Texaco is flaunting a possible flush. They're head-to-head, taunting and bluffing each other.

Pennzoil's legal judgment against Texaco for interrupting its deal with Getty is about $10 billion in claims and damages, the largest verdict in corporate history. Tough talk of huge security demands blasts forth from Pennzoil. Dark threats of bankruptcy filings emanate from Texaco. Relativity plays a role here, and the game is an artful one. For Pennzoil, it's a bonanza; the issue is how big. For Texaco, it's life and death; the issue is survival. What to do?

Strangely, the interests of both companies should suggest settling the suit. Both sides have too much to lose by not agreeing out of court. Texaco is not without resources nor is Pennzoil without fear. Let's see why.*

If Pennzoil does not settle, one of two things could happen: (1) Texaco could declare bankruptcy and Pennzoil would become just one of many unsecured creditors embroiled in a legal miasma or (2) a subsequent judicial appeal could overturn the verdict and Pennzoil would wind up with nothing. Furthermore, it is unlikely that Pennzoil would ever get everything. So Pennzoil should be highly motivated to settle, not gamble.

If Texaco does not settle, Pennzoil could win the appeal and exact the full $10 billion plus accumulated interest, virtually gobbling up Texaco in the process. Even if this worst case scenario does not happen, it is likely that Pennzoil would get more through the courts

---

*The situation is illustrative of game theory in action. Game theory is a method of using formal mathematical analysis to select the best available strategy in order to maximize one's potential gain and/or minimize one's potential losses under various circumstances and conditions. Applications range from battlefield strategy in warfare to pricing strategy in business.

than in a settlement. Thus Texaco, too, should be highly motivated to settle, not gamble.*

* *Note:* Following the failure of final negotiations between Texaco and Pennzoil, including face-to-face meetings between their chief executives, Texaco filed for protection from all creditors under Chapter 11 of the Federal Bankruptcy Code. Texaco, the United States' eighth-largest industrial company and its third-largest oil company, has become the largest bankruptcy in history. The court proceedings will be monstrously complex, the legal maneuverings tortured and twisted. Whereas all reason had demanded mutual agreement, the two oil giants were reduced to trading charges of greed and arrogance while the stock of both companies plummeted. There is no doubt that each firm is now far worse off—Texaco's business is debilitated and Pennzoil is scrambling to protect its rights in the overwhelmed courts. Logic had screamed "Settle!"—both companies would have been better served. (In a Chapter 11, the only real victors are the lawyers.) But logic, as we've seen, does not reign freely in organizations. Suffice it to say that managerial ego upstaged stockholder interests on both sides. There is no other conclusion. No matter the ultimate outcome, the risks were just not worth the rewards.

# 8 _DEAL SECRET_

# Establishing the Positions

_INITIAL POSITIONS SET CONSTANT TONE_

Most positions are predictable. An athlete coming off a brilliant season makes noises about contract problems. TASS, the Soviet Union's news service, reports the U.S. position to be "reactionary and imperialistic." The White House considers the Soviet position to be "propaganda and nothing new."

Establishing position is the opening engagement in a negotiating campaign. First posture is like an imprint, a permanent pattern of behavior. It sets the stage for subsequent conduct. Relationships are formed early. Once imprints are stamped they are difficult to alter.

Establishing deal-making positions for humans is akin to securing territorial control for animals. Consider a dominion battle between two male chimpanzees for regional rule (the area being marked off by urine). Who will take the lead? Who will mate the females? Once dominance and recessiveness are set, each chimp maintains its assigned role. (Now I do not mean to imply that dealmakers are apes, but those not-too-infrequent "pissing contests" among lawyers make one wonder. . . .)

## Positioning the Other Side

Establishing proper initial position is critical. It sets a mood that generally does not change during the rest of the negotiations. Initial positions are not set in the dark. Deals are not blind dates. Each side considers the other before going into the first meeting. It is important to know your opponents, understand their relationship to you, and have a general sense of how you are going to act with them.

1. *When Dealing with Equals.* Be open and direct. Build subtle dominance by aggressive concern for mutual interests (such as schedule, procedure, etc.). Control is achieved more easily by process assistance (e.g., setting the agenda) than by position assertion (e.g., insisting on your price).

2. *When Dealing with Superiors.* Confident respect is the key here. Your power is inferior and, face facts, it will remain so. A forced aggressiveness is at best shallow and at worst silly. A strong, friendly attitude is what you want to project.

3. *When Dealing with Subordinates.* Be respectful and listen seriously. Draw them out when they are not communicating forthrightly. Avoid haughty disdain or put-on deference. Maximize your superior position by not making it obvious.

4. *When Dealing with Buyers, Clients, and Customers.* Here's heresy: The power of buyers is overrated. The buyers' job is to buy. If they don't buy, they lose their job. After all, their firm needs what your firm has. Your relationship with buyers should be viewed this way: You enable buyers to keep their jobs.

5. *When Dealing with Sellers, Vendors, and Suppliers.* Now you write the check. You wield the Big Pencil, that fabled instrument of order-writing fame. You need to know your relative power versus that of other customers. However strong you are, never bully. A hand on the shoulder always beats a twist of the arm. Show your vendor the

importance of the relationship. Dangling this carrot—confidence in continuing business—will improve your position.

Remember, personality colors deals. Friendly, personable stances usually work better. Memorize first names. Effective dealmakers don't take themselves too seriously. Attitude is especially important when setting forth initial positions.

## After You, Please

A prime rule of deal making is, *"Always let the other side move first."* Maybe, if you're the buyer, the seller will set an initial price lower than what you would have offered. Maybe, if you're the seller, the buyer will offer an initial price higher than you would have set. You'll never know if you go first. You can't lose by not going first. If the other side's number is ludicrously out of line, you can always dismiss it with a laugh. This flips the question back to them.

A second rule is, *"Never bid against yourself."* Anxious buyers often get caught in the trap of increasing their offers when there are no other serious players in the game. The best antidote for this poison is patience. Wait a while before responding to a rejection of your last bid. Don't be quick to modify and change. Good sellers make an art of encouraging qualified buyers to up their offers.

## Aim for the Best Deal

You can't get across the street without walking across the road. Words of wisdom. The deal-making philosopher is Richard Grassgreen, president of Kindercare, Inc., the country's largest operator of day-care centers. He states that when he sends naive employees out to negotiate rental of a new location, they sometimes can get a better price than the experts. Comments Grassgreen, "They didn't know what they couldn't do. And they weren't afraid to ask." Asking is easy, it's cheap—and you can always say you were kidding. Too many people forget to ask.

There's another side to this tactic. If you take too aggressive an initial position, you run the risk of scaring off the other side. Sometimes buyers bid so far from reality that sellers think that the buyers are either (1) incapable of evaluating the situation and therefore not worth wasting time with or (2) downright insulting and not worth doing business with.

There are two ways of balancing these extreme positions.

1. Know the other side—the characters, their desire for the deal, and their other alternatives.

2. Ask high, but do it with a twinkle. Make that an enigmatic twinkle. Put a pixieish sparkle in your eyes, a Mona Lisa smile on your lips. A quixotic grin can mean either "Don't take me too seriously" (if the offer is outrageous) or "You can really hit this pitch" (if the offer is in the ballpark).

# When You Must Go First

Sometimes you can't avoid making the first offer. So maximize the positive benefits of going first. You control the opening issues and attitudes. It is in your power to decide what matters will be discussed and where initial negotiations will focus. For example, if you make an offer that allows something other than full cash payment up front, it makes a statement.

If standard terms in your industry are "net 30 days," and your initial offer is "net 90 days," you make terms and dating a real issue. If you make such an offer as the vendor, you may couple it with a higher than normal price. You are constructing a deal responsive to your customer's current cash bind, and the increased purchase price reflects not only the payment delay but also the inherent risk.

## When You Can Go Second

Counterpunching is always easier than throwing the first blow. You can see the specific interests of the other side. You now have great insight into their approach.

If, for example, they play lowball, you have a choice of responses: highball (an equal and opposite reaction), a mild laugh (as if to say, "That's funny, now let's get serious"), or a more formal dismissal ("There's no sense in countering").

If their first offer is reasonable, you again have a choice:

> You can play hardball and pretend that the offer is lowball, choose from the above responses, and await further developments. Maybe they'll go up.

> You can respond in kind. This is a better tactic. You want to make many deals, not exact every last cent from one deal. After all, you might be back for another bite.*

## When You're Exploring Boundaries

Making deal proposals that push limits must be done with care. You must avoid antagonism and quick rupture of relationships. A good approach is to vary one part of the deal at a time, while holding all other parts constant. Try to frame your offer in the context of honest inquiry.

For example, after discussing a complex deal that has many elements of consideration to be paid over long periods of time, switch

---

*I like the other side to do well. It's not pleasurable for me to find, after making a deal, that the other side paid too much as a buyer. If the other side received too little as seller, well, I must admit, that bothers me less. Why the double standard? When a buyer pays too much, they have the continuing burden of making the damn thing work. When a seller gets too little, that's a one-time event with few subsequent pains. I'm not sure my thinking's logical but that's the way I feel.

to all cash: "Let's say we could pay everything in hard dollars. How much could you reduce the price if we snap all greenbacks at closing?" This gives insight into the importance of cash and the lowest possible price within reason.

Conversely, a seller might switch from insistence on all cash at closing to very favorable terms. How much could the seller raise prices by giving such advantageous conditions? If the buyer can and will give acceptable guarantees, and if the seller does not need as much cash, such a deal could be better for both buyer and seller.

# When in Competition

### As Buyer

Buyers have two simple objectives:

Not getting knocked out early
Smoking out competitors' offers

When you're a buyer competing with others, offer a fat price—but with the open understanding that your numbers are subject to further analysis and checking. The seller has nothing to worry about because if everything turns out as claimed the higher price will be justified. (In reality, you can always find something wrong). Your juicy offer will keep you actively in the game, and may even scare off some competitors.

### As Seller

Sellers, too, have two simple objectives:

Keeping as many bidders as active as possible
Discovering the hottest candidates

Sellers might consider proposing a slightly lower price and then observing the reactions of potential buyers. If the price is like chum before sharks, and buyers start swirling around you in a craze, then you know you can really land a big one—and at an inflated price. Again, do not deceive. Put out your offer in a contingent manner: "Suppose we set a price of X; what would be your reaction?" You can then inform buyers that, on further reflection, your trial price was low. You hope that the blood-dazed predators hardly notice the difference. (See Deal Secret 28.)

## When You Really Mean It

Have no illusions: No one is going to believe that your first offer is your final offer. It's like bluffing in poker. You must go all the way a few times before anyone will take you seriously. Once in a while, you must stick to your guns.

Assume you have no flexibility whatsoever on a particular deal point. How do you build credibility if you've already modified other deal points? One strategy might be to tackle another, rather minor issue first and prove to the other side that you really mean it when you say that your first offer is "all she wrote."

## What to Do?

You are up against a real character. She is capricious and testy and her only consistency in deal making is making constant changes. She never actually lies, though she comes awfully close, and you can never seem to get a straight answer out of her. Unfortunately, her offer is the best you've got going. How to cage this bird? What to do?

A formal approach is the prescription here. Precision is necessary. Set strict ground rules at (or before) the first session. Insist that all offers be communicated in writing. React forthrightly to anything in print, but do not respond seriously to anything verbal. Allow trial balloons to float harmlessly into the wind, dismissed with mild humor. Suppose she says, "What would you do if we reduced our notes a bit, but made up for it by increasing the interest rate?" Your response might be, "I would look forward to reading a memo on the subject, with all the blanks filled in fully and fairly."

# 9 *DEAL SECRET*

# *Getting the Price*

*GETTING YOUR PRICE MEANS MAKING YOUR DEAL*

When asked why he was making more money than the president of the United States, Babe Ruth replied, "I had a better year."

Price is the crux of all deals. It is the way we keep score. Although price seems simple, straightforward, and easy to evaluate, it is not.

## How to Get Your Price as Seller

### How to Determine Price

The market generally sets the prices, but you do not have to be straitjacketed by the market. (Sure, if you're selling a commodity, the exact same stuff everyone else is selling, the market governs.) First, determine the selling price for products like yours. Next, you must position your specific stuff. Some aspects that boost the price are: brand recognition, special features, quality, custom design, and the like. Perceived value (e.g., Porsche 928S vs. Ford Mustang) makes for higher pricing.

### How to Differentiate Your Product

Your goal is to sustain maximum market share within a limited market. Seek control of a niche. In other words, be a big fish in a little pond. The way to do this is by making your stuff different. If you're the same, you get the same price. If your product is recognizably different, you can get a better price.

The key to making your products different is segmentation—carving out a particular area where you can claim uniqueness. Any uniqueness. It doesn't matter whether you differentiate by size, category, distribution system, varieties, quality, or customer. It doesn't matter which you choose. Any difference, if perceived to be important to the buyer, can command a higher price. Products must be tailored tightly to the market.

Assume you make furniture. There are lots of furniture manufacturers around. How to differentiate? Specialize. There are a thousand ways. Maybe you can serve a particular industry, such as banking. Maybe you can import from Scandinavia.

### How to Stimulate Bids

Shopping around without revealing your game is the best way to stimulate bids. Don't give the impression of handling picked-over merchandise. When it becomes known in Hollywood that a script is making the rounds of the studios no one will touch it—after all, who wants to be last in line? The same is true when selling a business. Pick your targets carefully.

When working with interested parties, get a bid—any bid. The only way to find the market is with real numbers. Your objective is to get the highest number on the table. Thus prospective buyers should be told that their bids should assume "everything presented is perfectly true." These bids are not morally or legally binding. Buyers can do their detailed analysis later and make any changes they want.

### How to Raise Prices

A positive change in your product should be made at the same time you raise the price.* The change doesn't have to be big, but customers and prospective buyers should feel they are getting something for their extra cash. For example, 2 percent of a 7 percent price increase should be plowed back into the product in a visible way (e.g., a slight redesign, some fresh colors, or a little extra service).

### How to Use Terms

Is it worth trading off better terms for the buyer in exchange for a higher price for the seller? For example, if a buyer is allowed to extend dating from "net 30 days" to "net 90 days," the seller can up the price. The seller must be compensated for the cost of money and the additional burden of carrying the longer receivable.

## How to Get Your Price as Buyer

### How to Determine Price

Shop around. The market is key. Compare all aspects of the products, not just the price. The cheapest products are not always the ones with the lowest price tags. For instance, the cost of financing the deal as well as any warranties and service responsibility should be figured into your price comparisons.

### How to Make Your Bids

Make an offer that you would love to be accepted. Judge the situation. If you're hot for the deal, make a reasonable first offer. If you're

---

*The opposite is devastating. Everytime a favorite restaurant kicks up prices, it seems, food quality falls flat. Is it my imagination? I think the same profit squeeze that triggers the price hike also provokes cost cuts. Unfortunately, you taste the latter while paying the former.

unsure, throw out a red herring. You never know who may bite. Don't be afraid to discuss your offer over and over again. The more you talk the more you learn.

### How to Adjust Prices

Every offer is made subject to appropriate due diligence. Deals should be bid as if everything presented is absolutely correct. Thus a fat first offer encourages the seller that the bidder is a prime candidate. The process may even drive out some competitors. Then, after making a detailed analysis, you can always change your mind ("take a haircut" or "move South" in deal-making parlance).

### How to Improve Terms

As discussed in Deal Skill 10, "your price, my terms" is a deal-maker's maxim. Deal terms are as important as price to the buyer.* The opposite is often true (at least psychologically) for the seller. Sellers like to brag about the price they got. Cater to this tendency: Trade off higher prices for better terms.

# When Parties Compete

Competition is great when you're a seller, not so when you're a buyer. The same tricks, I'm pleased to report, work in both situations.

### When Buying

As a buyer, never bid against yourself. Many buyers have upped their offers when no other parties were even in the running. Look for

---

*You'd be happy to pay a full asking price as long as it required little money down, all financed by the seller, and all cash payments to come from the company. If you could buy a business strictly from the cash flow of that business, say within four years, then no price, if you think about it, is too high.

situations where the sellers will acknowledge that your party is the only bidder. "Let's do a negotiated deal," you would say. "Let's proceed in good faith. If we can't reach a good deal for both of us, we'll back off with nothing lost." If necessary, agree to a time limit. Stretch as far as possible to eliminate competition.

### When Selling

As seller, try to deal with several interested (or, better yet, anxious) suitors simultaneously. Having other options around makes you a more confident negotiator. Alternatives stiffen backbones. Furthermore, there's a strange phenomenon in the buying and selling game. The great majority of offers cluster, as you'd expect, within a tight range. But then there are usually one or two outliers, parties who for their own reasons bid significantly higher. Your task is to find these fine folks.

# Buying and Selling in Auctions

### Bidding Theory

Recent research has confirmed what canny traders have known for some time: Most bidders in auctions harbor inflated opinions of their own judgment of value. Though they may do detailed analyses, the bottom line is that they generally go with their intuitions. Instincts lead the charge, and more often than not, it's a slaughter for the buyer (and a windfall for the seller).

New theory in bidding psychology shows that the structure of auctions molds strategies and influences behavior.* Major companies are monitoring the progress.

---

*Generating the highest bids from the seller's viewpoint depends on the characteristics of the assets being auctioned. If demand is not sensitive to price (inelastic), the highest price is produced by a normal auction in which the highest bidder pays the price he or she offered. If, however, demand is highly sensitive to price (elastic), then a "second-price" auction is recommended for the seller's benefit. Here the top bidder pays the price offered by the runner up. Buyer psychology encourages inflating the price since each buyer knows that he or she will not

### How to Handle Auctions as Sellers

**When to Auction Deals.** When you have an especially hot property, the rules change. Now you're in the driver's seat. Make wide contacts. Establish a date for bids to be submitted.

**Seller's Auction Strategy.** The optimal strategy for soliciting bids includes the following steps:

Encourage the maximum number of bidders; the greater the number of participants the higher the winning bid.

Make available before the auction as much information as possible about the object or asset to be auctioned. Trust the marketplace to squeeze out any windfall profits—but only if all relevant data is widely distributed to all potential bidders.

Do not give away any information about the bidders before the auction. Avoid all actions that will reveal the number, nature, or strategies of the rival bidders (e.g., use no prequalification procedures; keep your bidders totally blind).

Do not give away any information after the auction. Avoid giving bidders any hint of their competitors' strategies. (This applies both to second-round bids or future auctions.)

Consider a second round. This is delicate. Allow those bidders that came close to sweeten their offers. Since the first round winner would scream like hell, don't announce who won. Do not disclose the winning bid, either. However, a new floor for the final round should be established.

### How to Handle Auctions as Buyers

**When to Participate in Auctions?** Auctions should be avoided whenever possible. Only bid when you have specific competitive advan-

---

have to pay his or her own high price if he or she wins. Since all buyers think the same, the overall price pushes up. To demonstrate that different auction structures produce different results, Charles Plott of the California Institute of Technology auctioned off a dollar bill. How to get more than 100 cents? If the dollar is given to the highest bidder, but the second highest must pay for it, bidding skyrocketed (above $1.00!) since everyone had an incentive to outbid rivals.

---

tage. For example, an operating company that knows it can bring substantial new business to the firm being auctioned has an edge over an investment company looking purely at that firm's current cash flow. The operating company can afford to make a higher offer and still generate a similar return.

**Buyer's Auction Strategy.** The optimal strategy for making bids includes the following steps:

Only participate when the number of bidders is relatively small. Some companies will not even enter auctions with more than five hats in the ring.

Seek some competitive edge in the bidding. For example, look for synergies with your current operations. Or try to get special information about the object or asset to be auctioned. If you cannot go into the auction with some sort of comparative advantage, forget it.

Learn as much as possible before the auction about the number, nature, or strategies of the rival bidders. Put yourself in their shoes and plan alternative scenarios.

Learn as much as possible after the auction about your competitors' strategies. This will prove useful when bidding against the same rivals again, and it will be a benchmark against which to judge your own preauction evaluation techniques.

## Making Sure Buyers and Sellers Can Deliver

The most frustrating experience is to cut a good deal with a party that can't produce. You must establish confidence in the other side's credibility. Sometimes, the parties with the lowest credibility offer the best deals. This is logical, since weaker buyers must offer sellers something special to compensate for the uncertainty. Don't dismiss these flakes too quickly. They may be hungry enough to belly up to the table.

You always want to know how much the buyer can pay. It's like children selling candy to each other. "How much does the Mars Bar cost?" asked the wide-eyed six-year-old. "How much do you have in your pocket?," answered the street-smart eight-year-old.

## What to Do?

George Morgenstern, president of Defense Software and Systems Inc., is a remarkable man. An ordained rabbi in the Orthodox tradition, he has been a leading computer consultant for major U.S. military contractors for 25 years. Morgenstern is largely credited with introducing Talmudic scholars to computer programming as a profession, both in the United States and in Israel. ("There are three things similar between Talmudic learning and software programming," says Morgenstern. "One, you need to have a keen, analytical mind. Two, you need to be able to put up with some off-the-wall ideas. Three, you need to be able to sit on your rear end for a dozen hours straight.")

The story of how Morgenstern established his company in Israel (Decision Systems), today perhaps that country's leading defense-oriented software firm, is a story of price. It seems that after several years of consulting for the Israeli government, largely for no remuneration, Morgenstern was asked to set up a more formal operation to handle a specific aerospace contract.

Now this was different. He would have to pay employees and carry overheads. So for the first time, he would have to present a price for the contract. But how much to charge? What to do?

Morgenstern bid the contract essentially at cost. He was not a wealthy man, but this was his way of contributing to the homeland of his people. However, his proposal was rejected by the government officials. Why? It was not too high, they said, but too low. One wise man counseled:

> George, you *must* make a profit. Not for your sake but for ours. We need you to work on these projects. And while we can't be sure that your Zionism will remain as fervent in the future, we can be very sure that your interest in profits won't change.

# 10 DEAL SECRET

# Learning the Opening Game

*THERE IS NO SUBSTITUTE FOR PREPARATION*

What marvelous analogies come from chess! "Chess is life" expound the grandmasters, who speak of the "essence of a bishop" and the "elegance of a sacrifice." No grandmaster, it is said, has ever lost a game when feeling well.

Chess games are divided into three parts: the opening game, the middle game, and the end game. Each part, with its special attributes, teaches specific lessons about deal making. Each will be discussed in its own chapter.

1. *The opening game* is the first few moves in which all the pieces are put into play. Good opening-game strategy is characterized by well-prepared themes and variations.

2. *The middle game* is the play with the major pieces on the board. Good middle-game strategy is characterized by plans projected out many moves deep, positional strength, combinations, sacrifices, and mating attacks.

3. *The end game* begins when the major pieces come off the board. Here, through the promotion of pawns to queens, small advantages are transformed into winning positions. Good end-game strategy is characterized by precise calculations of tempo and timing.

## Kinds of Chess Openings

In chess, openings are patterns of moves. There are dozens of different openings with wonderfully colorful names.* There are also hundreds of variations which sport their own personalities.† Each of these patterns of moves has clear advantages and disadvantages— with the boundary between brilliance and blunder often being subtle. The same is true of deal making.

Gambits are important in both chess and deal making. A gambit gives up something, such as a pawn (in essence a fetal queen), to gain position and mobility. A gambit is a risk, trading something tangible for something intangible. If there's little compensation, if your opponent's pawn advantage is maintained to the end, you face a lost position.

Surprise is an important opening ploy. Shock can often overwhelm a superior system. Say your opponent chooses an older, inferior opening. If you haven't prepared for it and your opponent has, you could be in trouble. See an analogy to deal making?

## Principles of the Opening Game

There are certain ideas behind good chess openings. These principles correspond directly to deal making.

---

*Names are given for people (e.g., Morphy Attack, Evans Gambit, Reti Opening, Colle System, Falkbeer Counter-Gambit), countries (e.g., English Opening, Sicilian Defense, French Defense), and positions (e.g., Giuco Piano, King's and Queen's Indian, King's Gambit, Queen's Gambit Declined, Hypermodern).

†For example, the Sicilian Defense has numerous variations, including the Dragon, the Moscow, the Najdorf, the Scheveningen, and the Nimzowitsch.

1. *Develop Pieces Efficiently.* Each move should bring out a new piece. Developing your pieces by attacking your opponent's pieces is efficient. If the other side must defend after each move, he or she is less likely to develop an attack. Good dealmakers optimize their resources.

2. *Put Pieces on Good Squares.* Positioning of pieces is vital. Maximize move-making mobility.* Know the value of each piece in your arsenal. Good dealmakers understand how best to take advantage of their capabilities.

3. *Pieces Should Work Together.* Synergy is important.† Good dealmakers appreciate how their resources combine for maximum effectiveness.

4. *Control the Center.* Center control is the most important early principle. The greater your control of the center, the greater space for your pieces, and the more constricted the space for your opponent's. An offensive posture is always more desirable. Good dealmakers know that control of central issues is a critical factor for success.

5. *Protect the King.* The king is your vital piece. Lose it and you lose the game. What cannot be lost must be constantly protected. Good dealmakers never neglect their bottom-line vulnerability.

## Kinds of Deal Openings

Try the following openings of the deal-making game. (I've had some fun with these.)

> *Ronald Reagan Center Game.* Friendly and compelling. Moves are made for show and image, not content and substance.

---

*Knights, for example, should be positioned near the center, not the edge of the board (since they can jump over other pieces). Bishops, on the other hand, can rake the board from the edges, and should not be blocked by pawns.

†For example, lining up or connecting rooks reinforces their strength. Bishop pairs on long diagonals can skewer opposing pieces and dominate the board. Pawns should support one another on adjacent files.

*Cary Grant Suave Game.* Cultured and urbane. Moves are made to exude graciousness and charm.

*Jackie Kennedy Onassis System.* Elegant and refined. Moves are made for polished manners and social standing.

*Carl Sagan System.* Erudite and understandable. Moves are made to make hard concepts easy to digest.

*Don Rickles Attack.* Insulting and cutting. Moves are made to irritate and offend.

*Charles Bronson Attack.* Brutal and solitary. Moves are made to blow you away.

*Mr. T. Attack.* Intimidating and coercive. Moves are made to bounce you around.

*J.R. Ewing Gambit.* Tough and sneaky. Moves are made behind your back.

*Muammar Khaddafy Gambit.* Wild and dangerous. Moves are made without concern for consequences.

*Sylvester Stallone Gambit.* Powerful but superficial. Moves are made to accomplish simple purposes.

*Yogi Berra Countergambit.* Odd and wise. Moves are made that appear silly but contain real insight.

*Woody Allen Countergambit.* Witty and wise. Moves are made to convey profound truth in a lighthearted manner.

*Johnny Carson Defense.* Light and easy. Moves are made to put you asleep.

*Leonid Brezhnev Defense.* Stoic and blunt. Moves are made to maintain an iron curtain.

*Nikita Khrushchev Defense.* Boorish and uncouth. Moves are made to irritate and affront.

*Rodney Dangerfield Defense.* Hesitant and self-conscious. Moves are made with worry and uncertainty—sure not to get any respect.

# *What to Do?*

"You're in trouble, kid," said the high-pressure lawyer, barely concealing his glee. It was my first big business deal, certainly my first exposure to the tortuous maze of tax-loss law. I was sitting, by myself, in a large conference room of a major New York law firm, surrounded, it seemed, by all the attorneys infesting Park Avenue. I felt instant empathy with the gladiators of ancient Rome, alone in the arena encompassed by wild beasts.

My naiveté was as evident as an open zipper and I was being hustled by real pros. If I didn't virtually give my company away, I was warned, I could lose it all. (I didn't and I didn't, but that's another story.) If making me worry was the theme of their show, it was a smashing success. Their carrot-and-stick negotiating posture skewed well more to witches than to rabbits. What to do?

My problem was preparation, or more precisely, the lack of it. I like learning from others, but not, I quickly realized, from a dozen hostile lawyers smelling blood. The solution was to plan ahead of time, be prepped in the topic, and bring along expert counsel to even up the odds.

**11**

# Imaging the Middle Game

*ALWAYS CHECK, IT MAY BE MATE*

Let's start with a surprise: The trick in good deal making is often not what tactic you use but how well you use it. Specific strategy sometimes doesn't matter. Making that strategy work is what counts. It's like the middle game in chess where there are numerous strategies from which to choose. How well you execute the strategy is more important than which one you pick. Implementation, in other words, is more critical than formulation.

The current world champion of chess, Gari Kasparov of the Soviet Union, is a dynamic player known for explosive attacks that border on the reckless. The former world champion, Anatoly Karpov, also of the Soviet Union, is a positional player known for a suffocating style that has been likened to that of a boa constrictor. Kasparov is electrifying but erratic. Karpov is dull but consistent. The Super Ks are, without doubt, the two best players in the world. Their strategies differ widely, yet both are world class. Likewise in deal making: First-rate dealmakers evince diversity of strategy but commonality of excellence.

# Strategies for the Middle Game

The following strategic ideas fit the middle game. The general idea is to meld consistency and creativity in driving toward success. Most of these strategies can work together.

1. *Complete Development.* Finish the process begun in the opening. Get all your pieces activated; get all your issues on the table; get all your resources working as a unit. Be sure all moves support a clear plan.

2. *Plan an Attack.* Determine the best approach for mounting an offensive, whether a direct assault against the opponent's primary sticking point (such as price) or an indirect foray on an opposing flank (such as timing). In chess, the strategic decision is when to go after the king. In deal making, it's whether to go after vital or peripheral issues first.

3. *Combinations.* Look for ways and means to combine your resources. Moves must be thought through carefully. In chess, take advantage of the particular attribute of each piece. In deal making, it's the special character of each issue. Discover how several separate issues might be solved in one overall solution.*

4. *Sacrifices.* In chess, watch for unique opportunities where giving up a valuable piece can produce quick victory, normally by exposing the king's defensive position. The victory needs to be swift, since you are now down substantial material and would eventually lose if the position becomes simplified. In deal making, sacrifices are strategic concessions. Watch for unique opportunities where giving something up can induce swift closure on favorable terms. Maybe a sudden swing on price can cut through a morass of tangled problems.

5. *Develop Complications.* If you have the superior position, seek ways to increase complexity. In chess, a superior position is better-placed pieces, more focused resources, and more board control. In

---

*For example, consider a deal where the buyer does not want to pay the seller's price of $105 million, and the seller does not like taking back $20 million (of the $105) in long-term, high-risk notes. A proposed solution is to lower the amount to $92.5 million and make it all in cash. The buyer is pleased to save $12.5 million in value; the seller is pleased to get $7.5 million in cash.

deal making, it's less necessity to make the deal, larger size, and lower stakes. Here, for example, you should add additional issues and factors. Do not allow simplification.

6. *Simplify the Position.* If you have the inferior position, seek ways to decrease complexity. In chess, an inferior position is poorly placed pieces, dispersed resources, and less board control. In deal making, it's greater necessity to make the deal, smaller size, and higher stakes. Here, for example, you should eliminate current issues by exchanging or trading them off. Do not allow complications.

7. *Prepare for the End Game.* Few grandmaster matches end in the middle game. Few deals are consummated at this point, either. A concluding handshake with a room full of issues is rare. Instead, the preparations that begin in the middle of negotiations are what win the close. The key is to think out where you want to end up. Imaging the future is vital.

# Deal Tactics of the Middle Game

1. *Relative Value of Pieces.** Understand the comparative value of your issues and resources, strengths and weaknesses, so that you can trade them to your advantage. In deal making, however, there is no nice point system to count on your fingers. However, if you think in terms of relative value of issues, it can guide the trading process.

2. *Patterns and Positions.*† Familiarity with various deal positions is vital. Develop (1) a sense of circumstance and (2) limits around critical problems. Avoid being suckered by high pressure.

3. *Deep Calculations.*** Determining moves in deals is much the

---

*In chess it's easy; there's a point count to help: queens, 9; rooks, 5; bishops, 3¼; knights, 3; and pawns, 1. You would therefore exchange your queen and one knight (which total 12 points) for your opponent's 2 rooks and 1 bishop (13¼), but not your rook and 2 pawns (7) for two knights (6).

†Familiarity with various positions of pieces is vital. Develop a sense of position. Look for "mating nets" around the opposing king. Avoid "fool's mate" on your king.

**Determining moves in chess is simple to say, hard to do. What do I do, you ask yourself, if I make move X and my opponent makes move Y? You consider a move, then consider the various possible replies of your opponent, then your possible responses to each of those replies, same as in chess. You consider (1) a move, (2) your opponent's possible replies, and (3) your possible answers to each of those replies, and so on. You must learn to weed out the least likely scenarios quickly and concentrate on the most likely.

4. *Active People.** You want your people to be hard workers, doing all the things of which they are capable. Each element of deal making should be used where it works best: flexibility in the opening to build rapport, complexity in the middle game to add opportunity, and firmness in the end game to close the deal.

5. *Multiple Attacks.*[†] Applying multiple attacks to deal making can stimulate creativity. Two examples: "Pins," finding issues that your opponent can't be tough on for fear of uncovering a worse situation (e.g., a selling company might readily agree to pay extra money to eliminate a liability exposure for fear that the actual liability may be far more extensive); double attacks, simultaneously addressing more than one issue (e.g., giving your kids a weekly allowance can eliminate all disputes over financing their movies, new clothes, parties, etc.). Stress the strategy: Whenever you find a pinned issue, attack it! Whenever you can handle two issues at once, do it!

## What to Do?

A small company is willing to pay an excellent price for a group of businesses that would give them vital synergies, but they don't have

---

and so on. The variations branch rapidly and become impossibly complex. Assume that there are 10 reasonable moves for each side on every turn. This means, since each side must move on each turn, that considering your options just *six* moves out requires analyzing $10^{12}$ positions, or one *trillion* possible positions. (Incredibly, there are over $10^{115}$ possible 40-move games, far greater than the number of atomic particles in the universe.) The only solution is to limit drastically the options that you consider. Look at only the most likely. Which to study and which to ignore? This is where experience comes in.

*You want your pieces to be hard workers, doing all the things of which they are capable. Knights, remember, jump over other pieces, so they're especially valuable when the board is crowded. Bishops skewer like a sword, and work well with wide-open spaces. Rooks love to connect, especially on the seventh rank deep in your opponents camp.

[†]Pins, forks, double attacks, and discovered checks are chess tactics. A "pin" is when a piece can't move because if it does a more valuable piece will be lost (the strategy is to attack a

the financial horsepower to pull the whole thing off. The seller likes the buyer's valuation and enthusiasm. What to do?

Appreciate the common position, especially the relative power of the pieces in play. The seller should consider breaking up the businesses. The buyer should consider down-scaling objectives to purchase several but not all of the divisions. This is a deal that should be made: The price is too good for the seller, and the need too strong for the buyer.

---

pinned piece). A "double attack" is when a piece attacks two valuable pieces at the same time (and often it is impossible to defend them both). A "fork" is when a knight is the double attacker. A "discovered check" is a direct attack on the king by a piece that occurs when an interfering piece is moved out of the way. A discovered check is very powerful since it allows the moving piece a free move (say to attack a queen), since the king must be protected on the next move. In chess you are always on search for multiple attacks—to attack with or defend against.

# *12* DEAL SECRET

# Calculating the End Game

*TEMPO, NOT TEMPER*

In deal making, closing is what counts. You can be brilliant in finding, selecting, and structuring deals—but none of that matters if you can't finish them off.

In chess, the end game begins when all the heavy pieces (queens and rooks) are off the board. In deal making, the end game begins when most major issues are resolved. End game play takes on a different character. It must be very precise.

## Ideas for the End Game

1. *Wins* occur when you have clear superiority in material or position. At this point, it's all a matter of technique. In chess, exchange pieces—since the fewer pieces on the board the larger your advantage becomes. In deal making, trade out all remaining issues quickly.

Press your advantage with care. In deals, winning positions can be blown by high-handed manner.

2. *Forced wins* occur when you totally control the situation no matter what the other side does. In chess, it's just a matter of demonstrating your checkmate. In deal making, such occurrences are exceedingly rare, and flaunting your position can ruin it.

3. *Draws* are when the game is ended even. In chess, draws are declared when one side offers and the other accepts. (Protocol dictates that the side with the slight advantage should offer the draw.) Draws are usually duds in chess, though important when needed to clinch match victory. In deal making, draws occur when negotiations end in a tie. Draws are not duds in deals: If they mean closure, they are good; however, you may be disappointed if you sought more gain than you got.

4. *Forced draws** occur when any of the following happen: (a) all issues are resolved, (b) positions are repeated continuously without compromise or movement, (c) neither side can alter its position without conceding basic points, (d) a long period of time elapses without progress.

3. *Zugzwang* is a German word meaning move compulsion. It occurs when one side cannot make a move without giving away something important.[†] In chess, you have to move. In deals, you do not.

# Deal Strategies for the End Game

1. *Precise calculations* are needed to determine the exact sequence and timing of your final moves in negotiations. In chess, victory or loss is often measured in the tempo of a single move: Whoever would make the next move would win (generally by the promotion

---

*In chess, forced draws are when any of the following happen: (1) material is exchanged down so that checkmate is impossible (such as a king and a bishop against a king), (2) a position is repeated three times consecutively, (3) one side cannot move without moving into check, and (4) neither side has captured a piece or moved a pawn after 50 moves.

[†]In chess, these positions occur only in end games and are usually when pawns must move forward into being captured.

of a pawn to a queen). In deal making, completion or disruption is often calculated in terms of the resolution of a single issue.

2. *Mobility* is critical. In chess, it's position and timing: The king needs to shepherd its pawns down the board to become a queen. In deal making, it's attitudes and issues: Dealmakers need to shepherd their final points down to closing.

3. *Sacrifice* in the end game is more apparent than real, since you know exactly what you are getting for what you are giving. In chess, the benefits of an end-game sacrifice must happen in short order.* In deal making, the reason for the sacrifice is usually a quick trade to reach final agreement.

## How to Become an Expert

Developing world-class expertise is exceedingly difficult. One prominent management researcher—who did much of his work with chess grandmasters—believes that such expertise requires 10 years of concentrated experience and some 50,000 chunks of information.†

What's a chunk? A good bit more than a byte. A chunk is an integrated concept of knowledge—whole experiences—complete patterns of awareness that become the foundation for evaluating new situations. A chess example is a repeatable position of pieces. A deal example is handling an irritating personal affront.

## Chess Lingo

I am fascinated by the jargon of chess players. The talk sounds violent, yet has a whimsical touch. Some examples that relate to deal making follow.

---

*An example offensive sacrifice is when you give up two pawns for one so that another of your pawns can queen first. An example defensive sacrifice is when you are behind in material and trade your last minor piece (bishop or knight) for an opponent's last pawn, thereby assuring a draw.

†Simon, Herbert, "Understanding Creativity and Creative Management," in *Handbook for Creative and Innovative Managers*, Robert Lawrence Kuhn (Ed) (New York: McGraw-Hill, 1987).

### Hopelessly Lost

In chess, the winner is identified by default. If a player is winning, she is not declared a sure victor; rather her opponent is described as being hopelessly lost. In deal making, it's when one side just gives up the fight.

### Blunders

Clear mistakes—very bad moves made by very good players. A blunder to a grandmaster might be a decent move for normal mortals. We all blunder, even in deal making. Examples of the latter include giving away too much too soon and not compromising for ego's sake. Think about what chess players say about blunders: It's not the first mistake that kills you, but the second—the fatal flaw is often made while worrying over that initial, often minor, error. The message is clear: Don't fret about past failures; just concentrate on current issues.

### Stalemate

A forced draw—and a wonderful word. In chess, it's a would-be, should-be checkmate that has gone stale. Stalemates often occur when one side has a winning advantage and gets sloppy. Dealmakers who have negotiated a good deal must maintain full focus and not allow a minor issue to disrupt the transaction.

### Perpetual Check

In chess, when one side can continuously check the other side but never actually pull the mate. In deal making, when one side can keep the other side constantly off balance, say by harping on a sensitive subject. Perpetual check, in chess and in deals, is done by the weaker side and draws by repetition of moves.

### Adjournments

In chess, after 40 moves are made without victory, the players may take a recess to the next day—and all the strict rules of the game evaporate. Players are expected to work hard analyzing the numerous variations of the adjourned position. This is not like a take-home examination in college. There is no honor code to uphold. You may consult every expert, use every tool, and boot up every computer. Similarly in deal making, when negotiations are adjourned, it is vital to rethink strategy and plan your next moves carefully.

### Always Check, It May Be Mate

This is my favorite chess maxim. There are two points here: (1) you never know the impact of a strategy until you try it, and (2) you should always give luck a chance to weave its serendipitous magic.

# What to Do: When to Take Risks?

In both personal and business deal making, as in chess, you take risks when your position is either very good or very poor. In either position, a gamble can result in a profitable payoff. In chess, whether in the middle game or end game, you take risks under two opposite conditions:

> When you have a superior position with greater control of board space or better mobility for your pieces. Risk here may assure a quick victory.
> When your position is desperate and you have little to lose by trying something daring. Risk here may salvage a lost position.

### Superior Corporate Position

Assume you are discussing a promotion with your boss. You have just created a successful sales campaign (which gives you superior position) and have personally opened up several major accounts (which gives you greater control of space). As a result, several competitors are making attractive bids for your services (which gives you better mobility). What to do?

Now is the time to go for that promotion: The game is stacked in your favor.

### Inferior Corporate Position

If you are in a poor position, you can afford to take the same kind of risk because things couldn't get much worse. Suppose, for example, your department was decimated by budget cuts. Your boss has been fired and it is rumored that you are next. What to do?

It can't hurt to take an aggressive posture. March right into the division head's office, assert your positive contribution to the company, and state with confidence that you would like to be transferred to another department. At worst, you may be fired today instead of Friday. At best, you may be viewed as a take-charge person and a loyal employee.

### Superior Personal Position

Your mother-in-law has been bugging you for years. Not much of a provider, she laments. Not good enough for her daughter, she carps. Finally, you get a healthy raise. What to do?

Time to take a risk and put the lady linebacker in her place.

### Inferior Personal Position

Your marriage is falling apart; fighting is on the increase and divorce is in the winds. What to do?

Time to take a risk and put more adventure in the bedroom.

# 13 DEAL SECRET

## Stressing the Strengths

*WHEN YOU'VE GOT IT, USE IT (DON'T FLAUNT IT)*

Build strengths; avoid weaknesses—a good balance I like to avoid. The arena for doing deals is fiercely combative. Dealmakers must show their best stuff or be thrown out on their rears. It is better to be great at some things and poor at others than average at everything. Mediocrity just doesn't hold tough in competitive deal making.

## Strength and Weakness Assessment

Good dealmakers must know their own strengths and weaknesses, aptitudes and limitations. Check your personal balance sheet: What are your assets and liabilities?

The self-assessment process is tricky because it is so biased.* Thus the definition of one's strengths and weaknesses cannot be divorced

---

*A research study asked corporate executives to judge their firm's strengths and weaknesses. The results were startling: The assessment was based more on the executives' kind of job and

from one's position and responsibility. Objective analysis is difficult and one should never assume otherwise. However, performing the assessment in a comparative context can help.

### Inside Analysis

First, go internal. Compare your various departments or attributes among one another. For a company example, which is your firm's stronger division, marketing or manufacturing? For a personal example, which is your own better talent, technical or people skills?

### Outside Analysis

Next, go external. Compare your various departments or attributes to those of competitors. For a company example, how does your firm's distribution system compare to those of marketplace opponents? For a personal example, how good are you at outselling your rivals?

## Techniques for Maximizing Strengths

The following areas of deal-making strengths are matched with appropriate tactics to take advantage of these strengths.

1. *Size.* When your side is larger (and has more resources), take your time, strive for complexity, allow no pressure. However, above all, treat the other side as equals. Do not condescend. Do not chance antagonism.

---

level in the hierarchy than on the actual strengths and weaknesses of their particular company. In other words, perception had more influence than reality! Thus personnel and financial concerns (whether considered strength or weakness) peak at senior management, while marketing and technical concerns peak at middle management—*irrespective of the firm involved!* Senior managers all saw about the same strengths and weaknesses, as did all financial managers, as did all factory managers—and it didn't matter which company employed them. Stevenson, Howard H. "Defining Corporate Strengths and Weaknesses," *Sloan Management Review,* Spring 1976.

2. *Power.* When your side has more force (see Deal Secret 1), be slow to change on demand, quick to press agreement on your terms, and willing to allow face-saving concessions.

3. *Flexibility.* When your side is more adaptable, add complexities, alter issues, change agendas, move schedules, postpone meetings.

4. *Needs.* When your side has less demand for the deal, go slower, avoid pressure, be meticulous.

5. *Expertise.* When your side is more knowledgeable, use the impact of your advantage quietly. The less overt your content superiority, the stronger your influence.

6. *People.* When your side has stronger negotiators, have more face-to-face contact. Encourage larger, more frequent meetings. Discourage written communications.

7. *Time.* When your side has less schedule pressure, proceed properly. Do not slow the pace deliberately or you may infuriate the other side.

8. *Insight.* Sometimes you just know what to do; other times you just take a chance. Deal-making wisdom is the product of experience, natural gift, and trusting your own judgment.* Intuition can contradict logic. When you feel it, use it; when you believe it, do it.

## What to Do?

Assume that you are a group president in a large conglomerate. You have become embroiled in a competitive bidding battle to purchase a spin-off division of another conglomerate. The purchase is critical for one of your divisions. You've already reached the price limit set by the board's executive committee. You cannot go higher and you cannot win at this price. How can the offer be sweetened without violating the corporate rules? What to do?

---

*Not trusting my own insight, to be frank, has occasionally held me back from making dynamic advance. It's intimidating when you've been trained to respect quantitative, legal, or scientific reasoning to go forward with ideas that you cannot fully support.

Go with your strengths. Both conglomerates consist of large corporate groups with many diverse subsidiaries. In all likelihood, one of your company's other divisions can do business with one of the seller's other divisions. It may be worth a substantial amount to the selling corporation to secure a large, multiyear contract for its products. It may even be enough to give your group the acquisition as part of a larger deal.

# 14 *DEAL SECRET*

# *Skirting the Weaknesses*

*WHEN YOU HAVEN'T GOT IT, HIDE IT (DON'T IMPROVE IT)*

Improve your strengths—not your weaknesses. Deal making is not school. Bury those wobbly areas; never give in to them. (Why not strengthen your weaknesses? It's too expensive!)

## *Techniques for Minimizing Weaknesses*

The following areas of deal-making weaknesses are matched with appropriate tactics to downplay these weaknesses.

1. *Size.* When your side is smaller (and has less resources), propel the process, strive for simplicity, appeal to fairness. Above all, treat the other side as equals. Do not fawn.

2. *Power.* When your side has less force (see Deal Secret 1), be careful when conceding points. Be sure every concession really counts and that your concessions become progressively smaller. Try toughness as a surprise.

3. *Flexibility.* When your side is less adaptable, strive to simplify, contain issues, maintain agendas, keep to schedules.

4. *Needs.* When your side needs the deal more, try not to show it. Move the deal along without evincing nervousness. Showing anxiety is a serious lapse.

5. *Expertise.* When your side is less knowledgeable, try to learn quickly. Use your lack of information or experience as a negotiating ploy. "Now you can't expect me to understand you 'city boys' right away. . . ."

6. *People.* When your side has weaker negotiators, have less face-to-face contact. Encourage smaller, less frequent meetings. Communicate more in writing.

7. *Time.* When your side has more schedule pressure, move the deal along without showing anxiety. (Express nervous concern and you will be attacked like a wounded animal.)

8. *Insight.* When your side has less understanding of the deal, you can either let the other side lead and learn as you go or boldly suggest naive ideas and see what happens.

## Attitudes when Weak

Never succumb to weakness. Never evince resignation. A sullen, depressed demeanor invites stagnation; and rudeness, surliness, and sarcasm induce disruption. Consider the following:

Be hopeful, in outward attitude if not inward spirit.

Speak clearly and directly, not muffled and askance.

Sit erect and look well-pulled-together. Don't give yourself away with slumping, dejected posture—a slithering body conveys feebleness.

Eye contact is important. Don't fear eyeballs colliding across the table. Indeed, search out your opponents' pupils. You'll feel awkward at first, then good.

## *Weakness Can Be a Strength*

Used circumspectly, a help me posture can evoke concessions. Most dealmakers can fall prey to compassion. The key is to appeal to your opponents' human nature—not to their competitive instincts. (Naturally, when you're on the stronger side, beware of this tactic.) Some people, sadly, have a sadistic bent, and any sign of weakness will just encourage their rapacious behavior.

Finally, recall President Kennedy's words: "Let us never negotiate out of fear. But let us never fear to negotiate." We tend to overlook what he said beforehand: "So let us begin anew—remembering on both sides that civility is not a sign of weakness, and sincerity is always subject to proof."

## *What to Do?*

April-Marcus, the division of Eagle Clothes* that operates menswear stores for clients (see Deal Secret 30), is in the business of resuscitating troubled companies. It charges a fixed fee based on retail sales. However, what happens when a prospective client is unable to pay normal commissions because of cash flow difficulty? What to do?

Seek an alternative form of payment. One approach is to use the disputed difference to buy equity in the client company. This accomplishes several things at once. April-Marcus maintains its standard commissions and builds an equity position. The client preserves its cash and gains a strong partner.

*In the continuing spirit of full disclosure, the reader is advised that the author is a director of Eagle Clothes and one of its largest shareholders. One continues to debate the wisdom of mixing personal business with professional writing; one frets about conflicts, whether real or apparent. In the end I thought Eagle's several examples to be good ones, and that, to a writer, is the ultimate touchstone.

DEAL SECRET **15**

# Driving the Offense

## DOING THE DEAL MEANS MOVING THE PROCESS

Forward movement is vital for deal success. Stalling is as dangerous in making deals as it is in flying aircraft. Your object is to drive the offense without being offensive. Be a killer for the cause.

## Killer Instinct

A deal is never over, in Yogi Berra's immortal words, till it's over. Never be satisfied with good movement and proper direction. Never rest until papers are signed, money changes hands, and the deal is closed. Never be complacent.

Deals can stall because of inattention. Everyone, especially attorneys, pays more attention to those who complain. So growl, grumble, and grouse. Wail, lament, and moan. Talk to your people every day. Keep things hopping. If squeaky wheels get greased, then *squawk*, don't just squeak.

# Tips for Breaking Crises

There is a critical moment in most deals. It occurs when initial enthusiasm meets contentious disagreement. Progress slows, discouragement grows, and many deals abort. The problem has two solutions: (1) break through the crisis by resolving the issues or (2) close the deal before it reaches the crisis point. Following are techniques for achieving crisis breakthrough.

## Multiplying Options

Advancing is easiest when you have a choice of direction and method. The more alternatives you have, the more likely you'll find one that will work. Multiplying options is one of my major themes. The constant assessment of situations and the frequent search for new ideas facilitates breakthrough.

## Using the Team

It is not desirable for principals to confront each other too often. The top brass should get together only to resolve final issues. Other members of the negotiating team should be used for the nitty-gritty. Divide up duties—this technique allows communication to proceed at all levels.

## Going Off-the-Record

In off-the-record conversations, ideas can be suggested and opinions expressed without commitment. Don't misunderstand—there's no deception here; rarely are such discussions really off-the-record. Each side knows the technique, and both sides like using it. Off-the-record discussions give all parties a low-pressure opportunity to explore alternatives and fresh approaches.

### Setting Time Limits

There comes a moment when you know the deal is not happening. At that certain point you must crank up the heat. For example, if your offer as buyer is being shopped around or if your offer as seller is being delayed, you must increase pressure. Let the other side know your displeasure, that you're up to their tricks, that you have other options, and that you're prepared to take a walk.

## Using Written Communications

No matter what the circumstances or relationships, the agreement should always be put in writing. (See Deal Secret 37.) This puts the issues into clear view and reveals any hidden problems that must be resolved before the deal can get done.

Timing is important here. If the problems emerge too soon, they can kill the deal. For example, introducing technical difficulties early on might slow down momentum and cut off progress. The intrusions can divert energy and fragment focus. The solution is to reach agreement on the broad business matters before getting down to the details.

### Which Side Should Go First?

Generally the side that wants to control the deal will draw up the document. Then, any changes go on that side's original form (and word processor).

However, if there are some points of uncertainty, you might let the other side prepare the first draft. Perhaps they recollect the questionable areas in ways more favorable to you (see Deal Secret 37). Another approach is to draw up the memo or letter with blanks left for the key deal numbers.

### Types of Written Communications

*Memoranda of understanding* highlight all the primary deal points and are excellent instruments for moving a deal from talk to action. These memos are designed to confirm mutual understanding and are often composed by the parties involved—not their attorneys (however, an attorney should probably read over the memo). Since such memos are not legally binding, they enable both sides to express their thinking. Clear disclaimers are included and they need not be signed.

*Letters of intent* are more serious. They are signed instruments drawn up by attorneys. Both sides now affirm that they are committed to go ahead with the transactions according to the specified terms and conditions. You can still back out, but it's getting harder—and it might cost you something.

## Doing Nothing

Doing nothing is the hardest thing to do well. But often, there is no stronger offense. Going silent puts pressure on the other side, especially if they've invested time and effort in the deal (sunk costs) and need to get it done. Furthermore, as you may recall, silence protects your side from talking too much—a disease that can cause you to bid against yourself when there's no one else in the running.

## Wooing and Wowing

Time for your charm. Don't laugh. Everyone likes to be complimented, even flattered. If you're a buyer, tell the other side how well they've done with their business; if you're a seller, explain why they'll be satisfied owners.

Also everyone likes to associate with a winner. If the deal involves any continuing relationship between the parties, you should build your side's image in the eyes of the other side. You want to show, without being overt, that the association will be good for them.

## *What to Do?*

In negotiating to buy an equity interest in a small private firm, your terms and conditions remain inferior to competitive offers. What to do?

Take the offensive. Stress the increased likelihood of substantial asset appreciation for the remaining shares. The current owners would gain greater wealth, even though their percentage of ownership would be smaller, if your group brings more incremental value than would competitors. Such incremental value can take the form of additional business, better management, or stronger financial backup. For example, when such acquisitions are made by well-known investors, an initial public offering becomes more likely and valued higher.

# *16* *DEAL SECRET*

# *Buttressing the Defense*

*DOING THE DEAL MEANS CHANGING THE PROCESS*

"The best defense is a good offense" sounds great. When it works, it's nice. When your weak spot is attacked, don't defend, attack back. For example:

> If the other side demands that certain guarantees must be strengthened, tell them you are considering cutting them down.

> If your boss claims you are not spending enough time traveling to see customers, say, "What about those additional expense allowances you promised?"

Sounds like good strategy? Sure. The problem is that offense doesn't always work. The following are some ideas for counteracting adverse negotiating conditions.

# Counterpunching

Let the other side make the first proposals. It is easier to respond than to offer when defending a position. According to military theory, an attacking army needs far more soldiers than does a defending army. When you are the proposee, you have time for considered response. You learn more, too.

# Tag-Teaming

### Substitute Players

Put in some new folks. They may help, even if only slowing the process and shifting the momentum. This tactic is like calling a time-out to make a substitution in basketball—often used to break the other team's hot streak.

### Good-Guy-Bad-Guy Routine

Playing good-guy-bad-guy is always worth a shot. In deal making, this is also known as the black-hat-white-hat ritual. Note that taking the bad guy/black hat role means disagreeing—not being disagreeable. Creating a bad guy is often valuable because it makes the good guy stand out by contrast. He or she is someone with whom the other side can talk and in whom they can confide. Good guys can sometimes perform magic. This technique can be effective even if the other side is fully aware of your ruse.

# Stonewalling

Just say no. However much the facts demand change in your position, simply refuse to budge. Be obstinate. Keep a straight face and be stubborn and inflexible—mulish and bullheaded. Obviously, the strength of your stone and the height of your wall depends on the relative power of the parties. (See Deal Secret 1.)

If your side is the more powerful, stonewalling is easy to implement (though not necessarily good strategy).

If your side is the less powerful, stonewalling adds a touch of the irrational, which isn't all bad.*

Perhaps the most positive benefit of stonewalling is its impact. It can't be ignored. Furthermore, when you finally do make a change, however modest, the importance of the concession becomes exaggerated. Your efforts are much appreciated. The key is timing and relativity: People assess current events by comparing them with recent events. (See Deal Skill 2.)

## The Art of Bluffing

Bluffing is a common business practice. It is easy to do, but hard to do well. It's also dangerous, especially if the parties involved know your style; repeatable patterns are sensed quickly. If you bluff, you must be prepared to carry through with your threats.

## When Fighting Time

Take charge of the process. Schedule meetings. Set agendas. Energize attorneys. Produce paperwork. In other words, you assume re-

---

*Watch how irrationality helps the weaker side. Assume you're the stronger. How do you deal with people who won't make a decision that is clearly in their own best interest (as well as in your's)? How do you handle situations where normal logic, power and persuasion won't work? It can be disorienting, and sometimes you make a quick, unnecessary concession just to get the thorn out of your flesh. When dealmakers, however strong, confront illogical reaction, they may bend if they really want the deal.

sponsibility for movement. If the other side continues to delay, they either don't want to make a fair deal (in which case you'd rather know it sooner than later) or their effort to use time as a weapon is exposed.

Consider this less traditional approach. If the other side thinks it has you in a time squeeze, perhaps you should shock them by slowing negotiations yourself. It can disrupt their strategy and work to your advantage.

## When Fighting Bullies

Handling toughs and tyrants is risky because all options hold dangers.

> Pushing back hard can expose their cowardliness—but it may also trigger a blowout.

> Playing meek and defenseless can disarm the other side—but it may also invite mayhem.

> The best tactic is to sidestep ruffians. Allow their abuse to bounce off harmlessly, like a hot laser off a shiny mirror. If you don't react, their assaults don't penetrate.

## When Fighting Authority

Understand the character of the command structure you face and make your appeal accordingly.

> If the authority is based on merit and achievement, use logic and fact.

> If the authority is based on politics and gamesmanship, use ego and emotion.

The critical factor for manipulating authority is to show that taking your suggestions will enhance their leadership control, while not doing so will undermine their personal position.

## When Fighting Coercion

When the other side keeps trying to muscle you into making concessions, it is a mistake to assume they will stop. They won't stop until you stop them. So stop them!

## When Doing Nothing Is the Best Defense

Fickleness frustrates. Indecision can blunt the strongest attack. So be wishy washy. Force your opponents to try cornering you. Become loose like Jell-o®—attempting to nail Jell-o® to the wall can be nerve-racking. Doing nothing is sometimes the most aggressive move you can make.

Consider a protracted negotiating session where the other side, at the end of a long day, throws their final proposal at you. If that proposal is still well off the mark, perhaps you should do nothing. Be unable to schedule the next meeting; be unavailable for personal chats; be polite but vague during phone calls. The contrast will be sharp and the pressure maddening.

Generally, you don't have to do nothing for long to make your point. Nothing, please note, is not nothing.

## Personal Attacks

Threats, dares, insults, and the like are not good tactics. Little is gained from desperate acts of a personal nature. Deals are made because people want to make them, and if you antagonize the other side, you lose more than you gain.

## What to Do?

I admit I was rather panicked at the prospect of losing an important acquisition. The potential purchase could catapult a small company I had put together. The target firm was a spin-off of a large corporation, and management of the subsidiary held the key to the deal. All we could offer management was 20 percent of the stock, whereas they sought 50 percent, a number that competing bidders would approach. What to do?

Preparing for my visit with management, I was rehearsing the role of salesperson, articulating all the ways in which their company would benefit in coming with us (other than that stock percentage). The president of our company advised a different tack. He counseled me not to push. "Sometimes, oversell triggers an opposite effect," he advised. "The other side thinks, 'Why should he have to sell so hard?' Better to undersell and allow them to convince themselves."

I agreed with the approach—we had a strong story to tell. And then I saw the irony: I couldn't help but note the timing of the admonition—just as I, "the dealmaker," was struggling with this chapter. (The purchase, by the way, didn't work out for other reasons, though the undersell attitude was clearly correct.)

# 17 *DEAL SECRET*

# Surmounting the Setbacks

*THE FIRST FALL HURTS, THE SECOND ONE KILLS*

So you've had a setback. You're down. You're flat on your back. A setback is not the end of the world—or the deal. Maybe you've had to make some concessions. You're discouraged. The other side is pressing for more give. Your tendency is to let up, resign, and stay flat on your back.

Don't! Don't give in and don't succumb. Above all, don't make hasty decisions that can compound your first error. Recall the chess maxim about the second mistake, the one you make when lamenting the first mistake? Happens all the time in deal making.

## Containing the Problem

The first step is containment. Confine your losses to one location. Isolate the issue. Treat the setback as if it were an independent,

174

watertight compartment on a ship. The ship won't sink if one compartment ruptures.*

## Circling the Problem

The next step is flipping the focus away from the problem. Once having isolated the illness, you must move away from it. Change directions. Break stride. Make alterations of any kind. Pick yourself up and scout the lay of the land. Shift the theater of operations. You have several good options. For example:

Put new players on your negotiating team. Their freshness provides a convenient excuse to retard the pace or change the pattern of current negotiations.

Set a strange meeting time, perhaps later in the day. Such a switch suggests that you have more important activities earlier in the day.

Invite the other side out to a nice restaurant to continue talking. This shows confidence in your position.

Start talking about other issues. Pick an area where the other side is weak, or one that has not yet been discussed, or one in which the other side has a keen interest (e.g., if they've wanted to get a hands-on look at your plants, arrange the trip).

## Ultimatums

Declaring ultimatums is never an easy tactic to use or face. Too much self-image is involved and logic is often overrun by emotion. Yet few deals get done without a bit of brinkmanship.

Try this tactic right after a setback. It's the most unexpected moment. The threat may seem irrational, but not idle. It may scare the

---

*In fact, such a provision is a standard clause in most legal documents: If one provision of the contract is proven to be unenforceable, the other provisions are not affected.

other side into worrying whether you'll trash the deal. That's not so bad. Let them trade their iron mallet for kid gloves.


## Turning Lemons into Lemonade

No matter what happens, you can always improve the situation. Often, the embryo of a vital, new approach is buried within the carcass of the old approach. Being a little naive never hurts. If you don't know something can't be done, you might go out and do it.


## What to Do?

Eagle Clothes was an unsuccessful company having just emerged from bankruptcy but still losing money. Eagle had an excellent name as a fine men's suit manufacturer, but the men's suit market was flat and highly competitive. There was little hope in building back the wholesale business. A bold acquisition was needed. But finances were poor. What to do?

In a complex transaction,* Eagle purchased April-Marcus largely for seller notes. April-Marcus' profits would generate cash so that Eagle could pay off its notes. (Eagle's tax loss carryforward would help cash flow.) April-Marcus, a consulting company for off-price menswear stores, took over management and built up the Eagle name, including a division of Eagle-owned stores. Though not all sweetness and light, the creative deal transformed a bankrupt company with limited prospects into a profitable company controlling over $250 million in annual retail volume.

---

*The transaction was designed by attorney Walter Feldesman and the author.

# Breaking the Deadlocks

*CRACK THE TENSION, NOT YOUR HEAD*

Every deal reaches an impasse somewhere along the line. Breaking through that impasse is what you have to do. Stopping the standoff is what turns good dealmakers into great ones.

## Tips for Breaking Deadlocks

The following list describes various deadlock-breaking techniques:

*Change the Pace.* Switch topics, shift agendas, move meetings, or take a break. (Remember the time-out in basketball.)

*One-on-one Meetings.* Interrupt a larger meeting and go head-to-head with the other side's principal. Get the old, cynical attorneys and young, intense MBAs out of the room. Maybe out of the building.

177

*Play Mediator.* Take the good-guy role and put yourself in the middle. Try seeing the deal from both sides. (Play Solomon without the crown.)

*Bring in New Factors.* Generate fresh ideas. Introduce new concerns, matters, points, and problems. Reduce the importance of deadlocked issues by surrounding it with other issues. Substitute people. Bring in new people (someone off-the-bench—that substitute in basketball.)

*Go Senior.* A last resort. If you're not already dealing with the most senior person, reach up. Recognize that you are antagonizing your peers. Now they can't look good, no matter the outcome. If the deal works, the boss gets the credit; if the deal doesn't work, your peers get the blame.

*Do Nothing.* Often, the safest solution is to stand still. Be patient. When in doubt, don't do the wrong thing. Something can always be done tomorrow. You only lose your options when you use them.

# Art of Compromise

If you think compromise is splitting the difference—dividing negotiating positions evenly—you think wrong. Carving issues down the middle do not make the best deals. Compromise is a complex and surprisingly precarious process. Used properly, it closes deals. Used improperly, it causes disaster.

Compromise is the art of getting both sides to agree to a resolution that neither side likes. As long as everybody is unhappy, goes one adage, the deal is a fair one. The following principles should be used in making compromises.

1. *Don't Be the First to Concede a Major Issue.* Being the first to accept a substantial compromise is a sign of weakness. It can induce aggressive behavior across the table. The more you give, if given in the wrong way, the more they want. Feeding greed only breeds greater appetite.

2. *Suggest Only Minor Compromises First.* Offering minor compromises first is fine. It is a good way to encourage a reasonable solution. This tactic does not bring out the shark in your opponent.

3. *Don't Compromise Near Deadlines.* Don't give the impression of caving in to pressure. Compromise should always be combined with confidence. Offering a concession when a deadline approaches smacks of concern and collapse. Instead, you might inform the other side that you are ready to offer some new ideas—*after* their deadline has expired.

4. *Concede the Right Way.* It is vital that the other side interpret your concessions properly. You must communicate, in fact more than in statement, that your offers are minor and getting smaller. If your opposites think they can get more, they will push for more. That's the nature of negotiations. (Sometimes, being human means playing by jungle rules.)

5. *Milk Concessions.* When you've made a concession, no matter how small, make the most of it. Use your compromise to show your willingness to get the deal done. Use it to show what nice people you are. Talk about it seriously and with good humor. ("Now look how much you've squeezed out of us!")

6. *Skewing the Split.* Splitting the difference, please note, does not necessarily mean hacking the issue in half, nor must it always relate to price. Deals can be split, even though skewed to one side. A critical criterion is the test of mutually and relatively equal *unhappiness*. All issues are subject to such compromises, from features of product to terms of payment.

## *Finding the Right Angles*

If we assume that the two sides are 180 degrees opposed on outstanding issues, a 90 degree switch for both sides—each one moving half way toward the other side—sounds ideal. This would be true if we were limited to two dimensions. Since we aren't limited, the best solution might lie in three dimensions.

For example, if Company A (the seller) insists that it must receive $10 million for a certain division, whereas Company B (the buyer) asserts that it will only pay $8 million, they must negotiate. Assume the difference lies in disputed forecasts of next year's earnings. An even, split-the-difference compromise, which neither side will like and either may reject, is to pay $9 million. However, there is a better way. A three-dimensional solution would involve: (1) paying $8 million on closing and (2) an additional $2 million based on future earnings. A formula tied directly to those earnings will allocate the additional payments plus interest. Both sides should be happy. If the earnings will materialize, as the seller maintains, the buyer will be pleased to pay the full $10 million. If the earnings are not there, $8 million was the right price and the seller has no beef.

## Careful Concessions

Be cautious with concessions; they can cut both ways.

1. *When to Offer Concessions.* It is best to offer a concession when you are strong.* Concessions should be well-chosen and restrained— not arbitrary and unbounded. If the deal can be consummated with a final concession, go for it. A desperate concession to keep a deal alive generally has little value (but if you are desperate to do the deal . . .).

2. *How to Offer Concessions.* Proper style depends on underlying motivation. If you pull back your position out of strength, make a big deal of it. If out of weakness, underplay it. If you make a move that finalizes the deal, make it obvious that your offer benefits both sides.

3. *When to Accept Concessions.* It rarely hurts to accept concessions, unless some return action is expected or implied.

4. *How to Accept Concessions.* Don't gloat about them. Don't dwell on them. No one likes to give ground and the other side may be har-

---

*This was why President Sadat of Egypt could not attempt to make peace with Israel until after he had regained Egypt's pride with the semivictory of the 1973 Yom Kippur War.

boring second thoughts. It's a mistake to rub your opponent's nose in his or her weakness. Treat concessions as creative contribution rather than as erosions of strength.

## *What to Do?*

You have been transferred to a different job in a distant city. You've purchased a new home and must sell your old home quickly. (Carrying two mortgages is definitely one too many.) Your asking price is $150,000. After several weeks on the market, there are no offers— you are concerned. Finally, an offer comes in and you try not to appear too anxious—it's $120,000. You counter with $145,000. They respond with $130,000. Now worry gets the best of you—you *must* sell your house—and so you come down close to their price—you'll take $135,000. Suddenly, the prospective buyers sense your panic and reverse themselves—they drop back to their original $120,000! What to do?

What you've already done is wrong. Not necessarily the price you came down to, but how you got there. Since your first concession was $5,000 and your second was $10,000, you signaled to the other side, however inadvertently, that you could be moved even further down. Divergence in deal making is a dead giveaway for an anxious negotiator. However, if you were to have flipped the order of concessions, giving the $10,000 first and then the $5,000, you would have signaled that you were reaching your limit—even though you would have wound up at the exact same price. Try recouping by jacking *up* the price for a while—but your eggs have already been scrambled. Better to learn your lesson before opening the refrigerator. For the next buyer, converge your concessions.

# 19 <u>DEAL SECRET</u>

# Bridging the Gaps

## BRIDGES ARE MAN-MADE LINKS

What's the difference between Breaking the Deadlocks (Deal Secret 18) and Bridging the Gaps (Deal Secret 19)? The former concerns *process*, the means to get deals done, while the latter concerns *content*, the matter and substance of deals. This chapter discusses specific things you can do to span chasms in deal making.

## Give Both Sides Something

A bridge must have two sides; you can't cross a river without being anchored on both banks. It is surprising how many negotiators ignore the importance of giving something to the other side.

Ignore? They avoid it like a disease. To give is to fail, some deal-makers mistakenly believe. Concession is sacrilege, heresy, the unpardonable sin against the deal-making god. Such twisted thinking is nothing but the triumph of ego over action. In deal-making terms, you get more when you give a little. Always try to couple what your side wants to get with something the other side can receive in return.

# Seek Fresh Ideas

Even the appearance of newness is important. If nothing else, innovation is a face-saving device. If you attempt to exact concessions through brute force, you will breed resistance. No one wants to cave in. However, if you convince the other side that your approach is original, it will be easier for them to concede.

# Critical Issues

Critical issues make or break deals. They either build up or break up blockage. What you do with them depends on circumstances.

### When to Address Critical Issues

Sometimes you go right for the jugular. The deal is made or missed right here. You must have high confidence in the likelihood of success—or be under extreme pressure—to take this tactic.

### When to Avoid Critical Issues

It is more likely that you will skirt the major problems for a while. Get the other side into the habit of agreeing. Resolve the light issues first, then lay into the heavies.

# Eliminate Misunderstandings

Opposing sides view complex issues from opposite perspectives. Take, for example, the evaluation of inventory, a crucial part of most business acquisitions. A buyer may consider the downside scenario—what happens if the company goes out of business—and arrive at a low value. The seller, of course, takes inventory at full value. How to resolve the dispute? If the seller can demonstrate firm orders for most of the inventory, that would clear up the problem.

When to eliminate misunderstandings is a judgment call. You shouldn't do it too soon. Trying to mitigate a problem often exacerbates it. Attempting to cool down a smoldering altercation can actually flame it up. Open debate allows events to take their own course—actions and reactions become neither predictable nor controllable. Better let sleeping dogs lie, at least while working on other issues. When a major misconception stops a deal cold, you must handle it. Other times, take care.

## Postpone the Problem

When dealing with explosive situations, never slam the door shut. The risk is too high, the reward too low. For example, when negotiating ground rules for a hostile press interview, the attorney for a controversial organization was careful never to be the one actually stopping the interview, which was exactly what he wanted to do. By engaging in elaborate discussions, primarily by written correspondence, he was able to get the reporter to tire of the process and drop the story. A directly belligerent approach would have invoked wrath and assured a real hatchet job. (See Deal Secret 27.)

## Use a Contingency Formula

When a problem just cannot be solved, a contingent formula can give both sides what they seek. The unpleasant side effect of this strategy is the added complexity. For example, when the buyers of a business insist that $12 million is the maximum they will pay, and the sellers of that business insist that $15 million is the minimum they will accept, a compromise must be reached. Perhaps a deal can be structured as follows: a $12 million floor, a $15 million ceiling, and the $3 million difference contingent on something (e.g., collection of the seller's receivables).

The formulas, procedures, and policing methods needed to structure a contingent-based deal must be established. This is easier said than done. Often the contingent proposal bridges the gap during the negotiations, but is ultimately eliminated in the final agreement as being too complicated.

## Use Options

Try to give the other side alternatives. Allow them flexibility to choose from among various possibilities. As long as all of the available choices are good for you, you have nothing to lose and much to gain.

Array various options. The intent you show is more important than the specifics you offer. You evince serious interest to find solutions, to meet the other side's needs. This attitude creates an atmosphere conducive for making deals.

## Change Criteria

Whenever possible, reconsider the way you evaluate issues and problems. Can you reexamine your major needs? Have any shifted since the start of negotiations? Sometimes, resolution of one issue can help resolve another issue. For example, establishing an escrow account to cover any inventory shortfalls (which may be a minor concern) may be the solution to a heated dispute about the quality of receivables.

## Change Value or Consideration

Reconsider the material being transferred in the deal. If the sides are very far apart, try changing some basic assumptions. Altering the deal stuff—modifying what is being sold and/or how it is being bought—may give each side a fresh perspective.

## What to Do?

As a seller of some unusual personal property, you have been negotiating with one buyer for weeks. Price is the only issue to resolve, but it seems an insurmountable one. A wide gulf remains between the maximum he will offer and the minimum you will accept. Your problem is that the property is so specialized that it will be difficult to attract other buyers. What to do?

Make a valiant attempt to traverse the gulf between you and the buyer through a combination of fresh ideas. Give the buyer a choice of novel alternatives for bridging the price gap. For example:

Paying the disputed amount over time

Paying the disputed amount with assets other than cash

Binding arbitration with third-party appraisers

Appraising the property at some later date to determine today's fair market value with hindsight

The key is the choice: You allow the buyer to pick the option he prefers. At best, he will select one of your alternatives. At worst, he will come back with a new offer. Perhaps his offer will be more complicated. So what, it will get negotiations moving again.

# Taking the Control

*MANAGING HOW THINGS HAPPEN*
*MEANS MASTERING WHAT THINGS HAPPEN*

Leadership is vital for deal making. The process is both fascinating and subtle. What's going on over the table may mask what's going on below it.

Regulate how a deal gets made and you influence what deal gets done. In other words, the deal-making process controls the deal-doing content. Control is not a simple function of power, however. Even though the most powerful player starts out with greater control, the control can shift with subsequent events. Control is elusive and hard to pin down. Following are various techniques for asserting leadership of deals, for taking the control.

## Effect a Compromise

The point here is progress and process. Substance doesn't matter—the issue may be major or minor. It is vital for your side to initiate and effect some sort of compromise. You must be the catalyst—that's how you take charge. (Strangely, it is often better to effect a compromise than to receive a concession. The latter is a single event, the former a recurring attitude.)

## Get a Concession

Getting or giving a concession impacts other issues. Movement in your direction is great, and you should strive to achieve such positive action irrespective of the issue or its importance. Better to get a minor concession during negotiations than to start out with a major agreement.

However, if the other side has greater power, minimal largess, and only one concession to grant, don't squander the opportunity. Forget false pride and take what you can get.

## Set or Reject an Ultimatum

Ultimatums take charge. Little else is relevant once deal-busting conditions enter the scene. Setting an ultimatum is a powerful tactic. A typical case is declaring a time limit for concluding the deal: "Gentlemen: We have 48 hours to reach a conclusion—or we walk!"

Refusing to succumb to an ultimatum is just as powerful. When confronted with a buyer reducing his price, a wily seller deadpanned, "May I assume your lower offer voids my moral commitment not to speak with other buyers?"

## Sustain the Momentum

Having momentum means having control. If you've got it, preserve it. Keep doing what you're doing. Avoid disruption. Go with the flow. If you've lost it, the other side's probably got it. If that's the case, get it back. Try disruption—any break in the action. Again, the basketball time-out—usually called by the team that's falling behind. Break their rhythm and reverse momentum.

## Change the Schedule

It's amazing how deal schedules control deal momentum. Changing the schedule can be as simple as postponing a meeting for a day to as serious as recommending a week's hiatus. It can also include requesting a shift from verbal discussions to written communications.

## Change the Deal

Changing deal terms is never pleasant. But retrading is always expected. It establishes control at the same time it risks rupture. The other side is ticked off: They thought they had an agreement—suddenly they don't.

Altering prices is the obvious move. More often, price changes are couched in other terms. A buyer may delay payments or demand more features, while a seller may require faster payments or give fewer features.

## Bring in New Troops

In most deal-making situations, the participants become too familiar with one another. Sometimes you can break stride and take control by changing the players. For example:

1. Bringing in an unknown senior person with full decision-making authority can be quite disrupting. New relationships need to

be formed. In some ways, it's as if negotiations must be reset and started afresh.

2. Trotting in new professionals (e.g., your attorneys) accomplishes the same thing. The cozy negotiating group is suddenly invaded by aliens. Everyone has to back up in order to bring the new people up to date. As a result, the entire process slows to your speed.

## Request New Information

A call for additional data does more than give you further knowledge. It subtly communicates your lack of confidence in current direction and your need for verification. Since your side is doing the asking, the other side is put under pressure. (Calling for something substantial, like an in-depth audit, is a much more serious request and risks problems.)

If the information you request turns out to be unavailable or difficult to get, do not slough it off as unimportant. Doing so will send the wrong message. Not only will it imply that the request was frivolous, but also that you are shaky and unsure.

## Criticize Constructively

Constructive criticism of the other side can be effective. Before voicing the criticism, however, try to recognize a positive contribution they made, such as an insightful observation or a thoughtful suggestion. This creates the proper atmosphere.

Good dealmakers make points when they offer helpful critique. The action demonstrates a commitment to truth and a sincere desire to get the deal done. Made in the proper manner, criticism can build the other side's confidence in your personal integrity. "Do not reprove a scorner, lest he hate you; rebuke a wise man, and he will love you."*

# What to Do?

You are representing a financial institution that wants to coinvest with a venture partner in a leveraged buyout. Negotiations have stalled over several issues. Your required equity investment seems well secured. A primary problem is that although financial returns should be excellent over the life of the investment, you cannot afford to have assets deployed that do not generate income in the short run. But your venture partner maintains that cash cannot be paid by the debt-laden leveraged buyout for several years. How to make the investment? What to do?

Effect a compromise, giving both sides something. Since cash is not as important to your side as reported income, you make your investment as a zero-coupon note, which generates income for your profit and loss statement but does not pay cash until the note matures in several years. At that time you have the option of converting your note to the appropriate amount of stock.[†]

---

*Proverbs 9:8.

[†]This problem is based on the purchase of the Yellow Cab Company of Houston, Texas by Equus Investment in partnership with United Financial Group which put up the zero-coupon note. Yellow Cab, which is pioneering computerized taxi service, has a majority of the market in Houston; Austin; Colorado Springs; and Charlotte, North Carolina.

# 21 DEAL SECRET

## Following the Logic

*START WITH LOGIC NO MATTER WHERE YOU END*

Logic is a thought process in which each step dictates the next. Such thinking is built on facts, not opinion; truth, not belief. Well, that's the theory. But facts and truth in science are one thing; in deal making, they are something else again.

Consider this very simple example of logic:

1. All people are honest, and
2. All dealmakers are people, then
3. All dealmakers are honest.

Now let's get a bit more complicated: If some dealmakers are honest, and some honest people live in New York, it does *not* follow from logic that some dealmakers live in New York (though they do) or that the New York dealmakers in your deal are honest (though they probably are).

192

# How Logic Works

The scientific method is the application of logic to analyzing data and drawing conclusions. It seeks to understand how the world works from what can be observed. Proof involves the repeated testing of hypotheses against evidence, and the rejecting of those explanations that do not fit the facts. Theories are modified to match the findings as the process is repeated. Such repetition is essential.

Deal making follows a similar pattern:

1. In deal selection, you repeatedly test which of several possible deals looks better.

2. In deal negotiations, you repeatedly assess how well you can achieve your goals based on feedback from the other side.

3. As a result of such regular reassessments, you constantly modify your goals and strategies.

# How Logic Is Used

Logic is used to accomplish the following objectives:

1. *Demonstrating Correctness.* Logic can show why your position is the right one; why, for example, the price you're asking for your car, considering its fine bodywork, is appropriate.

2. *Demonstrating Incorrectness.* Logic can also show why the other side's position is not right; why, to flip sides in the car-selling example, the price is *not* appropriate since, although the bodywork looks good, the structure was damaged in a major accident.

3. *Moving Ahead.* Logic is a powerful device for getting and keeping deals going forward. *Let's stick to the facts.*

# How Logic Is Abused

To canonize logic is to deify a computer. A machine can be taught to assess mechanical truth but not to discern whole truth. There is more to making deals than accurate analysis.

People make deals, arguments do not. Logic has its place, but not the whole place. People are motivated by feelings and emotions; they do what they want, and logic may not change their attitudes. An owner of a business may not sell to the highest bidder just because she didn't like their negotiating tactics. Not logical? Though Star Trek's Dr. Spock wouldn't approve, it doesn't matter. No deal.

Proving your point with logic can even break a deal, if in the process the other side gets, to use the vernacular, pissed off. Logic is often a battle winner and war loser. Using logic, you can be right and still be wrong—right in your analysis of facts and wrong in how you used them.

The worst application of logic in deal making is to put down the other side. It can be tempting. Suddenly, after hours of contentious dispute, you find the winning argument or piercing fact—and you jam it right down those bastards' throats. It makes you feel good, sure, but it hurts more than helps your deal. Your opponents may concede that one issue but they will resist you more on every other issue. You made your point, but you also made an enemy.

Be careful when proving someone wrong in a meeting, especially a superior in front of subordinates. Consider presenting your argument in private. It will save face, and you will be appreciated.

# Techniques of Logic

The following are good ways to apply logic.

   1. *Be a Good Listener.*  You can't use logic's full strength unless you understand fully the other side's position. Concentrate on what your opponent says.

2. *Paraphrase.* Repeat back to the speaker in your own words what you think he or she is saying. Do it without judgment or critique. You make progress when you show that you really understand an opposing position.

3. *Fact Association.* Organize your information. Relate the data and ideas to the other side's argument. Look for those facts that undermine or subvert the opposing argument. There is a major difference between facts that do not confirm an argument and facts that destroy it. The former are common; the latter are rare.

4. *Coax, Don't Insult.* Unless you can blow the other side's argument out of the water, which is unlikely, proceed with caution. Take heed: You don't want to alienate the opposition—only thwart their attacks. Imagine yourself a surgeon, excising only those parts of the argument that are diseased. Start with positives before negatives. Approach the argument as one ripe for mutual improvement instead of coming on like gangbusters. Use developmental phrases such as, "What happens if we modify. . . ."

## Location of Logic

### When Logic Is on Your Side

With a winning position, you don't want to muck it up with bad feelings. The idea is to make your point and gain respect in the process. Don't make the other side look bad. Your mental image is mutual victory over faulty logic.

### When Logic Is on the Other Side

When your side has presented a failing argument, try to cloud the issue and lessen its impact. But avoid anxiety and obvious obfuscation. Heavy smoke screens are dead giveaways. Look for an excuse to move on to other topics. If the other side fumbles in explanation, be understanding. Your mental image is a minor matter of no consequence.

## *What to Do?*

Two legendary corporate dealmakers were negotiating the sale of a large division from one to the other. "I like the deal you're offering." said buyer to seller. "The companies are excellent—dominant market share, fine brand recognition, high quality, superb distribution, nice cash flow. I've only got one problem: If you're selling at a price, why should I be buying at that price? I've never known you to leave much on the plate." What to do?

Forget price. It's not the issue here. Seller motivation is what counts. The seller should give the buyer convincing reasons why he needs to divest the businesses. Perhaps the division to be disposed doesn't fit a new strategic posture; perhaps debt needs to be paid down; perhaps another cash-hungry acquisition has just been made; perhaps. . . .

# Feeling the Emotion

*EMOTION IS NOT SHAMEFUL—*
*IT IS NOBLE, WORTHY, AND VALID*

Emotion in deals is kingmaker, tipping the balance. It often decides issues at the end, even if it does not initiate them at the beginning. Emotion, never forget, makes deals.

## How Emotion Works

Emotions are nonrational, unplanned feelings. They are private knowledge, sensations we know ourselves but cannot demonstrate to others. They are outside the orbit of logic but do not contradict it. "Intellect [logic] is to emotion as our clothes are to our bodies." said Alfred North Whitehead. "We could not very well have civilized life without clothes, but we would be in a poor way if we had only clothes without bodies."

## *How Emotion Is Used*

Emotion affects the atmosphere of deal making, casting positive or negative spells, invoking spirits that uplift or depress. Good dealmakers encourage honest emotional expression. As long as respectful, nonthreatening behavior is maintained, there is nothing wrong with putting some volume behind your words. If you're upset, show it. If you're bothered, say it. What you are seeking is candid communication, and displaying emotion is part of that candor. In this sense, deal making is like group therapy; problems are discussed openly and emotion is expressed without shame.

## *How Emotion Is Abused*

Faking or flaunting emotions, on the other hand, is counterproductive. Fibbing or fabrication leads to more tricks than treats, and boisterous exhibitionism detracts from deal-closing solutions. Emotion shown should be sincere, or not shown at all. Don't plot artificial emotion, but don't be embarrassed to express the genuine variety.

## *Kinds of Emotion*

In what environment are you working? The deal-making atmosphere influences the dealmakers' attitudes. The following are some descriptions of deal-making climates. The further you can move to the left (no political pun intended), the better for getting deals done.

*Cooperative—Competitive.* Is the environment collaborative or cutthroat?

*Equality—Superiority.* Are the parties content with parity, or do they seek dominance?

*Factual—Judgmental.* Do the parties stick with simple data and information, or do they evaluate motives and imagine hidden agendas?

*Spontaneous—Calculating.* Do the parties react naturally to situations and events, or do they plot and scheme to get their way?

*Issue Exploring—Self-Certain.* Do the parties concentrate on examining points and solving problems, or are they arrogant and cocky in their private appraisals?

*Problem Sharing—Self-Protective.* Are the parties open and honest in investigating issues, or are they secretive and uncommunicative in their daily dealings?

*Solution Oriented—Ego Oriented.* Do the parties focus on resolving issues, or are they consumed by posturing and vanity?

*Empathetic—Callous.* Do the parties genuinely relate to the concerns of the other side, or are they cold-hearted and insensitive?

## Techniques of Emotion

The following are good ways to use emotion.

*Set a Baseline.* Get some sense of the normal emotional state of all deal participants. People are different—some are high charged, others low key. Good dealmakers come in all levels of intensity.

*Be a Good Listener.* Hear the nonverbal sounds—the tones and pitches of voices—being communicated. Receive the meta-messages.

*Be a Good Watcher.* Observe body language of the people on both sides. Note how people interact with one another.

*Control Your Own Emotions.* Control does not mean repression. Use your emotions to underscore meaning and conviction.

*Note Changes.* Any emotional shift may indicate a reaction to the current state of the deal. No matter what words are being said, whether the other side is conceding or stonewalling, emotional change indicates something's afoot.

# *Character of Emotions*

Emotions can influence deals. Once you understand what's happening, you can use it to your advantage.

### *Assess Commitment*

The depth of the other side's commitment to its stated position is the best clue to how hard you can push and how far you can go. An emotional upswing suggests increasing commitment while an emotional downswing indicates decreasing commitment.

### *When Emotion Is High*

Maximal emotion can cause deal volatility. Heightened intensity can either (1) help take control of the deal-making process or (2) disrupt progress. High emotion is like a catalyst in a chemical reaction: Whatever is supposed to happen will happen more swiftly. This can mean higher efficiency or bigger explosion.

### *When Emotion Is Low*

Minimal emotion can cause deal lethargy. Depressed intensity can either (1) lose control of the deal-making process or (2) allow momentum to run down. Deals languish with low emotion.

### *When Atmosphere Is too Tense*

High emotion generates tension, but tension in itself is not bad. Moderate tension may even be beneficial. Excessive tension, however, should be diffused, since it puts everyone on edge. Try humor, especially the self-deprecating kind. ("If I weren't such a masochist,

I'd enter a more relaxed profession, like risk arbitrage in the stock market.")

### When Atmosphere Is too Comfortable

Looseness and sloth do not close deals. A serene, untroubled environment is generally conducive to making deals, but sometimes a little zip is needed to prod things along. How to add zip? Try injecting some competition for your deal, or at least the threat of it.

# What to Do?

A church hierarchy threatened by schism summarily defrocked several leading ministers in an attempt to crush dissension. The ministers' complaint was both administrative and doctrinal, with charges of blasphemy and heresy being whispered. As the controversy bubbled and boiled, allegations of moral lapses on both sides started to surface. The confrontation was getting ugly and the media was getting interested. What to do?

Emotions must be contained before an explosive chain reaction uncorks and the split becomes public and permanent. Those ministers deemed essentially faithful should be reinstated and given a formal opportunity to present their grievances. Ground rules must assure a nonjudgmental, problem-sharing, solution-oriented atmosphere. Those ministers whose basic beliefs are no longer consistent with the church should be separated as amicably as possible, with proper appreciation shown for their past service. Vilification should be avoided at all costs.

# 23 *DEAL SECRET*

# *Changing the Attitudes*

*GOOD OR BAD ATTITUDES MEAN GOOD OR BAD DEALS*

Deal making begins under every conceivable circumstance. You never know what to expect when you first walk into the room: The other side may be desperate or unconcerned, ready to peel you apart or determined to play it straight. Your side also brings along a mixed bag of interests and attitudes.

Attitude is a frame of mind, within which the entire picture of deals are portrayed. The right attitude maximizes the chances of making a good deal. Even if the deal opens well, you must work at keeping it that way.

Good attitudes must be maintained throughout all of the deal's problems. This requires constant attention.

Bad attitudes must be changed from natural competition to mutual cooperation. This takes special talent.

# Types of Attitude Changes

The following are the different types of changes that occur in attitudes.

1. *Incremental Change*. This type of attitude is generally positive. It is a gradual, almost imperceptible shift. No major movement is noticed, but after a while you can see the difference. Positive changes are usually incremental.

2. *Sudden Change*. This type of attitude is more rare. It is usually triggered by a particular event that either destroys or enhances the party's confidence in the deal. For example, if something you said is proven false, trust is shattered. Conversely, a sudden step for the better can occur if the other side realizes it made a judgmental error. For example, if they thought you were holding back financial information, only to discover that their accountants had it all the time, their attitudes could mellow as a form of penance.

3. *Self-Induced Change*. Somtimes attitudes seem to improve by themselves. This can happen as confidence grows in the deal's progress. In this case, you don't interfere, but simply maintain the momentum.

Your attitude is a potent tool. The aura you project affects the strategy you plan. Your attitude toward the other side influences their attitude toward you. Smiling, for example, is contagious; it's also simple, cheap, and effective.

# Techniques for Changing Attitudes

The following are good ways to change attitudes.

1. *Build Trust*. Since the common assumption is that you will say anything and do anything to win your point, the only way to build trust is by being truthful and consistent. Trust is elusive in deal making. It takes time to build—and no time to destroy.

2. *Reduce Resentment.* Few deals start out with an overload of animosity although many wind up that way. Resentment is resilient and resourceful and extraordinarily hard to eradicate. If your deal is so afflicted, perhaps you can signal a change in attitude by reapproaching the issue from a different angle. Find the root of the problem. If it's a misunderstanding, be open about it. If it's real, work around it.

3. *Reduce Seriousness.* The best dealmakers work seriously but do not take themselves that way. A bloated sense of personal importance will antagonize, not impress. A light touch is the strongest pressure.

4. *Transfer Credit.* It is remarkable how much can be accomplished if you are willing to give others the recognition. In one organization where change was vital, I was the only one who really knew what to do but I was too young to do it myself. I had to work through the senior leadership, getting several executives to internalize my ideas and present them as their own. I didn't mind because I was deeply committed to that organization (normally I would mind!). Its success was all that mattered to me. You can change the world as long as you don't need the credit.

5. *Build Relationships.* The more impersonal and unapproachable you seem, the harder it will be to modify attitudes. Try looking and acting human, with problems as well as positions. Perfect, you're not.

6. *Use Informality.* Social settings are good environments to break ice and reduce tension. Sometimes, inviting your counterpart to an informal meal can help. A warm countenance can melt metal.

7. *Use Humor.* It is hard to get mad at someone funny. A good sense of humor is a marvelous asset in high-tension deal making. No tactic is better.

## What to Do?

After serving in World War II, my father, Louis Kuhn, decided to start his own business. He had been a successful men's outerwear salesman before the war, but feared following in the footsteps of

Willy Loman in Arthur Miller's *Death of a Salesman*.* My father had saved $15,000, and with another $10,000 borrowed from his new brother-in-law, he set up his new company. He wasn't starting cold, however, having amassed a sizable amount of initial orders from loyal customers. The business would flourish—if the merchandise could be delivered. The problem was money. How to get the clothing financed? How to pay for the raw materials, labor, manufacturing, shipping, and the like until receiving payment? A bank loan was essential. But a new company with little capital? Which bank would loan such a fledgling firm so much exposed cash? What to do?

One major bank did make the loan and the business grew into one of the largest in its industry segment. Why that bank took the gamble is the point of this story. It seems that when the bankers were inspecting my father's meager facilities, they noted that he would always turn out the lights when leaving each room. When in later years they recounted their critical observation, my father remarked: "But I didn't even pay for the electricity; that was part of the rent!" The banker smiled: "We knew that—that's why we made the loan. If you took that much care of your landlord's money, we figured you would do no less with ours."

---

*How my father entered the apparel trade is a different kind of deal-making story. He had been an excellent athlete, a top basketball and baseball player. Though academically talented, finishing high school at 16, he had to support his immigrant family. A jewelry job paying $8 a week was all he could land. Well, those were the days when union sports leagues were serious business. And so the garment union discovered my father's bat and arm, offering him $16 a week if he would play ball for their team. They hinted that he wouldn't need to work too hard, or for that matter have to show up all that often. (I call it the Depression's version of an athletic scholarship.) My father accepted the deal, but fooled them by not only going to work but working very hard.

# 24 *DEAL SECRET*

# Sensing the Changes

*CHANGE IS SURE—ONLY ITS DIRECTION IS UNCERTAIN*

"Fresh water runs on, and if you stop it, it becomes stagnant," observed Jawaharlal Nehru, former prime minister of India. "Nothing in the world that is alive remains unchanging."

Deal making is an environment of constant flux. Everything is flowing, altering, and being altered. These changes may be for better or worse. In either case, they affect the deal.

## Signs of Change

### Pregnant Questions

Questions are self-protecting mechanisms that allow negative response without loss of face. It's better to test waters with tiny toes before jumping in with large bodies. For example, if you want to break a deal deadlock by lowering your asking price, you might ask,

"What could we trade off if I were to reduce the price a bit?" This approach shows neither weakness nor concession.

### Trial Balloons

Trial balloons allow you to float ideas without actually committing to them. You test your thought by observing the reaction. If good, you can make it official. If not, you've learned another idea that won't work. The prime objective is self-protection. You certainly don't want to make a concession and then have it refused.

Trial balloons are released in numerous ways.* For example, the lower-level parties on your team can speak off-the-record to their peers on the other side. (Nothing, you must assume, is ever really off-the-record.) Alternatively, principals can go one-on-one and use a pregnant question.

### Mood Shifts

Most deal people aren't good poker players. Their moods are read easily. For example, I'd be concerned if a person's demeanor plummets when I've made a concession or we've concluded the deal. I'd wonder if there's more here than meets the eye.

### Tone or Body Shifts

Your sixth sense can tell you when the other side is more relaxed or more tense, more responsive or more obstinate, more inclined to compromise or more steadfast to stonewall. Direction is more telling than position: The way things are moving is more important than the ways things are.

Changes in voice tone and body language are the signals. You only have to listen and watch. Note fluctuations of voice and body, the subtle sounds and movements. For example, are the words more

---

*In politics, the most efficient trial balloon is a leak to the press—especially if accompanied by the adjective "confidential."

calming or cutting, the tones more comforting or sarcastic, the pitch more pleasant or high-strung? Are the torsos more straight or slumped, the hands more steady or shaky, the faces more open or crimped? Direction of change, remember, is the key.

### Increased Humor

A witty spirit cannot come forth from a sullen soul. Even a small, unfunny joke from a generally dour person is a positive sign. Conversely, silence from a generally ebullient sort screams a warning. If parties on the other side evince an uptick in humor, whether telling detailed jokes or making off-the-cuff drollery, you're making progress. I like to encourage humor during deal making. It makes the process more enjoyable; more important, it's a positive influence on emotions and outcomes.

### Indirect Expressions of Attitude

If some of the participants on their side are mixing freely with peers on your side, that's a good sign. If the sides maintain strict formality around the negotiating table in meeting after meeting, that's a bad sign. (If the latter, you might try breaking the spell by pulling up a chair on their side: "Thought I'd see how the deal looks from this side of the board.") Telephone calls are another sign. Some people obey protocol strictly regarding who calls whom. Any changes here should be noted.

### Increased Informality and Personal Rapport

If your opposite invites you to a business meal, gym workout, or weekend social visit, that's positive movement. During the deal-making process, such outings are a sign of success. The results for both sides might even be good enough to build a long-term relationship.* When a union official told Denys Henderson that he was

---

*In doing deals, you strive to build relationships. If friendship is budding with any of your opposites, that's good. It gives me great pleasure when someone with whom I've dealt re-

"friendly, fair, but bloody hard," the chairman of Imperial Chemical Industries (the United Kingdom's largest manufacturing firm) was flattered. "I would rest content with that on my gravestone," he noted.

## Change Within Organizations

Massive change is never made without turmoil and disruption, and deal making energizes the process. What happens to deal making within organizations beset by fundamental flux? This subject is a personal passion. It focuses on how changes are made within organizations in transition. The key is *commitment*, which I define as the link between personal meaning and organizational mission. How to study commitment? Much can be learned under conditions of intense religious fervor. The results show remarkable parallels between business and religion.*

### Change in Business and Religion

Which pieces of the past do you honor? Which traditions are so sacrosanct that they are forever above challenge? Such questions are addressed at critical times during the life cycles of both religious and business organizations, and the sets of answers that emerge have much in common.

Framing the issue for religion: When are doctrines and dogmas still fluid? When do they solidify? When do they ossify? How do beliefs

---

quests that, should the parties do another deal together, they'd like me to again be sitting on the other side of the table again. (Also nice is when opponents ask me to represent *them* in their next deal.)

*Dr. George Geis of UCLA and I examined organizations embroiled in fundamental transition while studying "commitment," the psychic knot that binds individuals and institutions. Our approach was that commitment could best be studied in extreme religious groups, such as apocalyptic sects and cults that believe in a near-term end-of-the-world. We investigated several such groups, building a model for commitment. We then derived principles that build or break commitment, techniques that can be applied to strengthening business organizations. See Kuhn, Robert L. and George T. Geis, *The Firm Bond: Linking Meaning and Mission in Business and Religion* (New York: Praeger, 1984), from which this section was derived.

define the boundary of spiritual groups, and what happens to internal deal making when some of those beliefs must change?

Framing the issue for business: When are strategies and policies still fluid? When do they solidify and ossify? How do corporate goals define the boundary of commercial groups, and what happens to internal deal making when some of those goals must change?

### The Life Cycle of Change

One might consider the issue of doctrinal or strategic change within the context of an organization's life cycle. In the early days of a religious movement or business company, there is generally free discussion between the founder and his or her first followers or employees. Doctrines or strategies are hammered out freely and openly, with opposing views vying for dominance.

Yet something happens as an organization matures. Doctrines or strategies stiffen, then harden. What was once considered loyal somehow becomes disloyal. Whereas at first it was supportive to challenge and prune, later it becomes supportive to defend and preserve. The more success an organization has, the more immobile its positions become. The cycle turns on itself, since such doctrinal or strategic rigidity facilitates fracture. The character of internal deal making changes in the process.

I have a story to tell. It illustrates the dynamics of deal making inside organizations when foundations shift and fundamentals change. What happens in religion happens in business. The parallels are powerful. And the root cause is commitment.

# What to Do?

### When Religious Truth Must Change

The devoted followers of Pastor John Philip Singer considered themselves the truest interpreters of the Holy Scriptures. They alone had the "spirit of understanding," hidden for two millennia. The pastor himself never claimed infallibility, although his disciples all but labeled his pronouncements perfect. His every word was recorded, transcribed, published, and studied. Nothing he ever said was allowed to be lost.

Great energy and growth characterized the movement. Men and women of intelligence and dedication were attracted by its clear, cosmic call. No other group, said the pastor, had such all-encompassing answers to the basic questions of human existence. Many were intrigued by his constant challenge to proselytes to read the Holy Book for themselves and discover the truth of everything he taught.

In the second decade of the movement's mission, as more converts took the pastor at his word, a number of doctrinal questions began arising. Nothing major, nothing to shake core beliefs, but questions nonetheless. One concerned when to celebrate a certain holiday. Others dealt with permitted manner and style of clothing and facial adornment.

The cases became heated. In each, the primary issue was scriptural fidelity. It was more symbolism than substance. Would the pastor follow the Scriptures and admit error? The pastor said he would change his teachings if the Scriptures would prove him wrong. But would he? The biblical proof was clear.

The pastor had come to conclusions no one else had ever come to before. Congregants used these examples to prove the unique inspiration of their leader. This explained the highly charged impact of the challenge. If the pastor could be off base here, however minor the doctrinal problems, where else might he have erred?

Those seeking to negotiate change were not being antagonistic or combative. They believed that the only way to truly support the pastor was to support him with whole truth. Wasn't that what the master always taught? How could one claim to be loyal and allow the master to reside in error? How could one remain passive when the entire movement was subject to scalding theological attack? Better to brave confrontation in order to protect his honor. Better to put life on the line in service of scripture.

But many surrounding the pastor felt their own position weakening. They defended the doctrinal status quo vigorously, overtly claiming inspiration for their leader while covertly solidifying their personal status quo. Here was their long-awaited opportunity to crack the upstarts. They took to ridiculing the questioners, twisting sincere inquiry into malicious divisiveness.

Others were torn between what they considered loyalty and what they believed to be truth. They would see the scriptural problems one day and support "our honest petitioners," only to swing suddenly the next day and condemn "these brazen heretics."

To the pastor's credit, and to the consternation of his more virulent defenders, he finally changed his teachings on several sensitive subjects. (His retinue of yes-men changed too, of course—although some, having spun around so quickly, were no doubt treated for whiplash.)

Those who had struggled for change were pleased that their movement would no longer be vulnerable, and that their basic beliefs would now shine forth more brightly. Protecting their pastor was worth the personal pain and prolonged anxiety.

It must be said, however, that those who promoted scriptural truth were always grieved by continued suspicion. Their pastor, although he recognized the accuracy of their logic, could not overcome the heat of their argument. He continued to believe, though he could not have been more wrong, that those who sought to bring about truth were more against him than for him. Those whose support went deepest were those whose motivations went questioned. They had defended their leader at great peril to themselves—and yet, though successful in correcting error and establishing truth, they remained permanently under a cloud of darkness.

The status quo defenders, on the other hand, always remained in the warmest of light and purest of favor. They supported the pastor when he refused to change, and they supported the pastor when he decided to change. They were always in support, always loyal, and consequently always safe and secure.

# What to Do?

### When Business Truth Must Change

ChemTech had been the darling of Wall Street. No one carried more clout in the financial community than its inventor–founder, Mark Chinn. But times had changed.

Chinn was a genius, having revolutionized the specialty chemical business with a continuous series of patented products during the 1950s and 1960s. The company attracted the brightest scientists, and could have become, with its talent and financial muscle, one of the world's leading high-tech companies.

By the early 1970s, however, many of ChemTech's strategic planners were forecasting an end of high growth for their current businesses. They felt that it was vital to move the company into the new high-growth areas of the 1970s and 1980s. The future, they warned, would not repeat the past.

Chinn asked his planners to find new growth areas *within* specialty chemicals. They could not. Chinn dismissed the rebels, abolishing the entire planning department. He stated his unequivocal position that ChemTech would only focus on specialty chemicals.

However, by the late 1970s, ChemTech stopped growing, and in 1980, for the first time in 20 years, the company suffered a loss. The recession had affected its primary customers. ChemTech's stock price plummeted and there was talk of a takeover. Throughout the tailspin, Chinn kept insisting that his company would remain in its corporate niche and that he would stay in his personal lab.

Frustrated with stagnation, many of the best people went elsewhere. Several started new companies in electronics and computers. Finally, Chinn acquiesced to a diversification program, but the company had lost forever its chance to become a true giant of our age.

# 25 DEAL SECRET

## Sending the Probes

*PROBES COAX—STATEMENTS COERCE*

What's your game? Puffing ego or doing deals? If the former, send barbs, not probes. If the latter, get smart.

Often, searching questions—probes—are needed to communicate serious intent in deal making. Probes explore limits and boundaries without risking insult and alienation. They are the best way to discover how far you can go in a deal.

## Objectives of Probes

The following are some purposes of probes.

*Solicit Information.* Get new knowledge from the other side: How old is the building?

*Transmit Information.* Give new knowledge to the other side: Did you know that our building was remodeled two years ago?

*Project an Attitude.* Show the other side your mood: Could you assist me in understanding these numbers? (beseeching). When are you going to stop retrading the deal? (showing irritation).

*Stimulate Reflection.* Encourage the other side to do some thinking: Assuming we can come close to your price, how much do you really need in cash up front?

*Focus Attention.* Make the other side concentrate on a fundamental issue: If you refuse to do any seller financing, is it worth continuing discussions?

*Finalize the Deal.* Bring the other side to a conclusion: If I agree to your last point, can we close in 30 days?

## Probes that Make Progress

These questions usually help. They inform and instruct, thus encouraging the deal-making process.

1. *Fact Probes.* Questions to gather data and information for building knowledge—asked with neutral emotions: How current is your inventory? What is the aging of your receivables? How much is that doggie in the window?

2. *No Limit Probes.* Questions that cannot be answered by a simple yes or no: What do you think the future strategy of the business should be? What is your opinion of current management?

3. *Sequential Probes.* Inquiries that are part of a step-by-step train of thought: If we were to solve the question of price, which issue would then become most important to you?

4. *Conclusion-Suggesting Probes.* Leading questions of the variety not allowed in court: Since you make money at $7.75 per item, why not sell them to us at that price even if we only buy 5000? You wouldn't have made such an absurd offer if my client weren't in Chapter 11, now would you?

5. *Introspective Probes.* Queries that peer into the inner sanctum of

one's mind: How do you feel about selling your business after 25 years? Would you like to consider a consulting contract after you sell?

6. *Solicitous Probes.* Questions that express an attitude of supplication and appeal: Would you mind if I ask your accountant for help in understanding these schedules?

7. *"What If . . ." Probes.* The easy entry for trial balloons. It's hard to get angry at a "What if . . ." It conveys personal uncertainty and mutual respect: What if we were to reduce your cash at closing, but more than make it up within two years?

8. *Questions that Deflect.* Bounce the ball of inquiry back to sender: Why should I accept less cash up front?


## Probes that Retard Progress

These questions usually don't help. They intimidate and alienate, thus fouling up the deal-making process.

*Deceptive Probes.* Any answer is wrong: The classic, when did you stop beating your wife? Or in business, when did you stop inflating your inventory?

*Bristle Probes.* The only purpose is to antagonize: Having made a public fool of yourself, don't you think you should apologize to your peers?

*Insulting Probes.* The respondent is put on the defensive: How dare you charge $450 for last year's model? What prompts you to make such an insolent offer?

*Spot-Putting Probes.* The respondent is put in an awkward or embarrassing situation: Since your boss is here now, tell him to his face why you said that his price was a sham.

*Intimidating Probes.* Confrontation, not information, is the objective: How can your projections be so perfect? Why do you think you're so much smarter than we are?

*Coercive Probes.* Forcing an answer to agree with your opinion: I think that your building is really run down, don't you?

## Responding to Probes

People answer questions in different ways, from complete truths to outright lies to clever evasions. Generally, the best way to answer is with targeted, unembroidered information. Everything you say is correct, but your objective is clear and your focus is sharp—there is no loose talk and no words are wasted.

Lies may solve the immediate problem, but they can cause bigger problems later. When you tell the truth you never have to remember what you said.

But what happens when you just can't answer a question? Side-stepping direct probes is difficult. Try using polite answers that convey sincerity and interest but little substance or information (e.g., "I know how you feel," or "I hear you").

## What to Do?

As a purchaser of small electronic components, you want to buy 5000. You are given a price. Let's say it's $10 each. Now, how do you get the best price from your vendor? What to do?

The trick is to discover the real costs of these products—incremental at the margin. First, you ask the price if you would buy 10,000. The price drops to $9 each. Then you ask about buying 50,000, exciting the vendor to no end. Suddenly the price plummets to $7.75. When you return to what you really want to buy, the 5000, you now know that at $7.75 per item the seller is still making some profit. (As a seller, avoid getting caught in this trap.)

# 26 *DEAL SECRET*

# *Lighting the Sparks*

*SPARKS START FIRES—FIRES WARM OR BURN*

In deals, as in forests, there are two kinds of sparks: controlled and uncontrolled. Controlled and used properly, sparks can start small fires that keep you comfortable. Uncontrolled and used improperly, sparks can ignite large conflagrations that scorch and destroy.

## *Sparks that Warm*

Helpful sparks are elusive to define and difficult to use. There's the ever-present danger of the fledgling flame flying out of control. In deal making, your intent can be taken out of context and blown out of proportion. Take care when making these sparks. You really are playing with fire.

### Kidding and Ribbing

You can often say humorously what you cannot say seriously. Jest is a marvelous form of communication, as long as you avoid sarcasm and sensitive subjects. A joshing remark can convey an important message. Do not pick on a single target. And be sure to sprinkle your humor with a healthy dose of self-mockery.

### Chiding and Chastening

This is a cross between constructive criticism and general kidding. The tone is sharper, but the spirit is still good-natured. Such remarks are intended to make a point. You can say, for example, "You are focusing so much on the tax issues that you are forgetting about the business. How about taking that trip to the plants?"

### Deadlines and Ultimatums

Used carefully, setting deadlines and giving ultimatums can push deals to conclusions. They remind everyone there's movement to be made. After all, you can't negotiate forever. Closure must happen or deals must collapse. Put the bad news nicely: "Well, my boss has given me the word. If we don't sign by next Tuesday, we're going to have to solicit other offers."

## Sparks that Burn

Harmful sparks are generated in two ways. Some people fly off the handle with minor provocation. Sometimes it's words they don't mean; sometimes it's words they do mean but shouldn't say. Other people plot and plan their rudeness. Thinking they can control the deal through coarse dominance, their malice is both insidious and premeditated.

## *Outbursts and Rudeness*

Loud disruptions and temper tantrums are very unpleasant. They might take control for a time, but they hardly create the proper climate. Negotiating with terrorists only encourages more of the same behavior. Don't cater to it. Don't give in to it. Just wait with a slightly annoyed, slightly bored look gracing your face.

## *Sarcasm and Insults*

Slurs and accusations heat emotions and compel retaliation. Try to avoid this natural reaction and encourage the decibel-producing party to calm down. If the ranting maniac does not cool off, the deal is over, anyway. If decorum is restored, you might gain an advantage as the rational party or gain sympathy as the injured party. You have nothing to lose by not jumping into the gutter.

## *Clashes and Confrontations*

These types of attacks are disagreeable, but they can be constructive. There is an issue to fight about. Try to get the other side to explain their position in detail. Ask complex questions about their views. It's hard to be analytical and scream at the same time.

## *Threats and Warnings*

These are the most distasteful of all. Here you are being browbeaten and coerced and perhaps intimidated and frightened. You are being accosted by lurid statements of what the other side is going to do to you if you do not agree to their terms. The threats, which are generally vague, should be taken seriously—irrespective of whether they are in fact serious. If the threats are real, it is better to back off from a deal than to stir such hostility. If the threats are only a ruse, you will force the other side to confront the unpleasant consequences of their inappropriate act.

# *What to Do?*

As a buyer, your purchase hinges on the quality of the seller's inventory. The stuff is obviously inflated well above its current market value. But when you bring up the subject, it's as if you were stepping on a land mine. Boom! Your intelligence is insulted and your character is impugned. You haven't heard so many four-letter words since Richard Pryor's last monologue. What to do?

First, keep a lid on your own emotions, which, understandably, may be bubbling over. Don't try to reason with the person until some calm is restored (or at least some quiet). Then start by confirming the behavior in a manner that enables the person to explain away his or her actions. Start by trying to find some reason—any reason—to justify the absurd outburst. Yes, justify! Make it easy for the ranter to recant. Even apologize for something you didn't do. Remember, you're trying to do a deal, not exact confessions. "You know, I think I understand what you're getting at," you might begin (with trepidation). "I didn't mean to suggest that you were overstating your inventory for *your* company, just that those goods aren't worth book value to *our* company. . . ."

# 27 *DEAL SECRET*

# *Defusing the Bombs*

*AVOIDING EXPLOSIONS IS DELICATE WORK*

There is a fine line between equilibrium and explosion. Dealmakers operate near the flash point where spontaneous combustion is an ever-present threat. Disaster is never far away as any disturbance can trigger a rapid rise in temperature.

## *Explosive Situations*

### *Deadlines*

Once a deadline is set, there's no going back. One of three things must happen:

1. The deal gets done despite adverse conditions for the party not setting the deadline.

2. The deadline is postponed, putting the setter of the deadline in an adverse position.

3. The deadline passes and the deal aborts.

Tough choice!

### Ultimatums

Ultimatums in deals focus on specific issues. Here, there are three possible outcomes:

1. The ultimatum is met and the deal progresses
2. The ultimatum is not met and the deal collapses
3. The ultimatum is not met but conditions are changed

Some examples of ultimatums are: From buyer to seller—"Either agree to guarantee the quality of your receivables or we reduce the price 50 cents on a dollar." Or from seller to buyer—"Put up $200,000 good-faith money by Friday or we're history."

### Verbal Attacks

When engulfed by a tidal-wave tirade, the issue is how to maintain personal dignity while not conceding deal control.* (See Deal Secret 26.) You have a choice of response tactics:

Answer softly, allowing the insults to wash on by

Answer in kind, confronting strength with strength

Proverbs* explains both sides of the question:

Answer not a fool according to his folly, lest you be like him

Answer a fool according to his folly, lest he be wise in his own conceit

† Proverbs 26:4–5.

# *Defusing Attitudes*

Attitude more than technique determines how to smooth the situation.

### *Keep Perspective*

How important is the overall deal? How important is the contentious point? Weigh relative values. Compare current pressure with desired results. Decouple the other side's behavior from your side's needs and wants. If the deal is still good for you in spite of any deadlines, ultimatums, or verbal attacks, stick with it.

### *Look for Negotiating Gain*

Is the deadline meetable? Is the ultimatum workable? Even if the answer to both questions is yes, try to exact concessions from the other side. After all, they threw down the gauntlet and might be feeling a bit badly. Before succumbing too quickly to their pressure, try to gain some deal trade-offs.

### *Never Judge the Motivation of Others*

You never know why other people do what they do. You don't know all their problems and pressures. It's tough enough to keep track of your own reasons for doing things. We tend to judge others as if they should be saints while giving ourselves every benefit of every doubt. Consider the boy with old shoes, who felt deprived until he saw a boy with no shoes, who felt deprived until he saw a boy with no feet. . . .

### Don't Take Yourself too Seriously

Throughout the struggle, keep in mind that this is just one deal. It's not your life. Salvation is not at stake. If you find yourself becoming overwhelmed by emotion, call a time-out.

## Techniques for Defusing

The following tactics reduce the likelihood of deal detonation.

### Deflate the Pressure

Try to throw the ball right back into your opponent's court. Say something like, "If my answer has to be now, my answer has to be 'no.'"

### Switch Issues

Substitute a viable option for a troublesome condition. For example, instead of guaranteeing all receivables as demanded by the buyer, you as the seller might suggest putting some of the purchase price into an escrow account to cover any possible shortfall. This satisfies the buyer while limiting your exposure. As another example, if a seller demands substantial good-faith money from you as the buyer, you might try softening the terms rather than reducing the amount. The idea is that you should have so many outs that it's hardly worth the seller's effort.

### Puncture Seriousness

Relieve the tension of the moment by injecting a little humor. Coaxing a smile from your opponent's face can facilitate a favorable trade-off. Get the other side to see themselves as human beings. Sure, they're professionals doing work, but they should also be people having fun. Humor is the most potent weapon to disarm the dreary. (See Deal Secrets 23, 24, and 40.)

### Give a Fair Reading

Restate the other side's ultimatum or deadline to reflect a position with which you could live. You are not being deceptive by modifying their statements—you are overtly trying to make it a livable offer. Assume the seller gives you a firm and final three weeks to close the deal. A fair reading might be "As long as our financial institution, as an independent third party, takes to complete its due diligence"—a more flexible time period. If they want to break off the deal, nothing will stop them. But if they really want to make the deal, they will listen to your fair reading.

# What to Do?

Often the most dangerous situations involve the falling out of trusted employees. As in a marriage and divorce, love and hate are strangely similar emotions. Your strongest advocates can turn into your most ardent adversaries. How to handle the severance of once-loyal employees? These are delicate cases and normal snapback reactions must be tempered. No one ever emerges clean from a mud-throwing contest. Granted, some may come out dirtier than others, but all get splattered if not smothered by filth. What to do?

Always continue talking. It's hard to fight when you're communicating. Look for compromises of pay and position. Often, the public posture of the severance is more important to the employees than the financial settlement. After all, future employment may depend on previous reputation (if not recommendations). No other company would want to hire a sore loser. Therefore, try to construct a respectable scenario of departure. Also, inject lightness into your talks. Try to recapture the personal part of your prior relationship. Recall the good days, the mutual accomplishments. Both sides gain by not losing.

# Playing the Tricks

## YOU CAN'T TRICK A TRICKSTER

I'm going to describe several dealmaking gambits. We've covered some of these tricks elsewhere; now we play them together. Learn how they work, how to recognize them when they're being played against you, and what you can do to thwart their impact. This Deal Secret—the "tricks"—are designed to be like karate moves—killers that are best used for self-defense. As in fencing, parry is what I offer, not thrust.

## Lowball

### Buyer's Version

As the buyer, keep a straight face and test the market by offering the lowest possible price. You never know, you might get lucky—recall the chess adage, "Give a check, it may be mate." The seller will scream, but how loud and how shrill will tell you where the deal is going. The greater your relative power the more serious lowball be-comes. This is especially true when the seller is under time pressure.

### Seller's Version

As the seller, lowball is less common. The object here is to attract as many potential buyers as possible in hopes that some will become seriously interested. This way, more parties will be around when you raise the price. If a lot of buyers are smoked out, it may pay to go into a formal auction. (See Deal Secret 9.)

# Highball

### Buyer's Version

As the buyer, highball is a competitive trick. You want to get the first shot at the deal and keep other bidders blocked out. Try entering into an arrangement with the seller that limits negotiations to you. Once you get all the inside information, you can make your actual proposal.

### Seller's Version

As the seller, you start by setting the highest possible price while still within the realm of reason. Test the market. Again, give luck a chance—give that check. Buyers will complain, but how strong and how long will tell you where the deal is going. The greater your rela-tive power, the more serious the game. This is especially true when you have no time pressure.

# Bait and Switch

The intent of this gambit is to attract—even entice—the other side with a deal they can't refuse. Once they're hooked, the gloves come off and the real offer is made. In a sense, this is similar to a buyer's game of highball and a seller's game of lowball.

# Bluffing

Bluffing is saying one thing and meaning another. Up to a point, it is an accepted part of deal making. For example, a buyer may tell a seller that the offer will only stay on the table for 48 hours. The buyer hopes to shut off other bids and prevent the seller from shopping the deal. A seller may tell the buyer that other bidders are offering more in hopes of getting the buyer to bid against himself or herself.

Bluffing is deception but not lying (although I am struggling to explain why not). It is easier to define where bluffing ends and lying begins. Giving false financials, for example, is clearly a lie. Speeding up last month's good reports while slowing down this month's bad reports—just as the deal is being consummated—is borderline. Perhaps a good analogy is that bluffing is pretending you've got great cards while lying is stacking the deck.

# Sandbagging

In sandbagging, one party strings the other side along, allowing (encouraging) them to think that they have a deal at their price. Only after they have invested substantial effort and resources (sunk costs)—really hooking themselves on the deal—are actual prices sprung.

If you find yourself on the receiving end of this trick, if you sense sandbags piling up, make the other side be as explicit as possible. Stop and confirm your understanding at every step, preferably in writing.

## Sting Operation

This is more dangerous. It involves the collusion of two or more parties who are conspiring to get the best of you. As buyers, their tactics may involve one of these set-ups to drive your price down:

One party lowballing the price to give the other feedback

One party highballing the price and then suddenly dropping out to disorient you

One party giving you discouraging reports to intimidate you into accepting their compatriot's offer

## New Entrant

As a deal moves toward completion, the other side introduces a new wrinkle to disrupt the deal. Often, the wrinkle is an actual person who has suddenly materialized to conduct the negotiations. The relationships carefully built up over the course of the discussions are shaken. Since you seem so close to closure, and you've sunk so much into the deal, there may be a tendency to give a little extra to placate this new person. (It's like paying an insurance premium.)

Sometimes, the new wrinkle is a fictitious third party who has unexpectedly made a better offer. The other side professes to be embarrassed, moaning about their fiduciary responsibility to accept the best offer. Although there is no binding contract, they avow a moral responsibility to you—consequently they will give you the option of matching the new offer. Keep your wits about you. The whole scene may be a ruse. The new entrant may only be a bluff.

## Appeal to Authority

Blaming an uncontrollable force is a favorite gimmick. If the person doesn't have the authority, a better offer can't be made. This tactic is especially useful when an intangible, such as the budget, is the target of the appeal. For example, what can you do if the other side says, "It's just not in my budget"? The answer lies in devising creative proposals. Suggest splitting your price, for instance, so that whatever is not in the budget this year can be paid out of the budget next year. Just make sure that your contract is enforceable and carrying costs are included.

# What to Do?

You are being recruited by an executive search firm for a high-level managerial job that you really want. There are five other finalists for the position. Credentials and experience seem about equal. One issue is compensation. What, you are asked, are your requirements? The industry scale at your level is very broad. What to do?

If you play highball, you could be deemed expensive or arrogant. If you play lowball, you could be judged cheap or insecure. So try a combination: Play lowball and highball at the same time. Be willing to take a minimal guaranteed salary, near the bottom end of the scale, and a relatively short contract. But couple it with a performance-based contingency that can produce the highest total compensation in your class. This way, they have the least risk—and you radiate confidence.

# 29 *DEAL SECRET*

# *Haggling the Trades*

*IT TAKES TWO TO MAKE WAR—OR MAKE LOVE*

There is an old Spanish proverb about getting rich: Buy from those who go to be executed, since they don't care how cheap they sell; and sell to those who go to be married, since they don't care how dear they buy. Unfortunately, we can rarely choose so carefully those with whom we trade.

Trading is the essence of deal making. One side gives something; the other side gives something. Both give a little; both get a lot. Bargains are struck. Agreements are made.

## *Dora in the Souk*

Middle Eastern markets, such as the souk in Old Jerusalem, are classic examples of nitty-gritty trading. This give-and-take maelstrom of swapping, exchanging, and bargaining can define the term.

In dickering to buy an old knife from a shopkeeper there, my wife Dora (who speaks some Arabic) learned of the knife's "long history in the Sinai" and of the "terrible consequences" for selling such a priceless relic so far under cost. When did the deal miraculously materialize? When my wife agreed to buy *two* knives at that same "horrendously low" price (which was, I think, about one-third the original asking price). Why if the shopkeeper was losing so much money selling one, he was so delighted selling two, my wife never asked.

Some dealmakers find the game more enjoyable than the results. Another shopkeeper in that same souk complained to us that the previous tourist had paid the sticker price and departed without so much as a disgruntled sound or exasperated gesture. (After my wife would leave, he would yearn for the serenity of that previous tourist.)

When haggling trades, whether over ancient relics in crowded markets or modern products in splendid offices, certain principles are universal.

## Value Is Relative

If you get what you want, don't worry about what the other side gets. My wife wanted those knives, both of them in fact, from the beginning. They were ornate, well made, and decorative; they were reminiscent of her childhood, and most important they would go well in our living room. Whether that sixteenth century Bedouin chieftain really used those bejeweled blades in heroic exploits, or more likely his far-removed descendent just made them last week, was irrelevant.

Only you can judge whether you are getting a good deal. It's difficult for anyone else to label your deal good or bad. One just doesn't know another's reasons and motives. Generally, if both sides get what they want, then the values are equivalent.

## Making Trades Count

When making trades, make them count. Surprisingly, much of what's offered in deals is more meaningful to the giving side than to the receiving side. Thus, to make good trades, it is imperative to know what's important to your opponents. Hit these hard. For example, if the seller needs cash, you can probably cut a better price by cutting a quick check. A cash-rich seller, however, might be happier with taking back part of the purchase price in high interest-bearing notes. Finding and pushing hot buttons is more art than science. It involves the senses of touch and smell more than sight and sound. It demands empathizing with opponents and thinking the unusual.

## First Offers

The original price of the knife that my wife bought in the souk had, shall we say, a healthy gross margin built in. At least two-thirds of the sticker was reserved for trading. But, in this case, the buyer and seller knew the same rules and both made a good deal.

Most people do not give their best offer up front. No one expects them to. It's just not done. You can't swim upstream, so you might as well start in a range where you can make some movement.

Corporate America is not much different from the Jerusalem souk. The percentage of reserves in deals may differ but the principle is the same. No fooling, it's the same. A prominent financier told me, "There's always 10 percent in every deal, maybe more."

## All Cards on the Table

Complicated deals contain so many issues that it's easy to fall prey to the salami technique. Each slice doesn't take too much off, but after many cuts you've lost a lot of meat. Getting nickel-and-dimed to death is a variation on the same theme. Here each little coin seems trivial, but the process never ends. Such deals can rupture more for the annoyance they cause than for the amount they lose.

The solution to this problem is to get all the issues out on the same table. Whenever I sense a salami slicer (especially if I hear the jingle of small change in his pockets), I stop discussing any minor matter, no matter how minor. "We are going to get all the issues out on the table," I proclaim, "and solve them all together, not one at a time." I stress that although every issue may be negotiable, they are only negotiable collectively, not individually. I must see the entire puzzle before altering any particular piece. (Gathering all points together is especially important when dealing with those most infamous of salami slicers—lawyers.)

## Playing the Game

In each deal-making situation you must play according to the rules. In the souk, you must at some point begin to walk out, even if you have no intentions of leaving. If you worry, "But I really want to buy," you're an easy-mark amateur.

Never forget that the buyer is the one spending the money. The buyer can walk out—and come back again. My wife made three forays out the shop door, one of which brought her 10 yards down the road, before being frantically called back to bargain. She swapped stories with the shopkeeper, each accompanied by verbal exuberance and visual flamboyance. He told her of all the fierce battles won by these knives, interspersed with heartrending accounts of sick parents and hungry children. She told him of just seeing 10 duplicates of the same one-of-a-kind knives in other stores at half the price (her lie was tinged with truth, his a little less so).

Each deal follows its own path to completion. If you go through the required ritual the deal will probably work out. Some corporate dealmakers use tough-talking attorneys to get in some additional whacks. Others blame faraway executives or nameless committees.

Preserving the honor of principals is always a primary objective.

Playing the deal-making game should be fun. My wife and the shop-keeper both enjoyed their 30 minute negotiation. I liked the show so much I almost gave the man a tip.

## *What to Do?*

In one corporate deal, the parties were about $10 million apart in a $50 million transaction. Negotiations had proceeded as far as possible without resolution. Here were two of the canniest traders in U.S. commerce; neither had budged in weeks and both had run out of ideas. What to do?

Suddenly, in the course of a casual conversation, it was discovered that the buyer, not in the real estate business, had a money-losing property that he was trying to dump. The property was worth, to the buyer, under $5 million. The seller, with a large real estate operation, could easily run such a property with minimal additional overhead. To the seller, the property was worth above $10 million. You guessed the outcome; the buyer's property was thrown in as additional payment to the seller and the deal made.

DEAL SECRET $30$

# Creating the Innovations

*BEING BETTER MEANS BEING DIFFERENT*

Deal making is competitive. To make deals that are better, you must make deals that are different. That's the purpose of creativity and innovation.

## Deal-Making Creativity and Innovation

Creativity is the generation of original ideas. Innovation is the transformation of such ideas into practical applications. Innovation, then, is the end result, and creativity is how you get there. Innovation affects all aspects of deal making, especially breaking deadlocks and bridging gaps. Almost every deal requires a few twists, some inventive ways to leap high hurdles.

Creativity, the process stimulator, and innovation, the deadlock breaker, should not be closeted until needed. They are capricious

237

characters, not accustomed to performing on cue. You must nurture them, caring for them regularly. Good dealmakers think often about novel and unusual ways of doing things.

Most people think that creativity and innovation are limited to high technology. This is wrong. The best business examples of creative and innovative management in action come from low-tech companies doing high-tech deal making.

## Principles of Creativity

### Develop a Climate for Creativity

A creative climate is supportive, with enough freedom to explore individual ideas and clear direction to maintain collective focus. People are told what to accomplish, but not how to do it. They speak openly, not worrying about voicing silly-sounding ideas.

### Encourage Everyone to Be Creative

The freshest ideas can come from the most unexpected sources. Creativity is no respecter of persons. Wide knowledge may not help. Ditto for seniority. Neither technical brilliance nor lengthy experience are sure generators of original proposals. In fact, both brilliance and experience may *inhibit* creativity by solidifying long-standing grooves of thinking.

### Reward Success, Don't Punish Failure

Creativity fails more often than it succeeds. To talk innovation but reward failure by personal penalty (or, worse, career wipeout) digs deep credibility gaps. To make your team comfortable with taking creative risks, give them a high ceiling for which to leap and a soft cushion on which to fall.

# Creative Techniques

The following are mechanisms and tools for generating original options and alternatives.* Most were developed by creativity specialists. They stress the composite character of ideas and the need for making new connections. Note that these techniques are methods for getting the ideas. As such, they are not the ideas themselves. They are the process, not the content. (See Deal Skill 6 to increase receptivity to new ideas.)

### Linear Techniques

Linear techniques apply step-by-step thinking to innovative problem solving. This is the so-called left-brain dominant mode where analytical reason rules. A logical progression builds the next idea on the previous idea. The following eight methods are linear.

**Break Apart.** This technique breaks down a problem into its component parts, lists all possible subparts under each part, and then develops new ideas by combining the subparts in odd and unusual combinations. Mix and match—and watch what happens. Figure 30.1 illustrates how a payment problem is broken apart.

**Matrix Squares.** This procedure lines up two lists of categories, across the top and down the side of the tic-tac-toe-like squares (on X and Y axes), and generates new ideas to fill in each box of the grid thus formed. Being forced to address each empty square stimulates thinking about relationships not heretofore considered. For example, payment schedule (down payment, at closing, in one year, etc.) may be paired with payment types (cash, notes, stock, etc.). Filling in the one year—stock box may suggest a novel contingent payment in common stock (see Figure 30.2).

*For further information and examples about these innovation-producing methods, see the Robert Lawrence Kuhn *Handbook for Creative and Innovative Managers* (New York: McGraw-Hill), 1987. Note Chapter 13, "Techniques for Stimulating New Ideas: A Matter of Fluency" by William C. Miller. Generating new ideas, alternatives, and options is vital for deal making.

| Payment Parts | | | | |
|---|---|---|---|---|
| Amount | Time | Type | Security | Source |
| Full | Up front | Cash | (Full guarantees) | (New subsidiary) |
| (Part) | One year | Notes | (Limited guarantees) | (Parent corporation) |
| Little | Two years | (Convertible notes) | No guarantees | Financial institution |
|  | Three years | Preferred stock |  |  |
|  | . | Common stock |  |  |
|  | . |  |  |  |
|  | . |  |  |  |
|  | Irregular |  |  |  |
|  | (Contingent) |  |  |  |

**Figure 30.1. Break apart creativity.** *Suppose payment is the problem in an acquisition. Perhaps you bridge the gap by issuing, for part of the purchase price, a convertible note contingent on future earnings, with full guarantees by the new subsidiary and limited guarantees by the parent corporation.*

Payment Schedule

| Payment Types | Down Payment | At Closing | One Year | Contingent |
|---|---|---|---|---|
| Cash |  |  |  |  |
| Notes |  |  |  |  |
| Preferred Stock |  |  |  |  |
| Common Stock |  |  | ✕ |  |

*Figure 30.2. Matrix square creativity.*

| Best State | | Issue | | Worst State |
|---|---|---|---|---|
| Being Promoted | | | | Being Fired |
| Continuous success | ← | Track record | → | Numerous failures |
| Trusted | ← | Customer relationships | → | Disliked |
| Well-respected | ← | Peer relationships | → | Irritating |
| Strong presence | ← | Leadership ability | → | No charisma |
| High commitment | ← | Dedication to job | → | Ritual and routine |
| Intense | ← | Energy level | → | Lackadaisical |
| Shows confidence | ← | Requesting a raise | → | Shows arrogance |

*Figure 30.3. Force field creativity.* The tug-of-war between best and worst states when dealing with your boss.

**Force Fields.** Here, a tug-of-war between two opposite conditions—often, the best and worst states imaginable—is used to understand the essence of the underlying issue. The battle fallout is a better understanding of the desired state. For example, assume you are discussing your career with your boss (see Figure 30.3). The best state is a promotion; the worst state is being fired. The procedure calls for pitting each condition against the other by specifying its pulls and powers. Evaluating which of the multiple opposite outcomes is more likely can give insight into what one should do to make the best state happen.

**Design Trees.** A design tree uses a central idea as the trunk and then develops successively more remote branch ideas. The fully developed tree becomes a dynamic portrait of your ideas in transformation. Figure 30.4 portrays a design tree for a salesperson who seeks to increase his or her sales for a major product line by 20 percent (the center box). Each branch is a separate idea; follow how each one forks and develops as one possibility triggers another.

**Confrontation.** Two teams are assigned—both on the same side of the deal—to work out different and conflicting solutions to the same deal-making problem. The confrontation between these teams highlights underlying assumptions and suggests creative synthesis. After tussling on your side, you are ready for the other side.

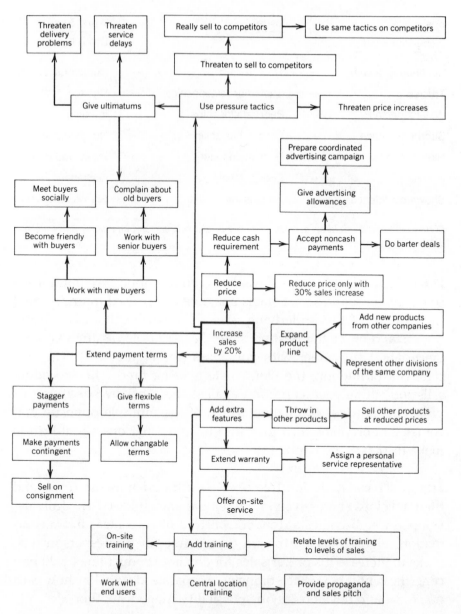

**Figure 30.4. Design tree creativity.** *One idea leads to another as a salesperson seeks to increase sales by 20%. Note the progressive branching and development of options outward from the central box.*

**Assumed Perfection.** This technique encourages participants to imagine the best possible deal conditions. The only restrictions are that the deals (or deal points) are technically feasible and operationally possible. A systems approach is used so that each new idea is integrated into a complete deal structure. This process has two purposes: It releases participants from unconscious limitations; and it can suggest ways to approach the ideal.

**Transforming Ideas.** This method uses checklists of concepts to trigger new thinking. Such lists, which can be broadly general or highly specific, are massaged by various verbal operations: Change? Use? Adapt? Modify? Maximize? Minimize? Substitute? Rearrange? Reverse? Combine?

**Alternative Scenarios.** This approach develops families of related plans to deal with sets of possible circumstances. Patterned after military war games, these contingency-based scenarios assume a radical change from the current expectation (i.e., a discontinuity). For example, the sudden surge of oil prices in the early 1970s and their precipitous decline in the mid-1980s are discontinuities that were ripe for scenario planning.

In deal making, alternative scenarios develop responses to diverse possible offers from the other side. What would we do, for example, if the other side unexpectedly offered to pay our price but demanded stiffer guarantees? Such exercises are good preparation for handling real offers. It can also trigger new ideas.

### Intuitive Techniques

Intuitive techniques apply holistic thinking patterns to innovative problem solving. This is the so-called right-brain dominant mode where emotional feelings and integrated images control. Logic is overruled. Whole solutions are swallowed in one gulp. Perception beats analysis. The next six categories are intuitive.

**Brainstorming.** Brainstorming sessions are meetings at which a group of people exchange ideas without fear of looking ridiculous.

Unconventional ideas are encouraged. The natural tendency to criticize is suppressed. No idea is too wild. No suggestion can be summarily rejected. Session participants use a free association technique in which one idea triggers another. These ideas are listed publicly (e.g., written on a blackboard) and the group is directed toward expanding the scope and outlandishness of concepts. Craziness should be contagious. The only thing forbidden is critical comment. The session's output is a checklist of ideas.

**Distant Analogies.** The technique of distant analogies (i.e., relating things from unrelated contexts) was pioneered by Synectics.* It joins together dissimilar and apparently irrelevant elements to suggest new solutions to old problems. These farfetched metaphors are rich sources of connection-making material and can cast new perspective on the problem at hand. For example, an executive who is drawing an analogy between her company and an octopus may seek deals that would attach divisions to customers through multiple tentacles.

The process should begin with "How to . . ." or "What if . . . ." Then, a field or domain should be chosen to draw the analogy. Bizarreness helps. A good rule of thumb is that the greater the distance between the field of the metaphor and the field of the problem the greater the chance for freshness. Analogies from nature—wind, water, sky, ocean, trees, forests—are common. "Making the familiar strange, and the strange familiar" is Synectics' maxim.

**Imagery.** This method uses symbols, scenes, sounds, or feelings as windows to your inner self. It can unlock ideas long in gestation. Imagery can be encouraged in guided fantasies conducted by experts when you are in a state of deep relaxation. It can be used to snap out of ruts and develop radically new approaches for breaking a deadlock in a deal.

**Dreams.** Daydreams and night dreams reflect the state of your subconscious. They can suggest remarkable ideas at the unlikeliest times.

*Synectics is a creativity facilitating company located in Cambridge, Massachusetts. See "Techniques for Fostering Innovation," by Richard Harriman, in *Handbook for Creative and Innovative Managers*, Robert Lawrence Kuhn, editor in chief (New York: McGraw-Hill), 1987.

The key is to write down whatever comes to mind—images, words, moods—before they are forgotten. Allow broad interpretation, since true insight may be hiding beneath the literal meaning.

**Wishing.** This technique surmounts current limitations by allowing you to imagine whatever outcome makes you happy. Idealize outcomes as you would want them. Visualize those marvelous scenarios. Then, while temporarily suspending judgment, verbalize a series of statements that start with "I wish . . . ." Wishing can free thought processes and galvanize imaginative thinking.

**Meditation.** Breathing, walking, chanting, listening to music, and guided fantasies are all meditation techniques. They can be used to tap into one's creative potential and unlock novel ways to get deals done.

## What to Do?

Many companies file for bankruptcy though loaded with high asset value, often in excess inventory. Though troubled by recent losses, these cash-starved firms are often viable. Given some breathing room, many could flourish. What to do?

April-Marcus is a firm that services troubled companies. "We turn slow inventory into quick cash," says Marvin Blumenfeld, president of April-Marcus. "That could be the difference between survival and extinction for cash-hungry companies. Our clients are the companies themselves, but we certainly assist their creditors in the process." Founded by Mortimer April, the firm resuscitates ailing businesses or liquidates dying businesses, primarily in soft-goods retail. It's all a matter of deal making. The client companies may or may not make an accounting profit as their balance sheet is liquified, but far more important is the fact they can now pay their bills. (Profits are generated when new merchandise is sold in successful sales.)

How does April-Marcus work? Every deal is different, though their fee structure is similar. A commission of 10 percent is paid on retail sales, though large chains such as Sakowitz in Texas, Godchaux in Louisiana, and Smiths in California will skew lower. Client companies more than make up the commission costs, since April-Marcus brings to the party huge buying power (resulting in lower costs of goods) as well as retail and promotional expertise. "It's not unusual for us to more than double a company's sales over a three to six month period," reports Blumenfeld.

April-Marcus insists on tight protection for its merchandise shipped into the stores, especially with respect to general creditors of those troubled retailers. Financial and business exposure will vary depending on circumstances. Here's where the deal making gets hot—figuring the risk-reward trade-off.

# Managing the Time

*TIME IS A DEALMAKER'S MOST VALUABLE RESOURCE*

Strength in sports means nothing without timing. In swinging, throwing, shooting, and hitting, *when* is more important than *how hard*. The same is true in doing deals.

## Functions of Time

Time serves various functions in deals:

It is the standard of progress against which milestones are measured.

It is an ally of the less pressured side and an enemy of the more pressured side.

It is a resource to be conserved and spent wisely.

Every deal has a critical period. There's a strange spirit in a deal, a mutual feeling of movement that engenders positive feelings. However, pass the critical period and trouble ensues—up emotions swing down and the entire transaction becomes less likely to happen.

To make deals, various things must be timed to occur simultaneously. When you are negotiating to buy a business, for example, you must reach agreement, arrange the financing, coordinate the legal work, audit the financial statements, and plan for future operations—not to mention maintain harmony and focus within your own organization.

## Principles of Timing

The following are suggestions for using timing in deals.

1. *Assign Specific Functional Responsibility.* Be sure that one individual is answerable for each independent activity (e.g., accounting due diligence, working with management, factory visits, appraisals, bank negotiations, etc.).

2. *Assign Specific Timing Coordination.* Be sure that one individual is responsible for controlling all independent activity. Whenever possible, this person should be the principal dealmaker.

3. *Monitor Progress Regularly.* Keep in close touch with the key people in each functional area of responsibility. Communicate on a regular basis. Require each area leader to maintain and update a detailed timetable of milestones and accomplishments. Using a personal computer can aid such project planning activities.*

## Deadlines

Deadlines add volatility to a deal and kick a series of events into motion. Your side may set the deadlines. You may need to force a fish-

*See George T. Geis and Robert L. Kuhn, *Micromanaging: Transforming Business Leaders With Personal Computers* (Englewood Cliff, NJ: Prentice-Hall), 1987.

or-cut-bait decision (also known as "____ or get off the pot"). If the other side sets the firm time limit, you must decide whether it's in your best interest. If it is, fine. If it isn't, what will happen if the deadline is not met?

A deadline must always be taken seriously. *Never* give the impression that you think it is a charade. You must convey the gravity of the act to the other side. Deadline setters must confront the consequences of their actions. However, if you are unsure about just how firm the deadline is, test its resilience. Ask a question such as: "Our lawyers can't close until three days after the deadline expires—so what can we do to bridge the time gap?" The answer will give you the clue you are looking for.

## Slowdowns

Slowdowns are one side's deliberate effort to stall. They may be playing out an alternative opportunity because they think it could be better. Or, they may be using a coercive tactic because they suspect you are under heavy pressure. It doesn't really matter. The bottom line is that the deal is not going anywhere.

What to do when faced with a slowdown? The best countertactic may be an ultimatum. If the other side is working another deal, you'll put them on the spot—right where they belong. If they're trying to pressure you to make concessions, they'll find out that the tables have been turned.

## Making Meetings Efficient

Time is a precious commodity—especially in deal making. Since dealmakers must monitor their time, they should follow these caveats:

Meetings need reasons
Brief telephone calls can replace long meetings

Everyone doesn't have to be at every meeting

Specialists (e.g., lawyers and accountants) can meet with their counterparts alone

A smaller team can often accomplish more in a shorter time than a larger team can in a longer time

Perhaps most important, your team's chief dealmaker must stay personally in touch with all participants working with the other side. Reports, even if brief, should be given after every meeting.

## *What to Do?*

The buyers willing to pay the most money for a property you must sell have questionable ability to finance the transaction. They have asked for an exclusive for a period of time in order to line up their sources of financing. You'd love to get the price they're offering, but you risk blowing off the other, financially capable buyers. What to do?

Give the questionable buyers a tight time frame in which to work. Make the outside date for closing the deal as short as possible. (You can always extend the deadline if the buyers almost have the money— but at that point it would be your option, not theirs.) Next, require a hefty, nonrefundable deposit to begin the exclusive period. This deposit must be sufficiently large so that it would be very painful for them to leave on the table. At the same time, require convincing evidence that a capable financial institution has serious interest.

*32*

# Maintaining the Momentum

*GO FOR MO!*

Recall the frustration of a faltering deal? We've all felt the fizzle. Suddenly, spirit seems sapped. Both sides lose enthusiasm in the process and confidence in the outcome. Commitment unravels. You don't know what went wrong. Deadlocks and gaps abound—but that's normal for deals. What happened here? Momentum was lost.

## What Is Momentum?

Momentum is the essence of deal making, giving impetus and generating action. It's what happens when the dead weight of inertia is overcome through the application of constant force. Momentum is exciting. Once started, it's hard to stop. Once stopped, it's hard to start.

Deal-making momentum is the exhilarating sense of energized activity. The payoff is twofold: (1) making the buy or closing the sale and (2) obtaining the personal pleasure of being a winner.

Momentum is more attitude than action. When seeking momentum, never be satisfied with the status quo and always be on the lookout for new ideas—new methods to bridge gaps, new ways to break deadlocks, new approaches to solve problems.

## Momentum and Progress

Momentum is movement. Progress is a step or steps toward an acceptable goal. Either can be present without the other. However, momentum without progress is too wild and progress without momentum is too tame. In deal making, momentum without progress runs the risk of running rampant and progress without momentum may falter short of the goal.

## Methods for Maintaining Momentum

Momentum won't maintain itself. That's contrary to the laws of physics (friction depletes it). Momentum requires force, force needs energy, and energy demands effort. It's no different in deal making. Three elements for maintaining momentum follow.

1. *Reach for Attainable Objectives.* Two concepts reside here: *reach for*, meaning exceeding current grasp; and *achievable*, meaning within your capacity to get done. Nothing slows momentum more than objectives too easy or objectives too hard. If you do not stretch, overconfidence sets in, or, worse, boredom. If you do not believe in the likelihood of success, discouragement sets in, or, worse, depression. Both suck out needed energy and momentum stops.

2. *Always Keep Moving.* Momentum has an odd cumulative quality. Once it begins to slow, it is hard to speed up. Just as a bicycler

must begin pedaling faster when approaching a steep hill, deal-makers must work harder when approaching sticky situations. It is your job to keep the action going.

Always have the next step planned before the last step ends. If you can't make progress on central issues, work on peripheral issues. If there are no easy problems to solve, look for odd ones or make some up. Sometimes the illusion of progress is enough to keep the deal rolling toward completion.

Consider the old airline joke where the pilot announces, "I have good news and bad news. The good news is that we're making excellent time. The bad news is that we're lost." While making excellent-time-though-lost is not too cool for a pilot, it isn't so bad for a deal-maker. Maintaining the atmosphere of forward motion contributes to the problem-solving spirit needed to handle those knotty, axial issues.

3. *Bypass Problems, then Circle Back.* It is not easy to keep moving forward, especially when unexpected obstacles crop up. If a seemingly insoluble problem arises, don't despair. Go on to simpler matters instead. You can always return to the thorny one later. In fact, it is often easier to resolve an open issue when it is the last one remaining on the table. Furthermore, the bare passage of time solves many problems by making them irrelevant.*

## Conveying Interest

How to show the other side that you really want to move the deal along—without looking like a supplicant? The following subtle actions can sustain momentum.

*Roll Up Your Sleeves.* Get to work. Dig into figures. As buyer, investigate what you'll receive. As seller, assist the buyer to make investigation.

---

*When I do not know what to do with some papers, I put them in a pile that sits for a while, perhaps several weeks, on, under, or over my desk. When I return to these little annoyances, the time having past, I usually find about half the issues are no longer relevant and much of the other half can be classified quickly.

*Go Kick the Tires.* Get out of the office and into the field. See the stuff.

*Give Compromise Hints.* Float trial balloons. Use pregnant questions. Offer tentative suggestions. Go off-the-record.

*Use Informal Occasions.* Invite the other side to more informal settings—meals, sporting events, or social activities.

# What to Do?

The year was 1975. Stanley Rader* and I were executive directors of the Ambassador International Cultural Foundation (AICF) which we created to operate, in addition to worldwide cultural projects,† a magnificent small concert hall in Pasadena, California. The AICF was nonsectarian, though it was funded by a Bible-believing church not without controversy.**

The church founder, Herbert W. Armstrong, believed that Ambassador Auditorium was an important part of his work and had spent significant sums of money on the inaugural concerts featuring the Vienna Symphony Orchestra conducted by Carlo Maria Guilini and a "Recital for Israel" by Arthur Rubinstein. The concerts were free since church policy was not to sell tickets.

It made little sense, in our opinion, to give tickets away. With the same subsidy allocated for the two concerts, we could present 50. More important, people respect only what they pay for (there were many no shows for those first free concerts), and the discipline of running revenues and expenses is the acid test of proper programming.

*Stanley R. Rader is a prominent Los Angeles attorney with high public profile. He worked closely with Herbert Armstrong for many years.

†Such as the archaeological excavations at the Temple Mount in Jerusalem in cooperation with the Hebrew University and the Israel Exploration Society.

**The Worldwide Church of God was founded by Herbert W. Armstrong, whose vision conceived Ambassador Auditorium. The church maintains a literal belief in the Bible, unifying Old Testament instructions (such as the Sabbath and Jewish holydays) with New Testament beliefs (such as salvation and prophecy). At the time, Garner Ted Armstrong was the church's media spokesperson. A later split between father and son resulted in Garner Ted starting his own church. The elder Armstrong died in 1986. The Worldwide Church, the Foundation, and the concert series continue.

Los Angeles institutions did not take kindly to the cultural upstart with so strange a heritage. Senior managers of the Los Angeles Philharmonic organization felt compelled to eliminate a potential competitor. "Present high school orchestras is what you people should do" was the greeting Rader and I received one midspring day. We had made a pilgrimage downtown trying to convince the Philharmonic to cooperate, not compete. Not a single performer was as yet signed for our rapidly approaching fall season.

Major artists had been booked solidly for months, so our self-serving advisors at the Philharmonic showed no real concern. But just to make sure, we were later informed (off-the-record), they let it be known that certain musicians shouldn't be playing with us. What artist, we worried, would risk incurring Philharmonic wrath to play our Pasadena hall?*

We had more problems. Obstacles sprung up from multiple sources—and still no performers had been booked! The *Los Angeles Times* enjoyed throwing barbs, some rather snobby, some rather deserved (the latter piercing the puffery that our organizations, to be frank, seemed incapable of avoiding). There was fear from area colleges, worrying about erosion of audiences. There was religious flack, dark suspicions of proselytizing plot—subliminal messages masked by the music, that supposedly our secret scheme, a theological Trojan horse in the guise of a classical concert hall.

Thus we had multiple goals: (1) to put Ambassador Auditorium to optimum use, presenting world-class concerts and series, (2) to convince the Church leadership that selling tickets was not bowing to mammon, (3) to achieve positive public awareness when the primary institutions were dubious at best, and (4) to attract world-class musicians to an unknown, controversial (and perhaps blackballed) hall.

Now this was a multiple deal. We were negotiating with wildly disparate interests all at the same time: already-booked concert artists, a cynical community, hostile competitors, and an uncertain

---

*During our fabled summit meeting with the Los Angeles Philharmonic, Rader and I joked that for every slur against the Foundation or the Church we would add five more concerts. Going into the meeting we had planned 20. We presented 65.

Church sponsor (laced with internal skeptics who could not see the founder's vision). The climb Rader and I faced was all up and all ice. But the stakes were equally high, the rewards well worth the risks. If we could run one good season, we thought, if we could only get the concert-going public exposed to the ease, beauty, and sonic excellence of Ambassador Auditorium, we could carve out a permanent place in the Southern California firmament. More important, the Ambassador Foundation would gain international visibility. Momentum was the key. What to do?

We needed movement. In a hurry. We did it with charity—"giving, not getting" in the words of Herbert Armstrong. The first season we gathered together as our co-sponsors several dozen leading Southern California charities—including United Way, Crippled Children's Society, March of Dimes, and the like. They would receive *all* the proceeds from ticket sales. Neither the AICF nor the Church would collect a dime.

This creative bombshell energized the vital momentum, accomplishing several things at once. First, great publicity was generated—no concert series had ever dreamed of such a strategy before. The participation of the charities encouraged many great virtuosos to perform. Next, these charities would promote their own patrons, a culturally astute group, and the Foundation would get a major publicity boost for its critical launch. Finally, the Church's position on ticket sales would be neatly finessed; after all, what religious leader could object to giving money to crippled children?

Another vital factor in determining success was our attitude toward artists that first season. Their schedules had been long finalized. We were terribly late in the season, and had powerful enemies seeking to abort our birth. We needed a breakthrough. Money, as they say, talks—sometimes a small amount can shout.

We decided to take a rather mild negotiating position regarding fees. Though only *slightly* less tough than the traditional encounters between promoters and agents, we made an impact sharp and convincing. In the end we probably paid 5 to 8 percent higher than others had. But we were new, controversial, and horrendously late. Artists, particularly their managers, loved booking dates with higher fees, and were more than willing to switch around schedules in order to squeeze us in.

Those higher fees, of course, had more symbolic power than dollar value. They would become benchmarks for the following season, the established prices from which the agents would sell their artists. We would be used against others when setting subsequent fees. The incremental cost to us was minimal. The incremental impact on artists was maximal. Furthermore, managers relished the thought of fresh, serious competition for their clients in the heretofore hegemony of Southern California. It was amazing how much leverage those few bucks bought.

The results were outstanding. In September 1975, AICF opened with Luciano Pavarotti, who was followed by Joan Sutherland, Yehudi Menuhin, and over 60 world-renowned artists and ensembles. The smashing highlight of the season was the coup of the decade. Our star attraction was the first West Coast performance in almost 25 years by Vladimir Horowitz.

How did we get the master pianist? We paid a little more—and then more than made up for it by promoting our other artists (i.e., allowing regular series subscribers first shot at The Horowitz Event). We also allowed Horowitz to play at the time most suitable to him, whereas the major institution in the city had been, we were told, less accommodating.

The artists, by the way, learned to love playing Ambassador Auditorium, and negotiations in subsequent seasons, we should note, became more traditional. The Church, as well, learned the benefits of selling tickets, not giving them away. The concert series remains one of the world's most illustrious.

# 33 DEAL SECRET

# Making the Close

## CLOSING DEALS IS THE BOTTOM LINE

Negotiating deals and not closing is like getting married and not mating. You can't be a good dealmaker unless you're a good deal closer. You can be weak in any of the other Skills or Secrets—but not this one. You must be able to put that final knot on the noose, that final nail in the coffin (Ugh!—I like love-making analogies far better).

Good deal closers focus on the desired outcomes. They see their goals clearly and keep them always in mind. Closing the deal takes a bit of bravado: You need guts to go for it—and the smarts to know when and how. You need not await a magical moment. You can end it all at any point. You can make the winning touchdown from any place on the playing field.

## Smell the Close

The best sign that a deal is ready to close is a suggested compromise on the critical outstanding issue. The offer should be made on the most contentious problem, the one that was most resistant to solution. Furthermore, it doesn't matter whether there are other unresolved issues still outstanding.

Other signs are certain telegraphic phrases, for example, "I think we can work this out . . ." in response to any offer you make; or "We need to rock this baby to sleep."

Watch for a lower tension level. A signal can be a change in tone of voice. Even before the final points are decided, conversation becomes more relaxed and informal, and humor picks up.

Often, you can test the waters by initiating such relaxed conversation yourself. If you do not get back reciprocal relaxation, you know you're not ready to close. Even if you get a positive response, you must judge whether you're really ready to close or the other person is just being friendly.

## Isolate Final Points

Closing deals means obtaining agreement on every issue. This is a formidable task. There are two general approaches:

1. Attack the major issues head on and leave the minor ones for later mop up
2. Solve all the minor issues first and then confront the now-isolated majors.

Which approach you choose depends on circumstances. When the deal looks relatively simple, or when the parties are not terribly far apart on the primary issues (such as price), you can go for a quick close by negotiating the major issues up front. When the deal is more complex, or when the parties remain far apart on the primary issues, then it is smarter to surround the problem by resolving the minor issues first.

## Who Makes the Push

Making the first move toward closure scares some dealmakers. They imagine it to be a sign of weakness. It isn't, although the possibilities of being rebuffed can be daunting.

I like to take the initiative. If it fails to get proper results for whatever reason (timing, offer, etc.), I make sure that the rejection does not affect my own self-image.

## Knowing when to Stop

There are two kinds of stops in deal making. Although they are opposite in intent, the same principle—sensing when to cease and desist—applies to both situations:

1. *When to Stop Pushing for More.* Work your tail off trying to maximize your value, but when you're finished, be finished. Some dealmakers never cease scheming. They're still negotiating as they sign the final documents. The sure sign of reaching the limit is an escalation of irritation on the other side. When you've gotten what you can get, call off the dogs.

2. *When to Stop Trying to Close.* Recognize that some deals never will be ready for signature. But some dealmakers press obliviously forward—annoying the other side and frustrating themselves. If at first you don't succeed, sure, try again—but not again and again, at least not in the same way.

## Looking Good

Human beings seek admiration in the eyes of their peers. There is no principle more fundamental in making deals. Remembering it makes you wise. Applying it makes you win.

Always strive to give the other side something they can repeat with pride to others. Consider their reactions as you plan the close. Think how they'll explain the deal to superiors, subordinates, even friends and family. A small concession, especially a cosmetic one, can work wonders.

## Problem Types

Lots of characters are dealmakers. Some give headaches by not being able to close. They always want to excise more flesh, to perpetually nibble your hide. These characters keep grinding for gain.

Nervous types are also unable to close deals. They are too scared to complete a transaction, worrying constantly about all the things that could go wrong. These characters keep looking for loopholes.

How to handle problem types? Nibblers must be smacked on the snout. A hard shot, this they understand. Just tell them categorically that, "If you want to close, close; if you want more, kiss off." The frightened types are more difficult to handle. Pressure will alienate, not coerce. You must give them room.

## After the Deal Closes

Good dealmakers do more than pack up their briefcases after the deal is done. They look for ways to express their appreciation for both the deal and the people doing it. Maintain contact for a while. Consider giving some needed assistance that is not covered in the contract.

The final point is what *not* to do. Never boast about besting. Crowing is for the birds. Even if you did get the better of the deal, forget it. Never make the other side feel beaten. If anything, do the opposite—show the other side some additional benefits of the transaction.

These actions will boost your reputation. They will also encourage the next deal. Good dealmakers view every just-completed deal as the forerunner of a yet-to-be-started deal.

## What to Do?

In selling a cooperative apartment to a tenant, the owner asked $230 per share. The tenant offered only $200. The tenant had occupying rights and could stay there indefinitely, paying below market-rate rent forever. What to do?

The owner knew that the tenant had greater power under these circumstances. The compromise at $210 per share was cut closer to the tenant's position. The owner encouraged the tenant by showing how unsold, unoccupied units were being advertised at $280 per share. However, both knew that comparable units were selling between $200 and $220, and that the actual price was fair. But making note of the higher asking prices made the tenant look good and helped close the deal.

# Employing the Pros

*THEY WORK FOR YOU—NOT YOU FOR THEM*

Attorneys are trained to break deals. Like Pavlov's dogs they are conditioned to salivate when hearing the bell of bad news. This is not slur; it is just fact. Negative attitudes of lawyers is as much a natural law of commerce as parental love for children is a natural law of biology. I cast no blame. They can't help it. It's the way the system is designed. Attorneys, you see, don't profit from deals that get done. But they sure take the heat for deals that get undone.

Listening to lawyers can turn optimists into pessimists, pollyannas into cynics. There are problems behind every deal point; there is no issue without peril. No deal, it can seem, should ever be made.

Deals, by definition, have risk. You accept risk in order to seek reward. The amount of reward must match the degree of risk, with the former well exceeding the latter. Attorneys and accountants explain the risk. Only you know the reward.

# Use Their Independent Judgment

Don't get the wrong idea: You must push your professionals to their limit. Ask them to go over the deal from top to bottom. Maximize the full extent of their expertise. Encourage them to be rough and tough, vigorous and vicious. Throw them raw meat. Exhort them to exercise independent judgment, to disagree with you and your deal. If they do anything less, they're not doing their job. "I am counting on you," I inform my attorneys and accountants solemnly, "to un-earth all the issues I've missed. Excavate and exhume if you must, but ferret out those problems."

# Due Diligence

Due diligence is the name given to the procedure that transpires between negotiating the deal and closing it. The process involves checking all books and records to determine if what has been represented to be true is indeed true. Normally, the buyer's team conducts due diligence on the seller's property. (The seller may conduct some due diligence if they are taking any of their consideration for the deal in buyer stock or notes.)

Risk assessment—lurking dangers and potential threats—is the primary role of attorneys and accountants. The due diligence process searches for skeletons; for example:

Undisclosed liabilities such as underfunded pension funds or contingent guarantees

Overvalued assets such as inflated inventories or improperly reserved receivables

Long-term contracts to sell goods and services priced below cost

Potential legal insults such as product liability suits not covered by insurance

Tax problems*

---

*One issue in acquisitions is the question of buying assets or stock. Generally buyers like to

Finding the problems is fine. But you should also ask the pros to suggest possible solutions. You do not want to change the deal more than once.

## Hidden Opportunities

While your attorneys and accountants are conducting their due diligence, prompt them to keep an eye out for hidden opportunities. A few examples:

Low-cost debt, such as industrial revenue bonds

LIFO (last-in first-out) inventories with a buried layer of low-cost raw materials

Law suits against vendors, customers, or insurance companies with likelihood of collection

Overfunded pension funds that can generate cash

Fully depreciated assets that have significant value

Raw land carried on the books at minuscule, long-ago costs

Investment assets such as minority ownership of other companies that have appreciated above book carrying costs.

## It's Your Deal

After the professionals have found all the problems (and then some), it's your turn. Never forget the big picture—why you wanted to do the deal in the first place. Although the deal may now look like a technical jungle—a thicket of legal thorns and tax bristles—don't despair. Instead, weigh the original benefits of the deal against

---

purchase assets, since they thereby avoid any undisclosed problems (e.g., tax, legal, etc.) associated with the prior company. Sometimes stock purchase is more desirable, such as with tax loss carryforwards, lease arrangements, and, most of the time, seller wishes.

Just how problematic the issues are,

Whether there are solutions to these problems, and

Whether you think the deal is still worth doing.

Balance the risks turned up by the pros against the rewards of the original idea. It is, after all, your deal and your decision. (If you decide to get out of the deal, the pros are your best resource. They can always find convincing reasons to back out.)

## Using Consultants

Consultants are freelance experts in a particular field; they are well positioned to give an unbiased assessment of the deal. (Their only bias is to recommend, as part of the first study, that you should continue with a second study.)

Consultants, it is said, will fly across the country to give a speech, but won't walk across the street to hear one. A less kind definition frames consultants as people who, having been fired from a previous job, can't seem to find a present one. My point is to be selective. There are numerous consultants around. Few are really good, but some are outstanding.

In appraising a potential deal (normally an acquisition), consultants should bring three strengths to the table: experience and expertise in the specific industry or field, a good nose for sniffing out opportunities and threats, and true independence of judgment.

Getting the most out of consultants means using them for highly specific purposes. Consultants are excellent for:

Technical analysis of products and markets

Assessing distinctive competencies of companies

Estimating competitive advantages of firms

Formulating alternative strategies

Evaluating diverse scenarios

A good analysis of a business should include detailed information on every critical aspect from product technology to cost structure to distribution systems. The more general the assignment the more nebulous the product. If you are not satisfied with a consultant's work, the blame should often fall on those who structured the task.


# What to Do?

How to overpay and get rich quick? Simple if you know what to buy and how to buy it. Mix financial leverage, managerial ownership, and professional structure. It's called a leveraged buyout (LBO), and what it does is cure the healthy. Take a sound company strong with equity. Sell it. Make it sick, heavy with debt. Make it better by re-building equity. Sell it again. Reap your profits. How can ordinary mortals offer $1.6 billion for Metromedia, Inc. the broadcasting chain, or $648 million for Dr Pepper, the soft-drink company? What to do?

An LBO looks like it's done with mirrors. Recall William Simon's $50+ million bonanza in a period so short he might have been caught for ordinary income, not capital gains. Simon simply bought Gibson Greeting Cards from a tired RCA and then sold part of it back to a ravenous public. Simon's timing was good, but his structure was better. What did the former Secretary of the Treasury put up? Only a few hundred thousand dollars, which, if you look closely, was hardly put up at all. (Would that he had performed such miracles with the national debt!)

How do LBOs work? Here's where you need attorneys. First, investors chip in a small amount of cash. This equity is then leveraged, 10, 20, even 50 times with debt. All senior funding—and this is the essential part—is secured by the acquired firm's *own* assets. Lending limits, for example, might be 80 percent of receivables, 50 percent of inventories, 25 percent of plant and equipment. The financial institutions get a nice premium for their risk, several points over prime. Often there needs to be a middle layer of subordinate debt, taken back by the seller or bought by a third party. (If bought by a third party, this mezzanine money demands a piece of the equity, called a "kicker," in addition to a higher rate of return.)

The touchstone of LBOs is cash flow. Here's where you need accountants. Almost nothing else matters. Profit and loss statements, surprisingly, are almost irrelevant. All that counts is whether, when, and with what safety you can meet interest coverage in the near term and can pay back principal in the long term. (Such payment schedules can be staged, with endless variation, to meet anticipated forecasts.) A nice feature in calculating cash flow is tax payments, or, more accurately, the lack thereof. Paying an inflated price can thus present no problems. The acquirer could merely (under the old tax law) write up company assets and generate higher write-offs for depreciation—in addition to already hefty interest deductions. Similarly, companies with tax losses have a competitive edge in LBO acquisitions.

You only have to watch the windows. Downdrafts in this business cause quick pneumonia. Sensitivity analysis is critical. What If games are not games. You had better be awfully sure you can weather any storm. Default sits right overhead in those low-altitude rain clouds, especially during the first few years. A slight change in market, pricing, margins, overheads, and especially interest rates, and in blow the banks with their liens in one hand and auction blocks in the other. (Or do they? When you owe small money, you have a creditor; when you owe big money, you have a partner!)

LBOs work, notwithstanding the extraordinary debt, because of the structure. Assets not being properly employed, such as current inventory, are shrunk down making a more efficient operation. Subsidiary businesses may be sold off for values far in excess of their cash-generating potential.

But the key to successful LBOs is management. LBO financiers insist that operating executives take part of the action. They require that management go at risk—making great gain on the upside and suffering serious loss on the downside. Savvy investors never do an LBO unless those who run target companies get a good hunk of the equity, at least 10 to 20 percent, and put up hard cash to buy it.

The critical transition, then, occurs inside the heads of these executives. Previously employees, they are suddenly owners. Professional managers with company-paid perks change mystically into personal entrepreneurs who turn out every light. Participation and commitment grab the essence of motivation. It is a remarkable transformation.

To be general manager of a conglomerate division managing public money is one thing. To be president of an independent company building private wealth is quite another. Take the decision-making process. Which will it be, a new corporate aircraft or an upgraded manufacturing facility? Think of the enhanced effort and reduced costs. When management is galvanized, the company is rejuvenated. And the key to the deal is professional structure.*

*Finally, my favorite lawyer joke: Why are medical researchers replacing white mice with lawyers in their experiments? First, there are more lawyers than white mice. Second, you don't get so attached to them.

# 35 *DEAL SECRET*

# Coaching the Team

Leverage in mechanics is the ability of a small force to move a large object. Leverage in finance is the ability of a small amount of equity to control a large amount of assets (see Deal Secret 34). Leverage also applies to deal making. Here, it is the ability of good deal-makers to multiply themselves by working with a group of key individuals. Just like a good surgeon uses assistants to open and close a patient, a good dealmaker uses assistants to handle various matters.

## Roles on the Team

Deal making has various parts, some of which should be delegated to members of your team. There is no sense having everyone do everything. There's no leverage in that.

Always staff for strength. Use each team member's talents for your advantage. Never allocate effort to improve weaknesses. Team members will vary in ability, experience, and interest. Give each one what he or she likes and does best. For instance, some people excel at the initial scouting of possible deals, others enjoy the due diligence process, and still others like coordinating the flow of activities.

Seek balance in assignment structure. Make your tasks too loose and you lose focused motivation and personal commitment of the individuals. Make your tasks too rigid and you lose innovative interaction and brainstorming dynamism of the group. Deal making is both art and science, and you need both creative types and analytical types on the team. You also need someone who knows where each type belongs.

## Coordinating the Team

One person should be responsible for assuring that all tasks are running in proper sequence and schedule. That person should be the principal dealmaker, or someone close to the key person. Progress should be monitored regularly. Few days should pass without communication.

## Ego and Attitude

There is one cardinal rule for deal teams: Never air your differences in public. (Exception: when the overt differences are part of a planned strategy.)

People who make deals have notoriously active egos. They think much of themselves, often more highly than they ought. They have strong opinions about things, and if those opinions are rejected, they may suffer or sulk.

Caring for a deal-making team can require the temperament of a opera impresario. Prima donnas abound—you never know when they will go manic or depressive. Deal-making types may be pampered and protected, though they shouldn't be coddled or spoiled.

## *Shuffling the Team*

Let's say you're in deal-making purgatory: Deadlocks can't be broken; gaps can't be bridged; momentum has stopped—and the deal has stalled. Worse, emotions have frayed on both sides and sparks are beginning to fly. You need to do something fast.

Try something different: Rotate your team. Break the accustomed relationships. Make each member of your side work with a new member of the other side. Go as far as having nonattorneys work with attorneys. The change in perspective can only be beneficial. After all, you have little left to lose.

## *What to Do?*

Two large military companies are negotiating to bid an advanced fighter aircraft. The contract will be worth billions. How to split the spoils is the issue. But these defense companies know that if they miss the deadline, neither gets anything. Furthermore, there's an enormous amount of preparatory work prior to bidding. What to do?

Coaching the team also applies to negotiating joint ventures. Win–win structures focus on areas of responsibility for the joint venture partners. The best solution would have each side desiring a different area (e.g., one might want the airframe construction and the other might like the electronic controls). If both want the same area, accommodations must be made. When a deadline is imposed by external circumstances, the two sides are on the same side. If an agreement can't be reached, new partners must be sought.

# Figuring the Numbers

*COUNTING COUNTS—BUT NOT TOO MUCH*

Figures lie, it is said, and liars figure. Numbers often appear to be statements of absolute truth. This is illusion. In doing deals, you must understand where numbers come from and how they are calculated. Equally important—and often forgotten—are the numbers that aren't available. Fooling around with numbers is really rather easy.

## Profits and Cash

Many a bankrupt company had a stellar record of steady profits until the day it filed Chapter 11. There have been companies, for example, that booked sales as "revenues" even though all they ever received for their products were weak promises to pay—uncollectible accounts receivable that eventually had to be written off as worthless. The "profits" were always on the books—but the cash was never in the bank.

When evaluating companies, stock analysts have come to realize that cash is king, and that watching the statements of changes in financial position, especially as they related to cash flow, can be more important than tracking profitability.* This is often proven by LBOs which may never show profits (due to high interest and depreciation)—but can eventually be sold for huge capital gains (see Deal Secret 34).

# Trends and How They Look

Using the same financial records, a company can be made to look either exceptionally desirable (if you're negotiating to sell it) or pitifully undesirable (if you're negotiating to buy it). Four principles come into play here: internal comparisons, external comparisons, choice of data, and choice of graphs. Buyers and sellers will view each differently.

### Internal Comparisons: Watch Your Base

Assume that Figure 36.1 charts your company's profit history. As a seller, you want to make the company look as good as possible by showing high growth. High growth will justify a high multiple of earnings. So you choose to present the four years of consecutive growth from 1984 through 1987. Four years seems fair—but does it present an accurate picture of the company? No matter, go get a premium price for this blazing star.

As a buyer, you want to make the company look as poor as possible. You want to show low growth, or, better yet, high volatility, in order to justify a low multiple of earnings. So you choose to evaluate the eight years from 1980 through 1987. Since the company's perfor-

---

*For companies, there is a great deal of difference between profits and cash. This is not so for individuals, who can calculate their personal profit for the year by simply adding up all the money they received and subtracting all that they spent. Businesses operate on the accrual system, which means that revenues and expenses are booked when realized—which is not when cash payments are received and disbursed. Furthermore, when a company buys new equipment, it is capitalized and therefore not an expense—although you can be sure that real payment was in cash or cash equivalents.

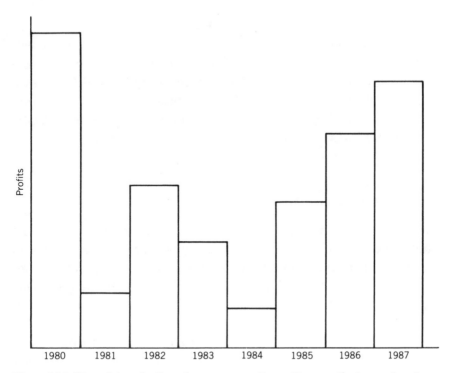

**Figure 36.1 How data selection changes perceptions.** *Compare the impression given by presenting only the last 4 years 1984–1987 with that of the full 8 years 1980–1987.*

mance varies greatly, the risk must be reflected in a lower price. Go get a deep discount for this panting dog.

The general rule: The seller puts his or her best foot forward by choosing the base years carefully. The buyer must be sure to look at all the years.

### External Comparisons: Watch Your Competition

If you are the buyer, compare the company to better-performing competitors. If you are the seller, look at poorer performers. If it is not obvious which companies are indeed competitors, the process gets tricky.*

---

*You can bet the seller will claim that the companies chosen by the buyer are somehow "in a different market," even though they do sell the same product in the same way. (Maybe they market in Maine but not in Massachusetts!)

A presentation we put together for the Pacific Lumber Company in marketing its long-term debt focused on increasing market control. We demonstrated that although its 1985 market share of upper-grade redwood lumber was a respectable 30 percent, it would rise to a dominant 60-plus percent by 1995. This was not wishful thinking: Competitors were running out of this unique resource and Pacific Lumber's holdings were the world's preeminent supply.


### Choice of Data: Watch Your Numbers

Deciding which numbers to highlight, and which to hide, is also part of the show. Say a public company is growing by making acquisitions for stock. The absolute amount of sales and profits might evince impressive growth, but if high prices were paid for the acquisitions (multiples of earnings for the acquired companies greater than that of the acquiring company), the earnings per share of the acquiring company would be declining and so might the stock price. Shareholders seeing the profit increases might be perplexed as to why their value was eroding.


### Choice of Graphs: Watch Your Scales

This one you see in the newspapers every day. Whether it's the trade imbalance or the national debt, how you draw the scales affects how you perceive the changes. Take a company whose sales were $100 million in 1985, $110 million in 1986, and $120 million in 1987 (see Figure 36.2). On a complete graph, the $20 million increase would appear as a 20 percent increase over the two years. If, however, the scale was drawn so that $90 million was the bottom and $120 million the top, the increase would appear to be 200 percent (the $20 million increase from 1985 to 1987 divided by the apparent $10 million size in 1985). When graphs are drawn with incomplete scales, all changes are exaggerated.*

---

* A complete scale must have 0 as the origin of the primary measurement axis.

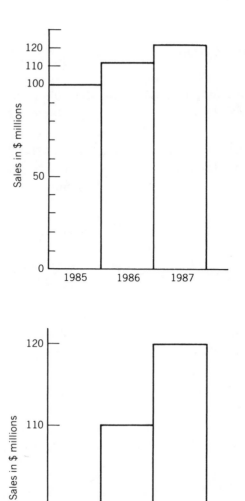

**Figure 36.2 How scale selection changes perceptions.** *Compare the different impressions given by presenting the same data on the two different graphs.*

# Equivalent Value

The key for understanding all financial numbers, especially in deals, is present value. All dealmakers must understand this pivotal concept that relates all future dollars back to a dollar value today. The process is simply the compounding of interest, either backward or forward in time. However, it becomes complex quickly. Dealmakers must be able to operate a financial calculator—or have someone handy who does.

# Return on Investment

Return on investment (ROI) over time is a trap for naive dealmakers. ROI demands more awareness and insight than many might think. Consider a deal where an investor group would loan $7 million at 13 percent interest and receive 25 percent of the company equity as an incentive kicker. The company would like to have the option of buying out the loan and equity for $9 million (plus interest) at the end of one year. The return for the year comes to almost 42 percent. Spectacular, you say? But ROI is more than numbers, and herein lies the problem.

There's high risk in the deal. Now the degree of risk in investments relates directly to the required rates of return. For example, venture capital deals must have very high returns in order to compensate for their very high risks—many of these business start-ups fail completely and the investors lose all their money. Therefore, returns of 40 percent or better are needed on the successful deals.

Furthermore, those returns must be compounded over many years to make the absolute number of dollars worthwhile. I'd much rather get 30 percent per year for three years than 42 percent for one year. In the above case, the profit over and above the 13 percent interest would be $5.6 million for the 30 percent over three years and $2 million for the 42 percent over one year.

# What to Do?

Assume that you have agreed to sell your business to a qualified seller. Part of the offer is $1 million now or $5 million in 10 years. How can you compare the alternatives? (For simplicity, we leave out tax considerations—but they really must be included.) What to do?

How to compare the equivalent value of $1 million paid today with $5 million paid in 10 years? You have to ask, in essence, how many dollars do I have to invest today, and at what interest rate (called the *discount rate*), in order to generate $5 million 10 years from now? Obviously, it depends on what interest rate you assume. If you use 7 percent interest, that $5 million out there is worth about $2.5 million back here. If you assume 10 percent, it's worth almost $2 million; if 17.5 percent, it's worth about the same $1 million; and if the interest rate is higher than 17.5 percent, then that glorious $5 million is actually worth less than $1 million is today.

How to determine a proper discount rate to use? You must add a risk premium to the riskless market rate (i.e., the interest on Treasury bills). A 17.5 percent interest rate compounded for 10 years seems like a terrific investment opportunity in today's world. Why not grab it? Be cautious. Proper determination of your required rate of return should include an evaluation of intangibles as well as present value cash equivalents. For instance, how do you know the company will be around in 10 years? What will happen to its market, its customers, its competitors? Then there's the issue of time itself: Do you really want to wait 10 years to collect? Believe me, as a seller I'll take my sure million right now. As a buyer, I'll try all day to convince you that you're walking away from a great deal.

# 37 *DEAL SECRET*

# *Crafting the Words*

*MEANING IS MORE THAN WORDS*

So you have a deal. Talking, you've done lots of. Writing, precious little. Now that you have an oral agreement, it's time to put the understanding into words on paper. It's amazing how different the deal looks in black and white.

## *Document Authorship*

Who prepares the documents? Which side takes the first cut? There are two approaches here. Generally, when you draw up the first draft, it's your outline and structure that controls the contract process. Thus it is better to prepare the document and have the other side offer suggestions for change.

However, if there are still some ambiguities in the deal, you face a dilemma. If your side prepares the papers, you might antagonize the other side—or give away something unnecessary. In this case, it might be better to have the other side write the first draft. Perhaps they'll state the ambiguity in your favor. If not, you can always discuss the matter. And, if you aren't happy with their draft, you can always rewrite it. If you do so, include at least some of their language to avoid a battle of wills among the lawyers.

# When to Start Writing

### Not Too Late

Sometimes it is wise to write up the deal elements at various stages of negotiations. Doing so can prevent misunderstandings from solidifying. By spelling out the deal points, you uncover problems not resolved and even issues not discussed.

### Not Too Early

Be aware, however, that a written document can highlight—even exacerbate—any real gaps between the parties. Sometimes it's better for such gaps to go unnoticed for a while. If focused on too soon, they may retard momentum and disrupt the deal. If ignored, these gaps might be narrowed through later discussions, or at least not interfere with the resolution of other issues.

# Types of Documents

### Term Sheets

Term sheets are two to three page summaries of deals. They are drawn up to confirm an oral agreement and only stress the major issues. Term sheets are generally neither morally binding nor legally enforceable. Thus they are rarely signed.

I find term sheets extremely useful in making deals—all parties can focus on each deal point without ambiguity or personality influence. Term sheets are so important that I write them myself—not trusting them to attorneys. Often there are good vibes and strong momentum at this stage, and lawyers can slow the process and confound the issues.

Don't misunderstand. Attorneys are essential for deals—but not for this function. The legal issues lawyers bring up are necessary and you'd be in thick soup if you ignored them—but term-sheet time is not the time to address these technicalities. Term sheets are tools for confirming agreement on the cardinal issues, and you don't want minutia impeding progress.

### Memoranda of Understanding (Letters of Agreement)

Memoranda of understanding (MOUs) are more official statements of the agreement between the parties. MOUs, which can run more than 10 pages, describe all essential elements of the deal. They facilitate the preparation of contracts by exposing most of the issues. It is often stated explicitly that the MOU must be replaced by a formal contract to be binding. Nonetheless, MOUs are often signed and the parties can begin to act as if the deal were in effect. Lawyers must prepare and critique MOUs.

### Formal Contracts

Formal contracts are the last step. Good attorneys shelter the principals from the ritual and tedium, but they always report any business change or difference from the expected structure, no matter how small. Attorneys from both sides generally work together to smooth the logistics of closing. Preclosings are often necessary to coordinate all the paperwork. Simply getting all of the signatures on all of the documents—some of which, we'd predict, will just have been changed—can take hours.

## Document Style

Documents can be prepared in many ways. Your approach depends on what position you're in.

If you feel that the deal is good for your side and should be done quickly, then go for documents that are straight, specific, simple, clear, and fast.

If there are still some points that need to be resolved and delay is to your benefit, then aim for documents that are tricky, general, complex, turgid, and slow. You can always trade off the ambiguity in a final give and take.

Keep in mind that turnaround time for documents is important in maintaining momentum. When you have an agreed deal, you must have a killer instinct to close it. More than one deal has died between lawyers' edits and choking word processors.

## What to Do?

You are one of several financial institutions competing for a lucrative loan to an investment group planning a complex acquisition. Negotiations, still only verbal, have been continuing for weeks and are a long way from final. You suspect that you are not offering the most competitive terms. Furthermore, due diligence has not been done. Suddenly, the deal materializes and, as usual, the investor group is in desperate need of an immediate letter of commitment for the loan. What to do?

Here, speed becomes a competitive weapon, replacing financial terms as the key element in getting the loan. You submit a draft commitment letter the next morning, delivered by overnight service or faxed by phone. You require aggressive financial compensation for upside return and include sufficient due diligence outs for downside protection. You need an attorney who is the rarest of the breed, a maker not a breaker of deals.

# 38 *DEAL SECRET*

# *Avoiding the Pitfalls*

*ONE FUMBLE SPOILS THE WHOLE GAME*

"Don't cough up the ball," coaches implore their teams. Football games are often determined by which side makes the fewer turnovers. The same is true in deal making: Whichever side makes the fewer mistakes is likely to achieve its objectives more easily.

Some common pitfalls are summarized here. (Several have been discussed in prior chapters.) Your goal is to understand these deal-making traps, watch for them, recognize them, and avoid them.

## *Faulty Information*

Errors of fact are an inexcusable gaffe. Any information used as a basis for a negotiating position should be both accurate and appropriate.*

---

*Note that information can be either accurate or appropriate without being the other. An ex-

## Premature Threats

Demands and ultimatums, whether blatant or subtle, are part of the deal-making process. But timing is critical. Shooting too soon looks ridiculous and has little effect. Worse, it ruins the potential power of these tactics at a later stage.

## Unplanned Anger

Showing anger without objective can adversely affect both the deal and your reputation. All dealmakers get a little hot at times. Frankly, it's not necessarily bad to show some viscera—it warns the other side that this stuff is important. But rage without reason does more harm than good.*

## Personal Insults

As for me, I never do it. I don't like to intimidate and I refuse to humiliate. No deal is that important. Also, it never works, not in the long run. Even if everything you say is true, you're building up resentment. What goes around, comes around.

## People Antagonisms

Friction between the sides sets up barriers to making deals. The only people you dislike, if you think about it, are the people you know.

---

ample of being appropriate and not accurate is when an appraisal of a property fails to take new zoning laws into consideration. An example of being accurate and not appropriate is when that appraisal is made of the land not the building, when the deal is for the building not the land.

*Do not jump to the opposite conclusion. I'm not advising you to plan your anger, to calculate

With big stakes involved (ego above all), it's easy to project your frustrations on to the other side, to blame them for your faults.* Control your personal feelings and get the job done.

## Cozy Relations

Getting too friendly with the other side can lead to conflicts of interest. These may not be either immoral or illegal, but it still could be a detriment to doing good deals. Avoid even the appearance of potential conflict or compromise.†

## Talking Too Much

A big mouth can lead to big trouble. Never forget that the other side is the opposition and you must watch what you say to them. You can be forthright, sure, but don't be foolish. You should be friendly, you can be informal, but always control your tongue. Everything said should be planned. (When reconsidering an investment after several months, an analyst on the other side confided that he thought the company was worse now than it was then. Well, I was 30 to 70 percent negative then, so his offhand comment short-circuited my reevaluation.)

---

your fury in advance as if playing some trick (though this may work on occasion). Rather, whenever your ire is triggered, be sure to consider the consequences of your actions and then direct your outbursts toward those goals.

*For example, my daughter just overslept and was late for work. At first, she blamed me for not answering *her* phone when her employer called. I wasn't answering any phones that day, not even my own, since the feared deadline of this manuscript was fast approaching.

†Occasionally during long negotiations, real friendships develop between members of opposing camps. Be careful to protect professional integrity. If business relationships develop, that's even worse. Co-investing in an unrelated deal, for example, is going too far.

## Fear of the Unknown

Never worry your way into deals. Concern about specifics can be helpful, but general agitation is detrimental. Good preparation is the best antidote against fear.

## Showing Anxiety*

Exposing nervousness among dealmakers is like spilling blood among sharks. Neither is recommended for continued well-being. Such apparent weakness invites aggressiveness.

## Feeling Inferior

This problem is more in the head than on the table. You may have less knowledge than the other side, or wield less power, but at the bargaining table all are equal. Everyone has the same ultimate weapon: The word is "no."

## Early Weakness

It's almost never good to show weakness in deal making, but it's disastrous at the outset. The emotional imprint for the entire negotiating process is formed up front. Even if your side has less power and control, hide it at first. Throw in some confusing signs, some swagger and brag if you must. You might even threaten an early abort.

---

*Anxiety is the outward expression of inner concern, an unspecific dread of the future, an uncontrollable consternation about upcoming events. It bespeaks a lack of confidence in outcomes. It reflects pressures that cannot be relieved.

## Being Nibbled

Giving up little by little can quickly turn into giving up more than you ever intended to concede. This salami technique of getting slivered by small slices must be avoided. State that all ideas and proposals will be considered, but simultaneously—not sequentially.

## Excessive Logic

When your head rules your heart, you can focus too much on facts and too little on feelings. People make deals for personal reasons. You can be right and still be wrong, winning battles while losing wars. Too much rational analysis of deals may slight the human factors. Too much numerical emphasis, too much quantitative decision making, can inhibit or destroy the insight and intuition needed to do deals. You can structure brilliantly, but if you don't also persuade pleasantly, you can lose what you should have won. Never forget, deal making is a people-intensive process.

## Excessive Emotion

When your heart rules your head, you may ignore facts and make emotional deals. Getting too attached to deals can lead to volatile decisions. Too much emphasis on intuition can dissipate or negate the detailed examinations needed to do a good job. Never make an emotional deal without knowing the logic behind it. Overriding logic with gut feelings is fine—as long as you remain fully aware of what you are doing. Never forget, deal making involves value and consideration measured in dollars and cents.

## Too Little Principle

A good reputation takes many years to build and a few minutes to destroy. Think about that in every deal you do.*

## Too Much Principle

Too much principle can also thwart a deal. Can't be too principled, you say, just like you can't be too rich or too thin? Well, that depends on definitions.

Having too much principle is a lot better than having too little. This is certain. Still, some people set standards that are spuriously high only because they seek to sustain their own lofty self-image. Ego, not morals, is the real stumbling block. Ego, remember, is the great killer of good deals.

## What to Do?

When I was lining up performing artists for a concert series' critical first season (see Deal Secret 32), I was subtly told that if I wanted to get a famous musician from an agent I would also have to take an up-and-comer from that same agent. The youngster, though reasonably good, was unnecessary. What to do?

So what's the big deal!

---

*A lack of principle can ruin a deal, or even a career, and doing hard time in the slammer isn't impossible (as several ex-Wall Streeters wouldn't be happy to confirm). Some dealmakers are steeped in conflicts of interest all the time. They know no other way. They represent one group overtly while participating in another group covertly. All their actions must be suspect. A typical example: purchasing agents receiving appreciation from vendors, however subtle the form of payment. Insider trading is but the latest, grotesque expression of one of the world's two oldest professions (which, by the way, have much in common).

# 39 *DEAL SECRET*

# *Doing the Work*

*WORK MUST BE FUN*

Work doesn't exist—not unless you would rather be doing something else. People do not suffer because of hard work; they break down due to worry, fear, tension, and anxiety.

The work of good deal making is exhilarating. It invigorates the spirit while engaging the mind. But have no illusions. Good deal making is hard—rigorous, arduous, strenuous, demanding, exacting, enervating, and exhausting. It is concentrated and intense, requiring both mental effort and social grace. It taxes all your resources, demanding people perception as well as technical precision. Doing deals is real work.

## *Taking Stock*

We're almost finished now. We've been through the 10 Deal Skills and just about 40 Deal Secrets. We've said so much about deal making that you may be a little shell-shocked. How to pull it all together?

Relax.

You don't have to memorize everything we've said. Absorbing the ideas and experiencing the stories doesn't mean instant recall of every point. Your subconscious is getting it, even if you feel a bit overwhelmed.

Perhaps it's like a first lesson in golf or tennis. The instructor tells you how, where, and when to move each limb. You can't remember it all, much less coordinate it together. But with practice, the diverse movements all begin to fall into place.

So take a deep breath and a step back. What follows is summary. If you remember and put these principles into practice, you'll be a good maker of deals.

## Be Committed and Focused

You must be dedicated, persevering, and intense. Good dealmakers are single-minded in pursuit of their clear goals. They have a great desire to succeed and always seek new solutions to old problems. They make better deals because they focus on objectives.

## Keep Flexible with Multiple Options

You must have various alternative deals from which you can select. Good dealmakers know that the most critical decision is often made up front, deciding in advance which deals are most doable. They know that maintaining other possible deals outside the current trans-action improves negotiating strength. They are creative in devising innovative strategies, structures, and bargaining ideas. They make better deals because they have greater choices.

## *Shoot Rifles, Not Shotguns*

You must hit the trunk of the tree, not fool with the branches. Good dealmakers go for the jugular, not to kill but to close. They know what issues are critical to resolve, what both sides need and want, what techniques bridge gaps and break deadlocks. They know where to find regions of win–win arrangements. They aim straight and true. They make better deals because they select the right problems to solve.

## *Seek Progress, Not Puff*

You must concentrate on doing the deal, not building your image. Good dealmakers focus on resolving issues, not enhancing power. They are socially aware, keeping track of characters and personalities on both sides of the table. They make better deals because private ego is subservient to collective benefit.

## *Have Fun*

You must like the action, not just the results. Good dealmakers love what they do as well as appreciate what they get. They relish the deal-making process and look forward to every new occasion. They find opportunities exciting and problems stimulating. They make better deals because they enjoy what they do.

## *So, Enjoy!*

Deal-doing work, above all else, requires deal-doing fun. Doing the work means having the fun.

# What to Do?

A private company was locked in severe strategic disputes that threatened to incite senior resignations and organizational fracture. The chief executive officer was maintaining an absolutely indefensible position. I was sitting with the top management group listening to the prime protector of current policy present a series of tortuously complex arguments that I was sure no one understood. Yet the older conservative executives, the keepers of the moribund status quo, reveled in watching the younger liberal executives, the proponents of constructive shift, finally being put down. "Well, that takes care of the rebel rousers," smirked a senior manager after the sinuous presentation. "We won't hear from that crowd again." I was furious. What to do?

The subject cut to the core of company mission. To keep the old ways would invite organizational collapse. So, corralling my overactive emotions and restraining any sarcasm in my voice, I put a question to this smug senior manager, "Of all the excellent arguments defending our current strategy, which did you think was the very best?"

The older manager, who couldn't possibly have understood what he had heard much less repeat any of it, fumbled a bit, then admitted, "You know, I never could follow anything that man ever said." Slinking away, he never discussed the matter again. Well-chosen words, even a few of them, can cut a sharp edge.

# 40 *DEAL SECRET*

# *Having the Fun*

*FUN TODAY MUST BE FUN TOMORROW*

If work is whatever you need to get done, then fun is whatever you like to be doing. Deal making must be both fun and work: You should like to do whatever you need to do.

A wealthy dealmaker was asked why he continued working so hard into his late 70s. "My friends play golf," he said, keeping his eyes glued to obscure financial notes; "I make deals." He explained that he likes doing what he's reasonably good at doing—a category that did not include driving, chipping, or putting.

Good dealmakers have fun doing their deals. What's to enjoy in deal making? How to have fun amidst the tension? The following attitudes should help.

## *Relax*

Manner and demeanor are important. How you feel governs how

you act. Don't allow pressures to overwhelm emotions. No deal is that vital. Cool beats hot. But the deal's getting away, you say? Don't be anxious. If a horse runs away, says a proverb, don't fret; if it's your horse, it will come back; if it's not yours, you don't want it back.

Being relaxed doesn't contradict being focused and committed. You can still be dedicated to deal making and work with ferocious intensity. The key is not to take yourself too seriously.

## Anticipate Newness

There's one special quality about doing deals that makes it exciting. Making deals is always new, always changing, always refreshing. Nothing is ever humdrum. Being bored never happens. So savor the always-present novelty.

When searching for new deals, look forward to each fresh possibility as if it were your first. Be eager. Sense the uniqueness, the expectation of surprise. What will the next deal bring? From where will it come? How will you do it?

When doing a particular deal, take pleasure in addressing each new problem. Problems have solutions. Solutions can be better or worse, and your task is to find those that are better. Make the search scintillating, invigorating, rejuvenating. Psych yourself and expect results!

## Keep Score

Whether your game is golf, tennis, chess, bridge, or Scrabble®, keeping score keeps your interest. You need a benchmark against which to judge performance. Winning may not be the only thing, but constant improvement helps maintain momentum. You don't practice your strokes or study your moves without testing them in live action. Part of the fun is charting your progress.

## *Enjoy the People*

To be a good dealmaker, you must like people. This is the first half of the bottom line. Good dealmakers enjoy engaging different personalities and handling different characters. They appreciate constructing deals in which the other side is satisfied. Good dealmakers never build resentment. New friendships, these they build often.

## *Enjoy the Process*

To be a good dealmaker, you must also like deal making. This is the second half of the bottom line. You must like what you do while you are doing it. The process should be pleasurable. Not just the result.

Now you can't really relish everything—conflicting opinions and stalled progress do not spark your spirit, nor do personality conflicts and disruptive threats give you big belly laughs. But even the aggravation can be fun if you view obstacles as challenges and problems as opportunities.

How to handle friction and strife? The trick is to see all action as part of a bigger picture. Keep end results in mind: Visualizing where you want to go facilitates how you are going to get there. Appreciate the quandaries and predicaments. Consider trouble the test of your mettle—the chance to devise creative solution.

## *Do What You Want*

A favorite story involves an exchange between two high school friends meeting after many years. One has become an enormously successful businessperson, controlling a huge industrial empire. The other remains an economic basketcase, teaching part time in a small college, reading good books, philosophizing with friends, and generally enjoying life.

"Why don't you get a real job?" asks the suave businessperson.

"Why should I?" answers the disheveled professor.

"Look, if you get a real job, you can make money."

"But why do I want to make money?"

"Because with money you can buy a business."

"But why do I want to buy a business?"

"So you can make even more money."

"But why do I want to make even more money?"

"So you can buy a bigger business."

"But why do I want to buy a bigger business?"

"So you can amass a huge amount of money."

"But why do I want to amass a huge amount of money?"

"Because then you can retire and do what you want!"

"But that's what I'm doing right now!"

## What I Want

Now I get personal: What I want to do I *am* doing right now. I love doing deals, deals of all kinds, deals of all sizes. I've made deals from Wall Street megamergers to entrepreneurial start-ups, from Hollywood's entertainment center to New York's garment district. I've strategized, structured, and struggled under conditions most riveting and most unusual. Financing new ventures, advising government agencies, mediating corporate conflicts, changing institutional directions, fighting famous lawyers, presenting temperamental artists—I've done them all. Sometimes I was hot, burning with personal passion. Other times I was cool, working with studied precision. At all times I was committed: Dealmaking lights my fire.

When I'm called in to make deals—to plan and put together novel transactions—I must quickly appraise what each side wants, needs, and can't live without. I'm under pressure—and I go for grit and gist. Although I don't like the analogy, having deal-making skill in today's world is like toting a fast gun in the Old West: "Have Skill, Will Travel" is the dealmaker's calling card.

Yet you can't always win. I like recounting the skyrocketing winners, but I won't forget the flame-out losers. I've agonized over deals hung up and second-guessed myself on deals gone sour. I've leaped for the stars and fallen in the dirt. But I always give it my best; sometimes that's good enough, sometimes not quite. I have a deal-making life and that's what I share in this book.

## *What to Do?*

Let's talk! Now it's your turn. At its core, *Dealmaker* is about having fun. The pleasures of doing deals are what this book is all about. If you've done some deals in which you've had special fun, whether in business or in life, how about telling me about them? I might like to use your deal in my next book.

If you like the idea, try writing up your stories and sending them to me. Don't worry about style. Just jot down the facts as you remember them. If you like, add your comments, opinions, thoughts, reflections. Mail them to me at the following address. (Let me know if you'd like your name noted should I present your deal in print.)

*Please Send Your Deals To:*

```
Dr. Robert Lawrence Kuhn
% John Mahaney
John Wiley & Sons
605 Third Avenue
New York, NY 10158
```

# The Components of Deals

It is important to understand the composition of deal terms and conditions in order to negotiate them effectively. We present the seven components needed to establish deal terms and conditions, followed by two example applications, one corporate and one personal.

## The Seven Component Questions

1. *What Kind of Stuff?* What is the nature and character of the value and consideration being exchanged in the transaction? This means the specific types of goods, services, assets, liabilities, ownerships, intangibles, rights, responsibilities, commitments, and the like.

2. *How Much of the Stuff?* What are the amounts of the value and consideration being exchanged? This means the precise number of the things, tangible and intangible, changing hands in the transaction.

3. *What's the Stuff Really Worth?* What is the relative benefit of the value and consideration being exchanged? How does each side of the transaction relate to the other.

4. *What's the Stuff Really Like?* What promises and assurances (representations and warranties) are given to the value and consideration? These are the legal declarations about the state of the value and consideration being exchanged; the mutual declarations by the respective parties, their rights to make the transaction, and the like.

5. *What's for Sure and What's Not?* Which terms and conditions cannot change (noncontingent) and which can change (contingent)? Contingent aspects of transactions depend on future events or conditions (such as income in later years in an acquisition). Noncontingent aspects are set forth absolutely and cannot be altered.

6. *How to Assure Compliance?* How to provide for each side living up to its side of the bargain? These are the mechanisms for generating confidence in deal completion by fulfilling the terms and conditions through security interests, guarantees, performance requirements, and the like.

7. *What's the Timing?* What is the schedule for completing the transaction? This describes the sequence of events for executing and activating each aspect of the terms and conditions, the time frame when exchanges and transfers of value and consideration all happen.

## Example of a Corporate Transaction

Assume Company A is buying a small subsidiary of Company B (call it SmallCo). How would each of the components fit and apply? The following is a simplified summary of the terms and conditions organized in answer to the seven questions.

1. *What Kind of Stuff?* Company A purchases from Company B all the assets and current liabilities of SmallCo for cash, notes, and profit participations; Company B keeps SmallCo's long-term debt and stock.

2. *How Much of the Stuff?* It costs $12 million, to be paid as follows: $2 million in cash at closing, $2 million in Company A stock, $5 million in promissory notes to be paid $1 million per year for five consecutive years, and $3 million in Company A stock to be paid as a percentage of future profits of the SmallCo division.

3. *What's the Stuff Really Worth?* The $2 million cash is easy; cash is cash. Company A stock is more difficult—it can be valued at market value if Company A is public, if the stock has a ready market, if there are no restrictions, and if there is reasonable stability in the stock— a lot of ifs. The $1 million for five consecutive years must be discounted to present value if no interest is being paid. Thus the $5 million of face value on the promissory notes would be only worth about $3.6 million (using a 12 percent discount factor). The $3 million based on profit participation is worth substantially less than its face value, since, in addition to the present value discount, its ultimate valuation is completely dependent on indeterminable elements: SmallCo's future prospects when controlled by other parties, and the double doubt of uncertain profits in the SmallCo division and uncertain real worth of Company A stock.

4. *What's the Stuff Really Like?* Company B asserts that all assets and liabilities being transferred are in good condition. Company A provides an acceptable method for determining SmallCo's future profitability. Each company assures the other of its legal right to do the transaction.

5. *What's for Sure and What's Not?* All but the profit participation is certain (noncontingent); the profit participation is dependent on uncertain events (and is highly contingent).

6. *How to Assure Compliance?* The $1 million per year for five years can carry the corporate guarantee of Company A. It may also be backed up by security interests in the assets being sold or even the independent guarantee of a financial institution (e.g., a letter of credit).

7. *What's the Timing?* The schedule for transfer of ownership of Company B value (SmallCo's assets) is stated clearly (usually at closing) as is the schedule for transfer of consideration (the various payments of cash and stock at closing and over time).

# Example of a Personal Transaction

These same components exist in every deal, although in smaller, more personal transactions, several are more implicit than explicit. For example, watch the seven components at work in a deal between you and your boss regarding last year's bonus.

1. *What Kind of Stuff?* You transfer to your employer last year's work product and the implied promise of next year's work product in exchange for certain financial consideration.

2. *How Much of the Stuff?* The length of your implied employment arrangement; say, one year. The quantity of each type of financial consideration is specified for your bonus; say, $10,000 in cash and $20,000 worth of stock options.

3. *What's the Stuff Really Worth?* A logical relationship should relate work performance to financial bonus.

4. *What's the Stuff Really Like?* Assertions are more assumed than stated. Each side (you and your boss) agrees to the exchange of bonus for previous and continued work.

5. *What's for Sure and What's Not?* The bonus is generally certain (noncontingent) for the previous year. It is usually uncertain (contingent) for the coming year (i.e., it is based on specific or unspecific factors such as the company's profitability, the relative performance of your division or department, your own personal productivity, and, often, the whim and caprice of your boss).

6. *How to Assure Compliance?* Confidence in receiving the bonus is often its verbal promise; confidence in your continued work effort is assumed. (However, it becomes problematic if you deem the bonus to be too low.)

7. *What Is the Timing?* The schedule for bonus payment is based on corporate tradition (e.g., at the end of the year when performance can be assessed).

APPENDIX *B*

# *The Domains of Deals*

Seeing deals from different viewpoints gives insight into their nature and character. To give sense for viewing (or cutting) deals from various perspectives (or angles), we present three disparate approaches: deal participants, deal locus, and deal sectors.

## *Deal Participants*

What's a deal participants perspective? Here, we look at the composition, numbers, and organization of the human characters on each side of the proposed transaction:

*One versus one* (e.g., discussions between husbands and wives or peers and friends, or negotiations between buyers and sellers of personal property)

*One versus group* (e.g., a spouse dealing with an ex-spouse's law firm, or a person buying a car from an automobile dealer)

*Group versus group* (e.g., law firm against law firm in corporate liti-

303

gation, or marketing department against manufacturing over new product responsibility)

*One versus institution* (e.g., a veteran fighting for promised benefits from his or her military service, or an inventor trying to free up corporate funds for high-risk research and development)

*Group versus institution* (e.g., individual investors planning to take over a public company, or union organizers seeking formal recognition)

*Institution versus institution* (e.g., the daily commerce of corporate buying and selling goods and services, or an acquisition battle for a desired target company).

## Deal Locus

What's a deal locus perspective? Here, we look at the proposed transaction from the individual dealmaker's vantage point. Where in one's own personal life spectrum, we ask, is the transaction taking place: On the job in the course of normal business? On the job affecting career potential (e.g., promotion opportunity)? Within the family altering relationships? Concerning one's private life (e.g., personal finance).

Deals in each different locus take on different auras and atmospheres. For example, deal making on the job is studied and professional. When one's career is on the line, count on overtones of tension and insecurity. Within the family, there's less inhibition and social restraint (e.g., screaming becomes an easy way to make your point more strongly). Concerning one's private life, never forget that you're still doing deals.

## Deal Sector

What's a deal sector perspective? Here, we look at the proposed transaction from the organization's vantage point. Where in society, we ask, is the transaction taking place? In commercial companies (i.e., the private sector)? Government agencies (i.e., the public sector)? Not-for-profit institutions (e.g., universities and charities)? Ideological institutions (e.g., religious and political movements)?

From this perspective, the issues are goals and strategies; that is, where we are going and how we are going to get there. In each sector, deals have their own special character and cast—influencing attitudes, objectives, and priorities. For example, in commerce, it's often money, career, and power. In politics, career and power. In not-for-profit institutions, organizational mission. In ideological institutions, transcendental mission (and, all-too-often, an unhealthy dose of power, career, and money thrown in for bad measure).

# C APPENDIX

## Symbols of Power

### Power Dressing

Asserting personal strength with clothing. In the world of high finance, elegant suits, preferably three-piece or double-breasted, are required. So are sharp shirts with white collars and cuffs, a small accent of expensive (but not-too-ostentatious) jewelry, and in some cycles, bright suspenders. In the world of entertainment, supercool always cops top honors.

### Power Eating

Where to dine to see and be seen. For example, in New York it's the Regency Hotel for breakfast, Four Seasons for lunch, Lutece among others for dinner. Each industry has its own hangouts.

# Power Puffing

Smoking large, imported cigars—clearly superior to munching small, crunchy apples.

# Power Living

Aboding on the right side of the tracks. Park or Fifth Avenue in New York whips First, Second, Third, or Lexington, and absolutely stomps anything on the West Side. In the arts, however, West Side wins.

# Power Talking

Using industry jargon and clever language. "Taking" meetings in Hollywood. Putting companies "in play" on Wall Street. "M&A" in one business (*m*ergers and *a*cquisitions in investment banking). "T&A" in another business (*t*its and *a*sses in motion pictures).

# Index

# About the Author

Dr. Robert Lawrence Kuhn is an investment banker and corporate strategist at home in the complementary worlds of business, academia, government, and media. He is editor in chief of the *Handbook for Creative and Innovative Managers* (published by McGraw-Hill) and the *Handbook of Investment Banking* (forthcoming from Dow Jones-Irwin). Trained as a scientist (brain research), Dr. Kuhn specializes in mergers and acquisitions, leveraged buyouts, new business formation, venture capital, organization strategy, corporate finance, and in structuring innovative financial transactions. He serves on several corporate boards.

Dr. Kuhn is Senior Fellow in Creative and Innovative Management at the IC² Institute of the University of Texas at Austin, and is Adjunct Professor of Management at the Graduate School of Business Administration of New York University. He holds an A.B. (Phi Beta Kappa) in human biology from Johns Hopkins University, a Ph.D. in neuroanatomy and neurophysiology from the University of California at Los Angeles, and an M.S. (Sloan Fellow) in management from the Massachusetts Institute of Technology.

Dr. Kuhn speaks and lectures frequently and is quoted and published widely. He teaches graduate courses in corporate strategy and business policy. He consults for several governments. He has written and edited more than a dozen books including *Micromanaging: Transforming Business Leaders with Personal Computers* (co-authored by Dr. George Geis and published by Prentice-Hall). His previous John Wiley book, *To Flourish Among Giants: Creative Management for Mid-Sized Firms,* was a main selection of the Macmillan Book Club and published in Japanese.